ARRESTED
BATTLING AMERICA'S CRIMINAL JUSTICE SYSTEM

ARRESTED
BATTLING AMERICA'S CRIMINAL JUSTICE SYSTEM

DAN CONAWAY, ESQUIRE

BASCOM HILL PUBLISHING GROUP | MINNEAPOLIS, MN

Copyright © 2014 by Dan Conaway, Esquire

BASCOM HILL
PUBLISHING GROUP

BASCOM HILL PUBLISHING GROUP
322 FIRST AVENUE N, 5TH FLOOR
MINNEAPOLIS, MN 55401
612.455.2294
WWW.BASCOMHILLBOOKS.COM

ALL RIGHTS RESERVED. NO PART OF THIS PUBLICATION MAY BE REPRODUCED, STORED IN A RETRIEVAL SYSTEM, OR TRANSMITTED, IN ANY FORM OR BY ANY MEANS, ELECTRONIC, MECHANICAL, PHOTOCOPYING, RECORDING, OR OTHERWISE, WITHOUT THE PRIOR WRITTEN PERMISSION OF THE AUTHOR.

ISBN-13: *978-1-62652-709-6*
LCCN: *2014905398*

DISTRIBUTED BY ITASCA BOOKS

COVER DESIGN BY ALAN PRANKE
TYPESET BY JENNI WHEELER

PRINTED IN THE UNITED STATES OF AMERICA

CONTENTS

PREFACE · · · vii

PART I: THE BEAST REVEALED—AN OVERVIEW OF AMERICA'S CRIMINAL JUSTICE SYSTEM · · · 1

Chapter One: The Nature of the Beast—*Law and Order* Is Not Reality TV · · · 5

Chapter Two: In the Belly of the Beast—Police, Prosecutors, Judges, and Defense Lawyers · · · 15

Chapter Three: Groups Influencing the Beast: Politicians, Special Interest Groups, Plaintiff's Lawyers, the Prison and Corrections Industry, and the Media · · · 37

PART II: BREEDING A MEANER BEAST—THE IMPACT OF ZERO TOLERANCE ON AMERICA'S CRIMINAL JUSTICE SYSTEM · · · 59

Chapter Four: A Book, a Movie, and a Magazine Article Lead to Zero Tolerance · · · 63

Chapter Five: How Zero Tolerance Impacts Police Investigations in America · · · 95

Chapter Six: The Impact of Zero Tolerance on Prosecution, Punishment, and Sentencing · · · 109

Chapter Seven: Signs of Hope—The Movement Toward Alternative Sentencing and Punishment Policies · · · 139

PART III:	BATTLING THE BEAST—YOUR CONSTITUTIONAL RIGHTS, BASIC PRINCIPLES OF CRIMINAL DEFENSE, AND SEVEN CASE STUDIES	145
Chapter Eight:	Your Constitutional Rights—The Bedrock of America's Criminal Justice System	147
Chapter Nine:	Basic Principles of Criminal Defense	179
Chapter Ten:	Defense Lawyers in Action—Seven Criminal Case Studies	195
Endnotes		245
Bibliography		255

PREFACE

As a practicing criminal defense lawyer for the past two decades, I wrote this book for three groups of people:

1. People who have been arrested or who are the targets of criminal investigations.
2. People who believe that, as good, decent, law-abiding citizens, they and their loved ones could never wind up in the first group.
3. Anyone who wants to know more about how America's criminal justice system really works.

Let's take a closer look at each group.

So you have been arrested. Or perhaps you have not been arrested yet, but you are the target of a criminal investigation by state or federal law enforcement. You are at one of the scariest and most critical moments in your life. You feel isolated, alone, and terrified. The world seems a dark and hostile place where "they"—the powers you thought were there to protect you and your family—are suddenly out to get you.

"They" are the police and the prosecutors. You know, the ones who always seem like the good guys on *Law & Order*, *Cold Case*, and *CSI* Except, right now, they are coming after you. You've become the "bad guy," and they are trying to take away your freedom, destroy your family, and generally wreck your life. What can you do to protect yourself? What information can help you make good decisions during the seemingly dark days ahead?

Or perhaps you haven't been arrested, but a close friend or family member has. My guess is you are experiencing many of the same thoughts and feelings we've just discussed. If the person arrested is an immediate family member—your spouse, your parent, or (especially) your child—my guess is your emotions are even stronger than if you were facing criminal prosecution yourself.

If you fall into the second group of people this book is written for, you probably feel absolutely sure that such a thing could never happen to you or a member of your family. The police only arrest *criminals*, and since neither you nor anyone close to you is a criminal, there is no chance that you will ever be arrested.

If this is your category, then this book is *especially* important for you to read. You are operating with blinders on, I'm afraid, and those blinders could lead you to make some very serious mistakes if you or a loved one winds up handcuffed and sitting in the back of a squad car. What will you do when your illusion that you and your family could never get into trouble with the law is shattered? How will you think clearly or rationally in the days and weeks and months—and possibly even years—ahead, as you have to make informed, intelligent decisions while your mind is clouded by fear and disbelief?

Not sure? Then this book is for you.

As for the third group, this book will provide you with "insider knowledge" about America's criminal justice system. This book goes deeper than the standard media coverage, which tends to skim the surface and—these days—to tell the story from the point of view of the police, prosecutors, and victims. This book will give you the perspective of a practicing criminal defense attorney who works within the courtrooms of America defending the rights of the accused.

I wrote this book to provide a basic guide for how to respond when you or your loved one is facing criminal charges. This book is in no way intended as a substitute for legal counsel. The information it contains is simply meant to help you understand what is going on and to give you insight as you work with your defense lawyer to face down today's criminal justice system—or, as I call it, "the Beast." The Beast is as disorganized, inefficient, and politically motivated as most other bureaucratic government organizations, and it has the power to take away your liberty and wreck your life. Since you should be prepared for battle before facing any monsters, a little knowledge is certainly required as you, your family, and your lawyer prepare to do battle with the Beast.

PART I: THE BEAST REVEALED—

AN OVERVIEW OF AMERICA'S CRIMINAL JUSTICE SYSTEM

Life can be messy. This is the fundamental truth that being a criminal defense lawyer has taught me. We all know what living in modern American society is like. Stressed-out and overworked, we all strive to pay the bills, raise our families, find love and happiness, maintain employment, stay away from abusing alcohol or drugs, and somehow keep juggling all the balls of day-to-day life. When an American citizen is arrested, it often means that one or more of those balls got dropped.

Working with my clients has taught me, better than any philosophy class, that as human beings we are all innately fallible. As a criminal defense lawyer, I have no need to be reminded that "to err is human"—I see it every day. My clients are people like these:

- **Sasha, a college student on an academic scholarship to an exclusive private college.** Under pressure to conform to the lifestyles of her wealthier friends, she succumbed to the pressure to shoplift a party dress "just this once." The store's policy against selective prosecution landed Sasha in jail, and her parents in my office.

- **Winston, a contractor, family man, and supporter of his local law-and-order politicians.** Pulled over one evening for failing to stop completely at a stop sign, he failed a Breathalyzer test and found himself in court on a charge of DUI, or "driving under the influence."

- **Martha, a bookkeeper and office manager for a privately held business, married to Mike, who worked at the local meat packing plant.** When Mike got laid off and Martha resorted to "borrowing" from the company accounts to make ends meet, the company fired her and had her arrested.

- **Jerry, a long-distance trucker with a wife and two kids.** The pressure to provide "just on time delivery" for his big corporate clients led Jerry to boost his drive time with crystal meth. Stopped for a moving violation, Jerry couldn't hide the signs of habitual drug use from the officer, who arrested him and took him to jail.

- **Jim and Janet, a married couple who got into a fight one night.** She got so angry that she threw a book at him. When he grabbed her by the shoulders, shook her, and threw her onto the couch, she called 911. The police came to find the fight had blown over, but they still arrested both Jim and Janet for domestic violence assault and battery.

I am always struck by the callousness and sanctimony of those who love to crow, "Well, they did the crime, so they should do the time." Yes, my clients many times did do what they are accused of. But the reason *why* they did whatever they were arrested for was not usually some deep criminal mind-set or an immoral soul. My clients are usually hardworking, decent, honest citizens who pay their taxes, raise their families, and try to follow the rules, but nonetheless have had their lives shattered by personal crisis and criminal arrest.

The politicians and the "law-and-order" radio and television talk show types boost their ratings by ranting and raving about our need to "lock everybody up who commits a crime, and throw away the key." They would be looking at things quite differently, I am sure, if it were they or their own sons or daughters standing in a courtroom accused of a criminal act and facing jail or prison and a lifetime of being branded a criminal. Then the notion that there exists some bright line between "us"—the good, decent, law-abiding citizens—and "them"—the criminals—would seem overly simplistic even to the most hard-core law-and-order advocate.

The reality is that it is much easier today for the average person to be arrested than it was twenty or thirty years ago. Many actions for which people are arrested nowadays would have been dealt with very differently a generation ago. Either they would not have involved the police at all, or they would have involved only a warning or some other conduct short of an arrest by a police officer. This "hyper-arresting" situation is a result of numerous changes in the criminal justice system over the past few decades, including the expanded definition of crimes, the creation of new classes of crimes, and the rise of "zero-tolerance" policies. These changes are affecting normal American citizens and their families in the marketplace, on the Internet, on the road, at home, and in their children's schools.

Regardless of the circumstances underlying an arrest, however, this is for certain: once you have been arrested, you and your family and friends are on a strict timeline, and the choices you make can, and will, ultimately affect the rest of your life. Ignoring the arrest will not make it go away, and the days when you could simply go to court by yourself and "deal with it in front of the judge" are long gone. America's criminal justice system is not "user friendly." The Beast is a highly politicized, adversarial, overwhelmed, inefficient, disorganized, and at times even predatory creature that must be tamed and slain if you, the person arrested and treated like a criminal, are going to come out at the end of the ordeal whole and able to move on—and not chewed into a million pieces with your life wrecked forever. If you have been arrested, I hope this book will help you and your loved ones as you prepare to battle the Beast.

CHAPTER ONE

THE NATURE OF THE BEAST—
LAW & ORDER IS NOT REALITY TV

Americans are fascinated with the world of criminal law. Turn on the television any day or night of the week and you can see hours upon hours of programming devoted to the criminal justice system—*Law & Order, CSI, Cold Case, NCIS,* and *Criminal Minds,* to name just a few of the available programs. Each night, millions of Americans—good, decent, law-abiding citizens all—sit riveted in front of their television sets watching lawyers, prosecutors, judges, police officers, victims and, of course, criminals navigate the Beast's labyrinth of rules and regulations, crime and punishment, sin and redemption. These shows are so popular that they keep producing spin-offs—the family of *Law & Order* and *CSI* programs alone now account for many hours of weekly programming. From the safety of our own living rooms, we keep a safe distance from the human drama that plays out nightly on our television screens. It's us—the good, decent, law-abiding citizens—against them—the no-good, low-down, scumbag criminals. But you may ask yourself, "Do these shows look like real life?" The answer is: not by a long shot.

Criminal Law as Entertainment

The public's fascination with criminal law is nothing new. Criminal courtrooms have always played a central role as a source of entertainment in America. In the years before television, entire communities would show up to watch trials at the local county courthouse. Go to any small-town county seat of government, and where do you find the old courthouse? Right in the middle of the town square. There is usually a grassy park surrounding the courthouse with lots of big shade trees. During trials, folks from the surrounding farms and villages would literally camp out on the courthouse square, have barbecues and picnics on the lawn, and catch up with their friends and fellow citizens.

Inside the courtroom, there was plenty of seating, usually with a balcony section as well, to accommodate as many local citizens as possible. Trial lawyers in the eighteenth, nineteenth, and early twentieth centuries were expected to be experts at the "art of oratory"—overblown theatrical displays of public speaking that were used as much to entertain the citizens in the gallery as they were to convince the judge of the rightness of their client's case.

Today, people still travel from all over to watch infamous trials. They wait hours in line hoping to get seats in the courtroom for a trial involving a celebrity or an especially heinous set of facts. Or they sit glued to their televisions awaiting the verdict for the likes of accused killers O. J. Simpson, Scott Peterson, the Menendez brothers, and Casey Anthony. When there are no real trials to grip us, the law-and-order television shows provide a close substitute.

The Three Types of Persons Generally Charged with Crimes

Three types of persons are arrested and charged with crimes every day in the United States. If you, like many people, get most of your information about America's criminal justice system from television shows, you know about the first two of these types. These first two types are the ones most of us think of as criminals. I call these two types the "unsuccessful criminal" and the "successful criminal."

The unsuccessful criminal commits small-time crimes on a regular basis. This person is repeatedly in and out of jail and prison for crimes ranging from basic drug charges to simple assaults and crimes of random violence to petty theft and property damage. He or she may be a repeat offender with a long list of purse-snatching charges, or someone with a history of domestic violence and aggravated stalking, or a small-time drug dealer with multiple arrests for selling small amounts of methamphetamine, marijuana, or crack cocaine.

Although I am generalizing somewhat, my experience as a criminal defense lawyer has led me to see three basic trends with the unsuccessful criminal. First, this person often has a severe substance abuse problem, such as an addiction to drugs and/or alcohol, and may also have other mental health problems. Second, the unsuccessful criminal is an opportunist when it comes to committing crimes: if this person sees a chance to commit a crime, he or she will do so, usually in order to get money or property to exchange for drugs, alcohol, food, or shelter. Third, the unsuccessful criminal is usually alone—having long since alienated family and friends, who were usually this person's first victims, stolen from to support an addiction or physically and mentally abused as a mental health problem spun out of control. The unsuccessful criminal is penniless, not only due to spending a lot of the time in jail, but also because he or she has become largely unemployable in normal society and spends whatever money becomes available on feeding an addiction. In fact, this person's family and friends may be glad to see their loved one in jail where he or she can at least "stay off the streets" and maybe get some help.

Unsuccessful criminals almost never retain the services of a private attorney. Public defenders usually end up representing these people for the simple reason that they have few financial means and cannot rely on family or friends to help out. The unsuccessful criminal is the person whose computerized "rap sheet" of prior convictions is so long that the prosecutor has to stretch it all the way across the courtroom table in order to read it to the judge. The unsuccessful criminal is that scary person hanging around the street corner, emerging from the back alley, or sitting aimlessly on the subway car with too much time on his or her hands. This is one of the two "criminal types" that we, the general public, think of when we ask ourselves the question, "What does a criminal look like?" They are the types often featured on the law-and-order television shows.

The most ironic aspect of the profile of most true unsuccessful criminals is that many were once good, decent, law-abiding citizens. Although some of the people in this category certainly started committing crimes at a very early age, many others had jobs and families and stable lives before ending up in the revolving door of the courthouse and the jail. These are folks who simply have never gotten out of the vicious cycle. The unsuccessful criminal typically:

1. suffers some type of addiction or mental illness,
2. gets arrested for the commission of a petty offense due to the illness or addiction and ends up in jail or prison,
3. is ultimately released,
4. does not make it "on the outside," and,
5. eventually repeats the cycle.

Even for those who want to return to mainstream life, it can be very difficult to get out of the clutches of the Beast once they have been arrested, imprisoned, and branded a criminal by society. (We will look at these issues more closely in Part II of this book.)

The second type of person who gets arrested and accused of crimes in America is a type I call the "successful criminal." Successful criminals are big-time drug dealers and persons involved in gang activity, organized crime, or sophisticated fraud. These criminals make up a small minority of total arrests every year, but they inflict a tremendous amount of damage on society and the lives of ordinary people. This is another group that you often see on television. These truly are career criminals, as their daily lives involve working at various illegal activities that often make them substantial sums of money. Organized crime figures are the most notorious examples of this type of criminal.

The "I Can't Believe It Happened to Me" Criminal

The third type of person arrested today is a person like my client Winston. Winston is a successful construction contractor and a member of the Rotary Club. He lives with his wife, Carole, and their three children in a nice suburban community. Carole is a housewife, a soccer mom, and president of the PTA chapter at their daughter's school. Until recently, Winston had never been arrested.

Winston and Carole belong to the local country club. Winston drinks socially at the club, but he is always careful to limit his alcohol intake, especially when he has to drive. He fully believes that "drunks" should be arrested if they are caught driving, and he always votes for the law-and-order candidate who promises to keep the streets safe by "locking the criminals away for good."

One night, Winston stays late at the club. He has had a couple of drinks, but he feels fine when he gets his car from the valet and starts his two-mile drive home. About halfway there, he is surprised to see flashing blue lights in his rearview mirror. He immediately pulls his car over and pulls his insurance card and driver's license from his wallet to have them ready for the officer when he approaches the car.

The police officer politely says good evening and then asks Winston if he realizes he failed to completely stop at the last stop sign. Winston knows he didn't completely stop—heck, nobody does this time of night with no traffic on the road—but he figures he better cooperate with the officer. So he answers truthfully that, yes, he realizes he did not come to a complete stop.

The police officer then politely asks Winston to step out of his vehicle and asks if he has been drinking. Once again, Winston—who is sure he is well under the legal limit—wants to fully cooperate and is sure he has nothing to fear from this very nice and respectful police officer, so he answers, "Yes, I have had a couple of drinks tonight, Officer, but I feel fine." The officer then asks Winston to "please perform some field sobriety tests." Winston, still wishing to fully cooperate, stands on one foot, walks an imaginary straight line, recites the alphabet, and tracks the officer's finger when it moves back and forth across his face.

The officer, who is stern but polite and professional, then asks Winston to blow into a hand-held alcohol-sensing device to determine the level of alcohol in his system. Winston is relieved to discover that he passes the test, "blowing" a .076 when the legal limit is .080. He is ready to get back into his car, wish the officer (who was "only doing his job") a good night, and drive home to bed. He is aghast, therefore, when the officer tells him to turn around, handcuffs him, informs him he is being charged with DUI, and escorts him into the back of the police cruiser. By the time Winston has been hauled down to the local jail, frisked, photographed, fingerprinted, and locked up in a foul-smelling holding cell to wait behind bars for his wife to bail him out, he has reached a state of despair.

Winston was out on bail when he walked through my office door. "I can't believe this happened to me," Winston said as he sat down shakily, nervously rubbing his hands together. "I mean, I can't believe I was arrested!" He took a deep breath and leaned forward in his chair. "Mr. Conaway, you have to understand, I'm not like all your other clients. I'm not a criminal!"

By "criminal," Winston meant, of course, those people who fall into the first two categories that I have described—people who intentionally set out to rob, cheat, or injure others. The rule-breaking, immoral, outside-the-bounds-of-decent-society, up-to-no-good hood who preys upon good, decent, law-abiding citizens like ourselves: this is the picture of "the criminal," which politicians conjure up when they urge us to vote for stricter criminal penalties and more prisons. The stereotypical criminal is someone we all fear—never the person we see in the mirror in the morning or, God help us, sleeping next to us or in our children's bedrooms at night.

I smiled at Winston and handed him a cup of coffee. "The vast majority of my clients are just like you," I said. "They're good, decent, law-abiding citizens who simply made a mistake or got unlucky."

"You mean what happened to me isn't that uncommon?" Winston asked in amazement.

"No," I continued, "it isn't. The truth of the matter is that many law-abiding citizens—folks who have never been in trouble with the law before—get arrested in America each and every month, year in, year out. This just happened to be your time. This is, unfortunately, your rainy day."

The fact is that the vast majority of my clients are people who have never been arrested before. They have no criminal records and have never been in trouble with the law. Or, if they have any records at all, they are for one other minor offense. My clients come from every walk of life. I have represented rich and poor and middle-class people, black and white, Asian and Hispanic, banker and bank teller, lawyer and legal secretary, corporate officer and mailroom clerk, college professor and high school dropout. All have walked through my door over the years, and the great majority had two things in common:

1. they had never been in trouble with the law before; and,
2. they could not believe it had happened to them.

Winston stared back at me earnestly. "But surely I'm the exception. I don't belong in your office. Only *criminals* hire defense lawyers!"

Contrary to the general public's perception, most people who retain my services have no prior arrests. Certainly, the stereotype of the "slick" criminal defense attorney—cynically representing the same core group of criminal characters over and over as a "hired gun"—is one we're all familiar with. On the law-and-order television shows, the criminal defense lawyer is often an oily character representing the worst dregs of society. They pay him in suitcases full of cash to "get them off the hook," and the lawyer spends his fees on designer shoes and Italian silk suits. So, when a new client like Winston walks in through my door, he is always shocked to learn that he—the good, decent, law-abiding citizen—is representative of my normal clients, and that my clientele is not a bunch of career criminals with their pockets stuffed full of ill-gotten gains. (I don't wear Italian suits or designer shoes, either!)

"I know," I finally said to Winston. "That's what everybody says who walks through my door. They can't believe it happened to them. But it did. So it's time to stop putting labels on yourself: you are not a criminal. You were, however, arrested and accused of a crime. We have to deal with that fact and prepare your defense."

By the time he left my office, Winston was still distressed, but at least his eyes had been opened. His shock was not unusual. For many people who find themselves under arrest, black is now white, day has turned into night, and the sun is no longer rising in the east and setting in the west. The same person who always clucked along with the law-and-order talk-radio types who were screaming about criminals getting away scot-free and the need for tougher laws to lock every one of them up—yes, indeed, the same person who nodded faithfully along whenever his local politician started preaching about the need for more jails and more prisons to lock away all those criminals roaming the streets of his suburban subdivision, ready to pounce on him and his family at a moment's notice—all of a sudden finds himself out on bail, charged with a crime, and trying to figure out how this all could ever have happened to him. I'm here to tell him: it happens all the time.

The Good, Decent, Law-Abiding Citizen Under Arrest

People like Winston who are law-abiding citizens make up many of the persons arrested and accused of crimes in America today. The television shows don't often depict people in trouble with the law for the first time. Hardened criminals make for better ratings.

I wrote this book mainly for people like Winston. These are folks who have no—or very little—prior experience with the criminal justice system. They work, go to school, raise families, pay taxes, and strive to obey the law in their normal, everyday lives. They are, in short, you and me and the vast majority of the people living in America today. The good, decent, law-abiding citizen who gets arrested usually ends up in my office because he or she makes a series of bad decisions, which lead to a personal crisis that ultimately leads to another really bad choice, landing him or her in trouble with the law.

In fact, if there is one common element in all of my clients' cases, it is chaos. My clients are in trouble with the law because their lives have spun out of control for one reason or another and they ended up doing something really stupid. This is not to say that some of my clients did not do what they are accused of doing. But even the wrongly accused typically put themselves in a bad situation by making a choice that they normally would not have made. Maybe, like Winston, they had too much to drink one night before driving home, even though they were usually careful about drinking and driving. Or they took a swing at their wives because things had heated up at the office. Or they pocketed a few bucks from the cash register at work because their kids' medicine was expensive and the rent was due.

The difference between a good, decent, law-abiding citizen who is arrested and charged with a crime and a criminal is that the former makes a bad choice (or series of choices) that are contrary to his ordinary character and lifestyle, while the latter chooses to engage in criminal activity on a regular basis in day-to-day life. In our society, it is the latter (the criminal) who gets all the headlines and media attention, but it is the former (the law-abiding citizen) who gets arrested much of the time.

There are at least two other factors, beyond making bad personal decisions, that contribute to the arrests of so many good, decent, law-abiding citizens today. The first of these factors involves the general expansion of what constitutes "criminal behavior" in American society. Our state and federal legislatures have broadened the definition of criminal behavior by both creating new laws and expanding the scope of existing laws. With tougher laws relating to everything from DUI to domestic violence, shoplifting to stalking, embezzlement to Internet crimes, it's a lot easier to get arrested today than it was twenty or thirty years ago.

The second factor that is leading to the arrests of so many people is the widespread public policy of "zero tolerance." This policy often limits a police officer's discretion as to whether or not to make an arrest at the end of a criminal investigation—even when the results of the investigation are inconclusive, at best. Zero tolerance operates in police stations, courtrooms, workplaces, retail stores, schools, and just about every other nook and cranny of our society, as I will explain in Part II of this book.

These two factors—the expansion of criminal laws and the rise of zero-tolerance policies—mean that the margin of error for the citizen trying to navigate his or her way through the rules and regulations of American life today is much slimmer than it used to be. These two factors—combined with the bad choices people make in the midst of a period of personal crisis—are usually the reasons why so many good, decent, law-abiding citizens are finding themselves ensnared by the Beast.

Another factor is, of course, just plain bad luck and being wrongfully accused without having done anything stupid to begin with. Although this happens—much more often than it should—it accounts for a minority of the clients that I deal with. Even in these circumstances, however, a better understanding of how America's criminal justice system works might very well have saved these clients from getting into a situation where "bad luck prevailed" and they were wrongfully arrested in the first place.

Good, decent, law-abiding citizens make up the vast majority of clients whom I have defended against criminal charges for almost two decades—as well as many of the people arrested in America today. Year in and year out, the trend continues. My typical client is not the greasy, rag-tag, petty thief who breaks into cars and houses; nor is he the big-time successful crook, his pockets bulging with loot. Nope, not at all. My typical client looks just like most everybody else—us—and not "them," the low-down, no-good criminals the politicians and television shows would have you believe are committing all the crimes in this country.

CHAPTER TWO

IN THE BELLY OF THE BEAST—POLICE, PROSECUTORS, JUDGES, AND DEFENSE LAWYERS

Why do I compare America's criminal justice system to a beast? For anyone who has ever been scooped up in its giant paws; for anyone who has ever had their rights, freedom, and reputation trampled; for anyone who has ever looked into the red-rimmed eyes and the snarling mouth of "criminal justice"; for anyone who has spent even an hour or two in a stinking, windowless, barricaded county jail holding cell; for anyone who has ever had their hands pulled behind them by a uniformed, gun-toting government official, been manacled with stainless steel handcuffs, then been stuffed like a helpless animal into the caged and sealed back of a police cruiser; in short, for anyone who has ever been arrested for any reason and had to do business with America's criminal justice system as the accused, I am sure the nickname "the Beast," makes absolute sense.

For everyone else, it is my way of describing, as succinctly as possible, the vast complex of government institutions, state and federal bureaucracies, private contractors, corporations, politicians, news media, lawyers, and public interest groups that make up America's criminal justice system. In this chapter, we will look at some of the key players in this system so that you, the reader, can begin to have a full understanding of how America's criminal justice system really works. Once we get a clear picture of how the system operates, we can take a look at how best to do battle with the

Beast. Let's take a closer look at what the Beast looks like by examining some of its essential players: police, prosecutors, judges, and defense lawyers.

Police and Prosecutors on Television

The vast majority of Americans think of the criminal justice system as consisting of two basic groups of people. First, the police—the men and women who work at the police station, carry guns and badges, drive around in cars with sirens, investigate crimes, and arrest criminals—and second, the lawyers: the prosecutors and defense lawyers who spend their days in courtrooms trying cases in front of juries.

The police and prosecutors, in most Americans' minds today, are the good guys. Passionate defenders of justice and protectors of innocent victims, they zealously put criminals in jail. In the minds of the vast majority of the TV-watching public, the police "wear the white hats" and protect ordinary people from the riff-raff. Prosecutors are the white knights of the courtroom, standing tall against packs of snarling, vicious criminals and their slick, oily defense lawyers.

This simplistic and fanciful way of looking at America's criminal justice system is, of course, largely based upon what people see on television. Most crime dramas center on the police who are investigating the crimes or the prosecutors who are trying the cases. In these shows, the prosecutors are routinely engaged in dramatic jury trials where the bad guy almost always gets convicted. Over the past ten to fifteen years, and—I would argue—especially since September 11, 2001, television shows featuring heroic prosecutors have become the most popular on television.

Television shows like *Law & Order* depict their police and prosecutors as cardboard cutouts of the stereotypical American hero: square-jawed, fit, confident, organized, and morally virtuous. Often we know almost nothing about their personal lives—they appear simply to emerge from nowhere, well dressed and sporting Hollywood good looks (but not too good; we don't really want our policemen and prosecutors to be sexy), ready to do battle with society's evildoers.

Gone from today's television shows are the rumpled, troubled, nicotine-addicted, sometimes-alcoholic cops and detectives of the 1960s, '70s, and '80s. Gone too are the bumbling, burned-out, or politically motivated prosecutors of yesteryear, who were too tired or cynical or lazy to bother investigating the case and who often prosecuted the wrong person. Television shows from *Perry Mason* to *Columbo*, from *Barney Miller* to *Hill Street Blues*, from *LA Law* and *The Practice* to *NYPD Blue*, all depicted police officers, detectives, and prosecutors as ordinary people—flawed, careworn, sometimes honest, sometimes cynically immoral and corrupt, sometimes brilliant, sometimes inept or, worst, dishonest, in their jobs—but always with an air of reality and imperfection.

In the past ten to fifteen years, this has changed as the police, detectives, and prosecutors on television are more and more often portrayed, night after night, as uniformly perfect. Most actors who play these parts are now young, attractive, well-dressed, blow-dried, flawless supermen and superwomen of justice who, with an almost mechanical, scientific precision, track down evildoers and protect all of us good, decent, law-abiding citizens from "them"—the criminals.

So, when average law-abiding citizens are being questioned by the police or standing in a criminal courtroom in America, accused of committing a crime, their understanding of the system—shaped by endless hours of pro-police and pro-prosecution movies and television—is almost always dangerously incomplete and inaccurate. Consequently, they blunder around the Beast with blinders on, unaware of the dangers to their life and liberty until it is too late.

Police and Prosecutors: In the Real World, They Are Your Adversaries

In order to get a better understanding of what the Beast really looks like, we need to take our blinders off, stand back, and take a hard look at those persons and institutions that operate in the belly of the Beast: the police and the prosecutors.

The average person's first encounter with the Beast is through the local or state police. These government employees, along with the Federal

Bureau of Investigation (FBI) and other federal law enforcement officers (and state and federal prosecutors), routinely investigate crimes and work within America's criminal courts resolving cases. The police and prosecutors are the groups that we, the voters and citizens represented by our local, state, and federal governments, have empowered with the responsibility to investigate, prosecute, punish, and prevent crime in our country.

I am going to now repeat those four key words: **investigate**, **prosecute**, **punish**, and **prevent**. None of those words says anything about "defending." The police and prosecutors are responsible for investigating crimes, and then prosecuting and punishing those persons they believe have committed the crimes being investigated. This is the only job of the police and prosecutors. The last of the four duties, to prevent crime, is achieved by doing the first three. Ask any prosecutors or police officers, and they will tell you that they prevent crime by investigating, prosecuting, and punishing criminals. This is not a bad thing; it is their job. The police and prosecutors of America have some of the toughest jobs in our country, and we, through our laws, have entrusted these men and women to handle those very important responsibilities.

What this means for you, however, as a good, decent, law-abiding citizen, is that if you find yourself in the middle of a police investigation or accused of a crime, these people—police and prosecutors alike—will be your adversaries. This is true whether you are simply being questioned about a crime as part of a police investigation or you are arrested and accused of a crime and have to go to court to defend yourself against the charges. Why are the police and prosecutors your adversaries? Because America's criminal justice system is an **adversarial system**. So the police and prosecutors are your adversaries but not because they are mean or corrupt or simply don't like you. They are your adversaries because the entire system is set up to be that way, and the police and prosecutors are simply doing their jobs.

What is an "adversary?" *Oxford English Dictionary* defines an adversary as "an opponent, an enemy." Related to the word adversary is *adversity*, which *Oxford Dictionary* defines as "misfortune or trouble." The related adjective is *adverse*, which is defined as "unfavorable, bringing misfortune or harm." Obviously, none of these "adversarial" things are good for you. Most of us don't go walking through life hoping to have trouble, harm, and misfortune rain down upon us from our enemies or opponents. Yet when most of us are approached by a member of the police force—whether by a uniformed officer or a plain-clothes detective—and the officer or detective flashes a badge and says, "Excuse me, sir, but I want you to answer a few questions for me," we almost always start talking right away, dutifully answering all of the police officer's potentially adversarial questions.

Police Questioning: Just Say "No"

Just why is it that most good, decent, law-abiding citizens immediately begin cooperating with a government official flashing a badge or dressed in uniform, who is their adversary by operation of law? Why do these citizens begin spouting whatever that government law enforcement official wants to hear without consulting a lawyer first, when it is their constitutional right to remain silent and immediately obtain an attorney? Most people in this situation simply can't get it through their heads that the government official with the badge standing before them and asking them "just a few questions, sir" always—no matter how informal and friendly the official may seem (or formal and unfriendly, for that matter)—is their adversary from the moment he approaches them. So if it happens to you, don't take it personally—remember: the officer is just doing his or her job. Then wake up, get a clue, and ask for a lawyer before you answer a single question!

If you are a typical good, decent, law-abiding citizen, you are probably thinking to yourself just about now: "Yes . . . but . . . ." If you are, your thoughts are the same as those of many of my clients when they have been questioned by the police, just before they provided immediate answers to the officer's inquiries, and not long before they have found themselves arrested, handcuffed, and thrown into a holding cell down at the local jail. The "Yes . . . but . . ." reasoning goes basically like this:

"**Yes**, I know this police officer is asking me questions and I have a right to a lawyer, **but** I think I should go ahead and cooperate and answer his questions right now, because I am a good, decent, law-abiding citizen and have nothing to hide. Only criminals have to fear the police. I am not a criminal, so I have nothing to fear."

When they eventually wind up in my office, I inevitably ask these clients why they talked to the police. They always say, "But, Mr. Conaway, I thought it was the right thing to do. Yes, I know I shouldn't have talked to the police without a lawyer, but . . . etc., etc."

Well, you get the idea.

Let me ask you something. If you suddenly found yourself in a boxing ring against a prizefighter, you wouldn't just stand there and smile while your opponent beat you to a bloody pulp, would you? Or, to take another example, what would you think if you went to see your favorite football team play and your team's quarterback was being rushed by the opposing team's snarling, swearing, 300-pound defensive linemen, and instead of scrambling out of the way or throwing the football downfield, your team's quarterback just stood there, held onto the ball, and let himself be sacked and smashed into the turf? Wouldn't you think he was nuts? Wouldn't you boo and jeer him off the field?

Imagine an Olympic sprinter who, at the start of the 100-meter race, smiled and cooperated with the other runners by letting them race ahead of him and cross the finish line first. Wouldn't you think he was about the sorriest runner you had ever seen? What would you think of a soldier who, when fired upon by the enemy, just stood up and let himself be shot in the head without firing a shot back? Would you want to go into battle alongside such a dim-witted soldier with no sense of common self-preservation?

So what do you think of a good, decent, law-abiding citizen who is approached by the police and is asked to "just answer a few questions" and immediately starts blabbing away, telling the police everything they want to hear and answering all of their questions without first speaking with a lawyer?

Now that you understand that the approaching officer is that citizen's adversary, wouldn't you consider the person who chooses to answer those questions without advice of legal counsel to be utterly insane and lacking even a shred of self-preservation?

And this is, of course, where we get back to the old "Yes . . . but . . ." response. Take Martha, for example. Martha is a bookkeeper who gave in to the temptation to steal some money from the petty cash account at work to pay her overdue bills. When Martha's employer discovered $525 missing from the account, he called the police. A police officer arrived unannounced at the company's office and started questioning everyone.

Martha was afraid that she would look guilty if she did not talk to the police, so she spoke with the detective when he approached her. The detective was nice at first and told her she simply needed to answer some routine questions. She did not ask to speak with a lawyer first—instead she just started answering his questions. The detective, who was trained at questioning people, soon saw that Martha was nervous and hedging her answers and so the detective began to bore into her aggressively. After a few minutes of this treatment, Martha admitted to the theft and signed a full confession.

The police officer arrested Martha and took her to jail. When she finally consulted a lawyer (let's call him Mr. Jones), she explained, "Yes, I know I shouldn't have talked to the policeman, but I was afraid he would think I was guilty." At that point, there was little Mr. Jones could do to help Martha. She ended up losing her job under her employer's policy of zero tolerance for crime. With a felony conviction on her record, she had little hope of ever working as a bookkeeper again. A mistake she made in her twenties would haunt her for the rest of her natural working life. And, of course, she faced possible jail or prison time and lengthy supervised probation, fines, and community service work involving tasks such as picking up trash in a prison uniform on the side of the highway or working in a recycling factory.

What if Martha had talked to a lawyer before talking to the police? It turned out the police did not have any other evidence against her aside from her confession, so she might never have been charged at all. If she had wanted to confess and make amends for what she did, she still could have done it, but with a lawyer's help the consequences would probably have been less catastrophic for her. For example, the lawyer might have been able to negotiate an arrangement with the employer to let her repay the money and—although she probably still would have lost her job—she might have avoided a criminal conviction.

The root of the problem is not that most people are crazy or self-destructive, but rather that they have a hard time seeing any police officer as an adversary. Approached by a badge-carrying government agent, most people want to believe that the government agent is on their side, that they are "on the same team," so to speak, and as long as they cooperate, the government agent will remain on their side. The police play this up by being friendly at first, and then turning ugly if you refuse to answer their questions. They may make vague threats like, "You better start cooperating now, or it will be hard on you later." Or, "Well, sir, if you don't answer my questions now, we can do so down at the station." Or, "You better talk now while I can help you, or I'll have to get a warrant for your arrest."

Most Americans don't want to see the police in the role of adversary because they have too much emotional and psychological investment in the concept of the police as their protectors. We are taught to think this way from grade school on up through all types of overt and implied messages put out by our schools, politicians, and community leaders. Remember the friendly uniformed police officer who came to your elementary school classroom when you were a kid? Remember how you got to play with the smiling officer's hat while he talked about growing up to be a "good, decent, upstanding citizen" by always cooperating with the police? Such public relations efforts are constantly around us in our communities. The police, we are told, are not our adversaries but our friends and our protectors; they keep us safe from the criminals.

This image is reinforced over and over again in our media, especially on television. In countless television shows, the police and prosecutors are portrayed as the good guys who are on our side and are there to protect us from harm. When we watch these shows, we quite naturally put ourselves in the shoes of the victim, not the slimeball criminal whom we are all rooting against.

We are taught from an early age that the police are there to protect us. Indeed, many police cruisers in this country are emblazoned with the motto that we all know so well: "to protect and serve."

Generally, of course, this is true. The police are there to protect and serve you, me, and everybody else in the community. It is tough, dangerous work at times, and all of us owe a large measure of gratitude and respect to those men and women who work to prevent crime in our communities.

The problem arises when you, the good, decent, law-abiding citizen, become a target of the police. This can be in a situation as simple as being stopped for speeding or as complex as being questioned as part of a major criminal investigation. Point number one to remember is that whenever a police officer, detective, or other government agent approaches you and wants to ask you a question, that person is conducting an investigation and is, by law, your adversary.

OK, in case that flew right in one ear and out the other, I will repeat it: **whenever a police officer or detective approaches you and starts asking you any questions, that person is conducting a police investigation**. Did that sink in the second time around?

Don't agree with me? OK, fine. Ask yourself: When was the last time a police officer stopped to ask you questions when it did not involve the commission of some type of breach of the law? Has a police officer ever stopped you on the side of the road just to say hi? Or has a police detective ever knocked on your door to deliver a few home-baked cookies his wife made that morning? Or has an FBI agent stopped by your job anytime recently to discuss whether the local college team was going to win the division that year? My guess is that they probably have not. Why do I know this? Because, by law, government agents are not allowed to detain you unless either they have probable cause that a crime has taken or may be taking place or, under some very specific exceptions, they are detaining the general public briefly for purposes of maintaining public safety. (The police roadblock is probably the best example of this type of exception.)

So now that I have persuaded you (I hope) of point number one, let's look at basic point number two: anyone being questioned by the police as part of a criminal investigation is automatically a potential witness *and* a potential suspect. Did that second part stick? Let me repeat it: **anyone being questioned by the police as part of a criminal investigation is automatically both a potential witness *and* a potential suspect**. If you put point one and point two together, the message is clear: **anyone being questioned by the police is automatically a potential witness and a potential suspect *in a criminal investigation***. What does this mean? It means that whenever any police officer or detective approaches you and starts asking you questions, he or she is your adversary. That's right: you've got it! That officer is your adversary, your opponent, your enemy—he or she is there with the potential to do you harm and to bring misfortune down upon you and your family.

One reason people have such a hard time seeing the criminal justice system as truly adversarial is that we live in a world that so heavily emphasizes the idea that all values are relative and that there is always a way to "work things out." This idea underlies much of American society. It helps explain the popularity of mediation and "alternative dispute resolution"—the idea being that if you get people with competing interests together in the same room and give them long enough to talk a problem out, they can always come up with a solution where "everybody wins." Nations today are urged not to go to war but to settle their disputes diplomatically. Many people believe that war should never be necessary because nations should always be able to work out their differences.

But America's adversarial criminal justice system is based on a very old approach. It was set up in the eighteenth century by our founding fathers, who borrowed centuries-old Anglo-Saxon legal concepts dating back to medieval England. Our entire criminal justice system is based upon the old-fashioned concept that the best results in a criminal justice system—truth and justice—come out through pure conflict. Hence, whenever the police question you, you are, quite literally, in a state of conflict with them. They are your adversaries from the moment they pull you over to the side of the road, knock on your door, or call you on the phone.

The adversarial system of criminal justice is, in fact, part of the philosophical bedrock of our American republic, serving as a bulwark against government tyranny while promoting a free and open society. Better a determination of guilt or innocence as a result of conflict in open court than a pronouncement of the king's henchmen in secret session.

It is to his or her dismay, nevertheless, that the good, decent, law-abiding citizen becomes enmeshed in an ancient system of justice created by men from centuries before who believed that conflict was the best way to find truth and justice. Conflict, battle, yes, *war*, was in the minds of the creators of our criminal justice system. They believed the best way for the police, the prosecutors and the defense lawyers, and, ultimately, the judges and the juries, to find truth and administer justice was to have the two opposing sides—the police and prosecutors on one side and the accused citizen and his lawyer on the other—fight it out in a court of law. No willy-nilly, namby-pamby, "why can't we all just get along and cooperate with each other?" kind of reasoning here. Instead, when you are a private citizen being questioned by a police officer you must realize that the officer is your adversary as legally defined under the rules of the Beast.

A Look at the Prosecutor

Let's assume, for argument's sake, that you have been arrested. You have been questioned by the police, handcuffed, thrown in jail, accused of a crime, and ordered to appear in court. What are you in for? What will the prosecutor be like? You know, that guy or gal who "rides in on a white horse" and puts away all those nasty criminals night after night on your favorite TV show? Certainly, the prosecutor will understand that you are a good, decent, law-abiding citizen and not a criminal. Even if that mean police detective who arrested you didn't see your side of the matter, surely the prosecutor will set things right.

If you are thinking this, then I'm sorry to bring you a little further into the real world, but—guess what—you are wrong! The prosecutor is not your friend, either. He or she—that fine, upstanding person you root for on TV and now see standing before you when you walk into the courtroom as a criminal defendant—is your adversary. Once you step into that courtroom, you are in what I like to call "the Belly of the Beast," and the prosecutor, by rule of law, is your adversary. Just like the police officer who "just had a few questions" and then proceeded to handcuff you and throw you in jail, the well-dressed, articulate man or woman taking the lead in the courtroom proceedings does not represent you or your interests, either. Prosecutors represent the state. They are not on your side. Is this because they are bad people? Is it because they are cold and mean? Is it because their shoes are too tight? No. It simply means that their job within the criminal justice system is to be your adversary from the moment you walk into a courtroom accused of a crime.

Prosecutors do this job professionally and objectively. They represent the State—or, more formally, "the People of the state" (in federal court, "the People of the United States"). You, the criminal defendant, are the prosecutor's sworn adversary. Prosecutors do not care about you, your family, your friends, or your future. They have taken an oath under the law to be your opponent in the courtroom and—provided they believe that they have evidence against you—to do battle and emerge victorious against you, regardless of the personal cost to you or your family or friends. Prosecutors take their oaths very, very seriously, and they will prosecute you—the accused—to the greatest extent possible under the law, regardless of the impact this has on your own life, liberty, and future. Again, don't take it personally. They are just doing their job.

Judges Are Human, Too

Now let's take a look at the judge. Patient, righteous, just, and fair—that is how we like to think of the judges who sit in America's criminal courtrooms. The judge enters the courtroom with an announcement from the bailiff, who cries out, "All rise, this court is now in session, the Honorable I. M. Justice presiding." Then a man or woman dressed in a long black robe enters the courtroom, usually from a back door behind the judge's bench. The judge sits down in a big, leather, high-backed chair and commands in a stern voice, "Be seated, everyone."

The judges in most American courtrooms sit up several feet higher than everyone else in the court, usually behind a big mahogany desk called a "bench." The visual and physical effect of this is to place the judge, with the black robe and the big chair, in a lofty position, high above and in a superior physical position vis-à-vis everyone else in the courtroom. As a lawyer, when you "approach the bench" (which you only do after asking for and receiving permission to do so from the judge), the visual effect is one of looking up at a man or woman who is staring down at you from over a big, high, wooden desk. The effect is similar to being in the first grade and having the teacher tower over you from behind her desk in the classroom—or even worse, the principal, if you ever had the misfortune to end up in his or her office. I have had clients literally start shaking the moment the judge entered the courtroom, so awe-inspiring and magisterial is the visual and auditory effect upon the simple citizen who has been ordered to appear in court and now, cowed and chastised, watches this billowing-black-robed authoritarian figure glowering down from behind a mahogany desk way up on high.

This effect of the judge's total dominance and superiority over everyone else in the courtroom is, of course, intentional. The visual effect simply reflects the position the judge is in. A first-year law professor of mine at Emory University told our class that judges are, in essence, the last true dictators of the Western world. The key thing to remember when entering a courtroom is this: the judge is in charge, period, end of story—and "game over" if you fail to remember and respect this basic truth.

I have had clients deeply resent this fact or, even worse, not take it seriously. In our modern American world, there aren't many situations in our day-to-day life where we come up against the type of traditional values that are still firmly in place in courtrooms all over the land. Americans tend to think of everyone as being on equal footing in their everyday lives. Everything is casual. Many corporate employers promote an atmosphere of equality and informality in dress and interactions among their employees. Men wear khaki pants and polo shirts—or even jeans and T-shirts—instead of suits and ties to the office. Women no longer wear suits or pantyhose. Corporate interaction is casual—bosses and employees are generally on a first-name basis. Under today's corporate approach, everyone has a say in the decision process. Corporate decisions are reached "by consensus," in a world where "everyone has an equal voice" and "we're all a team." These are the types of messages most people are used to hearing at work in today's America.

This kind of modern American thinking is a type of cultural relativism that seeks to remove barriers between people in traditional formal settings such as the workplace or school. But this lack of formality causes problems for Americans when they walk into a modern American courtroom. As I explained earlier, the courtroom still operates with all the formality and hierarchy that it had in the eighteenth and nineteenth centuries. The average American workplace today may thrive on a first-name-basis, everyone-dressed-in-blue-jeans kind of informality. The American courtroom, I can assure you, does not.

As a practicing attorney, for example, I would never think of entering a courtroom unless I was wearing a full suit and tie. I remember one hot summer day when the air conditioner died in a courtroom in Atlanta in which I was arguing a case. The temperature became overwhelmingly hot very quickly, yet none of us lawyers ever thought to remove our jackets or loosen our ties—or even to ask permission from the judge to do so. This would have been tantamount to heresy, as one simply never takes off a jacket or loosens a tie in a court of law. Doing so would be looked upon as a sign of disrespect to the court, to the judge, and to the entire legal process. The judge finally ordered all of us lawyers in the courtroom to "remove [our] jackets," which we did with great relief, but only after receiving express permission from the judge.

This is an example of the level of formality that still exists in American courtrooms. Outside America's courtrooms, it may be the second decade of the twenty-first century, but inside America's courtrooms the clock has stopped somewhere between Thomas Jefferson and Dwight D. Eisenhower. This is a critical piece of information for folks to understand when they attend court. I always tell my teen and twenty-something clients to speak with a grandparent—if they have one living—to get a sense of how important proper dress and proper formal manners are when walking into a courtroom and addressing a judge.

In our legal process, the judges are at the top of this formal, rigid, hierarchical system. They are placed in full power and authority in the courtroom. It is *the judge's* courtroom. They have the full power of the law behind them. They are the ones who will apply the law in each case, and they can put anyone in jail. This is the first thing to remember about judges. You need to respect the position they are in and the power they hold over you and your fate.

As well as to offer an air of formality to the proceedings, the judges also sit above the other parties because they are supposed to be impartial. They are like the referees in a tennis match. The prosecutor and the defense attorney are adversaries, on opposite sides of the net, so to speak, and the judge sits in the middle of the court in a raised chair high above the two sides. The referee's job is to make sure the playing field is even and the contest fair between the two opposing sides. As a referee, then, what the judge says stands, and if you don't follow the rules of his court you can end up thrown out of the game—except that instead of being tossed off of a tennis court and into the dressing room, you end up tossed out of the court of law and into jail after being held "in contempt of court" by the judge.

The ideal vision of the courtroom, of course, is that the judge will be the perfect referee. The judge is a dictator, yes, but hopefully a fair, kind, and wise man or woman who will understand your "side of things" and will make a decision favorable to you—or at least one that is fair. Most judges do work hard and do their best to render justice fairly. They often have years and years of experience and they take their jobs deeply seriously.

At the same time, however, judges are people, too. They are subject to all of the same pressures and stresses and biases the rest of us have. They are also, despite all of their endowed judicial authority, not entirely in charge of how they make decisions on a particular criminal case—or what sentence they are able to hand down against a person accused of a particular crime. They may look omnipotent sitting up there on their raised platforms, clad in black, but they are also under a variety of outside pressures and restraints from groups and individuals that seek to influence how they make their decisions, as well as how much latitude they have when reaching a decision as to what the "just and fair" outcome in a particular person's criminal case should be. When I walk into a courtroom and look up at the judge seated on the bench, I see more than just a man or woman sitting alone in the big leather chair behind the bench. I see all of the special interest groups and other political and social forces that are doing their utmost *outside* the courtroom to bring legal and/or political pressure to bear on the judge to lead him or her to decide criminal cases in a particular way.

Judges are under a lot of political pressure. Many judges are elected, and to keep their jobs they need to deliver what the voting public wants. In today's local elections—in which usually only a small percentage of the general public votes—that often means satisfying the goals of special interest political groups or powerful grassroots lobbying organizations that deliver predictable and large blocks of votes in local elections. Many of these groups actually "grade" judges to make sure they are "tough on crime," or at least tough on the particular type of crime that is the focus of that interest group. In today's law-and-order society, that means these groups are looking for more convictions and harsher sentences, and woe to the judge who does not deliver a steady number of convictions in a criminal courtroom. The law-and-order watchdog groups are doing just that—watching; and they will vote out of office, quicker than you can say "due process," any judge foolish enough not to toe their particular political line. These special interest groups aim to stamp out a variety of social ills such as drunk driving, domestic violence, white-collar fraud, child pornography, and illegal drug use. These goals are, of course, perfectly laudable; however, these groups also have a tremendous impact upon the way judges make decisions in our courtrooms.

Other groups that have worked hard to restrict the power of judges in their own courtrooms are our state and federal legislative bodies. Within the past generation, judicial discretion—the power of our judges to make independent decisions on a case-by-case basis—has been greatly restricted by Congress and by state legislatures. In today's American courtrooms, the judge's hands are often tied by zero-tolerance policies and mandatory sentencing laws that limit their discretion when it comes to ruling on any case, deciding what the sentence will be, or deciding whether certain charges should be dismissed or taken to trial. State and federal politicians know that law-and-order politics in the form of tougher sentences, mandatory minimum sentencing, and zero-tolerance policies are popular with voters—and especially with those special interest groups whose members actually vote in local elections. Thus, in each annual legislative session both in Congress and in our state legislatures across the land, there can be heard politicians standing up and calling for new ways of eradicating or restricting judicial discretion, thus limiting the amount and scope of our judges' power to make independent decisions in individual cases.

When I see a judge sitting in an American courtroom, I also see a man or woman who is overworked—inundated with cases—of which yours would be only one on a long list. The watchdog special interest groups grade judges in part on their "judicial economy," which means how fast they "move their case loads." This pressures judges to make judgments quickly and to use the resources of the court economically. The judge may be the dictator of the court, but it is the taxpayers who are footing the bill for its operation, and as the old saying goes, "time is money."

Finally, judges are just plain human. The day you come to court, the judge may not be prepared to focus all of his or her attention on your special case. He may be worried about paying his kid's college tuition bill. She may be worrying about her court docket getting too overloaded with new cases. He may be fretting about his upcoming election. Maybe a week earlier he got a bad "report card" from one of those special interest groups warning him to "get tough on crime," or maybe he faces a well-funded political opponent at the next election. She may be thinking that her robes are itchy.

The problem for you, the good, decent, law-abiding citizen in court because you have been accused of a crime, is that once the judge rules on your case, he or she is moving on to the next case, while you may be headed to jail. So remember, when you walk into an American courtroom—the Belly of the Beast—don't be so foolish as to believe that you will be able to rely on the judge's good graces to get you "off the hook." Don't expect the judge to show you mercy just because he or she likes you and believes you are not a criminal. In today's American courtroom, behaving in this way is like, well, a blind man walking up to a wild elephant and relying on the elephant not to crush the life out of him. The elephant may not mean to do it, but, hey, as the saying goes, it may just be "the nature of the beast."

Criminal Defense Lawyers

So now that we have looked at the role of the police, prosecutors, and judges in the courtroom, it is time to look at the last set of major courtroom players—the defense lawyers. You know, those slick, dastardly, Italian-suit-wearing, Porsche-driving villains of so many courtroom television and movie dramas. In many people's minds, criminal defense lawyers are the worst characters in America's courtrooms.

I do not agree with this assessment, of course. I am very proud of my work and the role we defense lawyers play in America's criminal justice system. As I see it, being a criminal defense lawyer is one if the most difficult and *noble* jobs in America. We defend the rights and liberties of persons accused of crimes, and by doing so protect the constitutional rights and liberties of all Americans. Beyond this, defense lawyers work hard to keep people from being convicted of crimes and to keep them out of jail and prison. There is nothing more tragic than when someone is convicted of a crime or goes to prison or jail. Yes, there are times when people have broken the law and there is no alternative for them other than a criminal conviction and period of incarceration, but it represents a tragedy, nonetheless.

We maintain law and order and protect our personal safety, property, and wealth by arresting people who break the law and throwing them into cages. This we call justice. At times, it may be necessary and even *just*—that is, based upon how we define justice at the beginning of the twenty-first century. This does not mean throwing people in jail or prison is not harsh. (If you don't agree, go visit your local jail or, even better, a state or federal prison.) But these conditions are not exactly surprising. I mean, would you want prison or jail to *not* be harsh? After all, that's the point of putting someone in jail or prison—punishment. But our jails and prisons should be safe, and, unfortunately, many are not.

I do not have an alternative to imprisonment to propose for those convicted of the most serious of crimes. But whenever we arrest someone, convict him, brand him a criminal, take away his freedom, and put him in a steel cage, a human tragedy occurs. We justify it by saying that it is "justice" and that the person who did the crime must "do the time." It is his fault he is in prison, because he committed the act that put him there. But even if we accept this rationale as truth, it is still a tragedy. When we put criminals in prison, we—as a society—essentially give up on them. Whatever they have done, the court or the legislature has determined it was so bad that we have no other alternative than to put them in prison or, in the most extreme and heinous cases, kill them. That may very well be so, at least at this point in human history. But in a system that puts people in prison and then calls it justice, the defense lawyer is the last line of defense for the individual who is facing this kind of cruel outcome. I think this is one reason why many people do not like criminal defense lawyers: they want criminals to be punished. The defense lawyer is the last person standing in the way of that outcome.

I believe another reason why many people don't like criminal defense lawyers is that they don't really understand how anyone could do the job of defending someone charged with a serious crime. The most basic answer is that a defense lawyer is *trained* to do it. In the 1970s movie *The Paper Chase*, the professor walks into the courtroom and announces to the first-year students, "You walk in here with a mind full of mush, and you leave here thinking like a lawyer."

What did that law professor mean? What he meant is that lawyers are trained to do their job representing their clients—period. A defense lawyer's job is to zealously defend his or her client within the bounds of the law. That's it, that's the whole job description. So it does not matter what the person did. Defense lawyers set aside their personal feelings and represent their clients. They may not like or admire their clients. They may even truly *dislike* their clients. It does not matter. Prosecutors do the same thing. They may feel sympathy for a particular defendant, but they still do their jobs. As lawyers, both sides are simply trained to put their personal feelings aside and do their jobs.

To illustrate the job of a defense attorney, let's go back to the example of Martha the bookkeeper and Mr. Jones, her lawyer—both of whom we met earlier in this chapter. If you will recall, Martha stole $525 from her employer's safe. Let's assume that Martha did not talk to the detective but instead invoked her right to legal counsel. She hires Mr. Jones and confesses to him confidentially that she stole the $525 from her employer. What does Mr. Jones do? Does he start yelling at her and giving her a lecture on the immorality of stealing money? No. Does he pick up the phone and call the police? No. Does he tell Martha he won't represent her, because he considers it immoral to represent someone who actually committed the crime they are accused of committing? No.

What does Mr. Jones do? He represents Martha, of course. Perhaps he is able to resolve the whole issue by negotiating a deal with her employer that she will pay the money back, no questions asked. Martha has to resign, and she pays back the $525, but—without her confession—the police don't have enough evidence to arrest Martha and charge her with a crime. Martha gets a second chance in life and her employer is made whole. So far, it seems like a fairly good outcome, especially if Martha learns her lesson and doesn't do such a foolish thing again.

OK, now let's change the facts a little bit. Suppose that, instead of stealing $525 dollars, Martha steals $5,000 and gambles it all away during a weekend trip to Las Vegas. Or suppose she steals $500,000 from the company by "cooking the books" and wiring all of the stolen proceeds to an offshore account, then she gets arrested just as she is getting ready to board a plane for Brazil. Even worse, what if Martha, instead of being a bookkeeper, is the CEO of a major corporation and embezzles $500 million from the company pension fund and then does make it to Brazil? The company goes bankrupt over the scandal, and thousands of hardworking employees lose their jobs and retirement pensions due to Martha's theft. Meanwhile, Martha hangs out in Brazil fighting extradition through her lawyer, Mr. Jones, while hanging out by the pool of her multimillion-dollar mansion—all paid for by the stolen pension fund money. Hmm, what do you think of "poor ol' Martha" now?

My guess is you don't like her very much. But guess what? Mr. Jones does exactly the same thing he did in the first example, where Martha was a penniless bookkeeper. He defends her. For Mr. Jones, it does not matter what the facts of the case are. He just keeps doing his job—defending his client, Martha. That's why people have a hard time with criminal defense lawyers. They just keep doing their jobs, regardless of the severity of each particular client's alleged actions. It's just the nature of the Beast.

CHAPTER THREE

GROUPS INFLUENCING THE BEAST: POLITICIANS, SPECIAL INTEREST GROUPS, PLAINTIFF'S LAWYERS, THE PRISON AND CORRECTIONS INDUSTRY, AND THE MEDIA

Aside from the people at the police station and in the courtroom—the police, judges, prosecutors, and defense lawyers—there are numerous other groups, largely unseen and unnoticed by the average citizen, who have an enormous stake in America's criminal justice system. From politicians like district attorneys and state and federal legislators, to special interest groups like Mothers Against Drunk Driving (MADD); from operators and employees of prisons, probation offices, and other members of "the law-and-order industrial complex," to plaintiff's lawyers and the media, these individuals and organizations have their own agendas for how persons accused of crimes should be dealt with. These groups are not in the courtroom when the average American walks into court facing criminal charges. No, these groups operate behind the scenes, working their influence and shaping the laws, punishments, and rules of America's criminal justice system. All of these players, however, have a huge impact on how you—the good, decent, law-abiding citizen—will be treated once you find yourself inside one of America's criminal courtrooms.

This chapter rounds out the picture of the host of influences that are making America's criminal justice system a harsh, intolerant, dangerous place—not only for criminals, but for everyone else as well. Let's take a look at each one of these entities that are working to influence the criminal justice system to make it more and more punitive, merciless, restrictive, and intolerant toward persons accused of crimes—while also working overtime to destroy our most sacred civil rights and liberties as American citizens.

Politicians

District attorneys, state judges, members of Congress, and local public officials all have one thing in common: they are elected to their positions either directly or indirectly. By "directly elected," I mean that they have to run in an election as a politician against other politicians and then win the election in order to get the job to begin with. Then they have to keep winning elections in order to keep their jobs. An example of a directly elected person would be a person who runs for and gets elected as a local district attorney or county judge. By "indirectly elected," I mean that an elected public official "higher up the political food chain" appoints the person to a particular public office. The appointed (or indirectly elected) public official is then beholden to the elected public official for that job. An example of this would be when the president appoints any U.S. attorney.

What does this method of job-filling mean to you if you are accused of a crime? It means the prosecutor in your case—such as the local district attorney or county solicitor or local U.S. attorney—and the state or local judge in your case—must constantly please the voters in order to get elected and stay elected. And the easiest way to get elected is to appear "tough on crime." That's right. The best way for the public officials presiding over your criminal case to stay in office is *not* to show "leniency and mercy" toward you, the person standing in a courtroom accused of a crime. Nope, the best way for them to remain popular with the voters is to be as tough and mean and merci*less* as possible. Yes, indeed, the best thing for them to do for their careers is to prosecute you to the fullest extent of the law and throw your butt in jail for as long a time as they can possibly get away with under that law. Sound harsh? Cruel? Inhumane?

Maybe it is, or maybe not—that is a political debate, which is not what this book is about. This book is simply about telling you, the law-abiding citizen, what America's criminal justice system is really like.

You might ask, "Why is it like this today?" Well, imagine for a moment that you are an average voter in a local election. Suppose you go to one of those local county fairs where they serve funnel cakes and real lemonade (not that powdered stuff loaded with artificial sweetener) and true blueberry pie with vanilla ice cream from the local dairy, and you sit on a metal folding chair in front of an outdoor stage set up in the middle of the fairground on a warm, sunny Sunday afternoon. As you sit there with your wife and children, eating your pie and enjoying the sunny weather, you look and see two local politicians, each dressed in the obligatory blue suit with a white shirt and solid red necktie, with a little plastic American flag pinned to his lapel. They are running for the vacant office of district attorney. Both of them are about to give their speeches explaining why you, the voter, should elect them to be the new DA. Both guys look pretty much the same, neither one of them has a horn growing out of the front of his head or anything, they both have shined shoes and seem reasonably intelligent, so you decide you want to hear what each one of these politicians has to say before you decide which one you will vote for in the next local election.

The first guy stands up, walks over to the microphone at the front of the stage, and after telling everyone in the audience how "proud and happy" he is to have the opportunity "to talk to all you fine people today," and stuff like that, he makes the following statement about how he will perform the job of district attorney if you, the voter, are gracious enough to elect him:

> Ladies and gentlemen, if I am elected to the county office of district attorney, I am going to make sure no innocent person goes to jail and that no one accused of a crime ever has to prove his or her innocence. I will work hard to prosecute crime, but I will adhere to the principle of our founding fathers: better that a hundred

> guilty men go free than one innocent man be convicted of a crime he didn't commit.

After making his speech, the first guy sits down, and there is a smattering of polite applause.

The second guy stands up. After thanking everyone again for being there to listen to him make his speech, he gets down to business and says the following:

> Ladies and gentlemen, if you elect me to the position of your county's district attorney, I will protect you, your home, your community, and, most of all, your children through every means possible under the law from each and every dirty, rotten, low-down criminal who has had the audacity to invade and infest our fair community. I will make sure that every criminal is arrested, prosecuted, and locked up for as long as possible under the law. There is an epidemic of crime in our community, ladies and gentlemen. We face rape and pillage from ruthless criminals. Around every street corner lurks some nefarious evildoer who is out to rape and rob our wives and children. Ladies and gentlemen, I will protect you and your families from these vile, lawless thugs who need to be removed from the streets of our fair city and thrown in prison where they can rot and hopefully die.

The audience erupts in applause. Eureka, the good voters have found their candidate! The applause rises like the roar of an oncoming locomotive, growing stronger and louder. Candidate number two, the self-proclaimed "law-and-order candidate," is rushed off the podium on the shoulders of well-wishers, who carry him away for a big slice of blueberry pie. The law-and-order candidate goes on to win a landslide election and becomes the next district attorney for your county.

Sound crazy? I mean, c'mon, really, which one of these candidates would you vote for? The first may, on some enlightened level, appeal to your sense of idealism concerning democratic government and the protection of civil liberties. The first speech certainly sounds nice. But the speech given by the second candidate, the law-and-order candidate, appeals to what psychologists and psychiatrists like to describe as the reptilian portion of our brains—or, stated more simply, what most of us call "just plain common sense." Whether you call it reptilian reasoning or common sense, it is that cold and calculating part of all of us that is constantly on guard for risks and dangers and looking out for our own survival. It is vitally important to the perpetuation of the human race, and it exists in our brains to keep us safe from harm. It is the part of the brain that senses danger and reflexively chooses the option that will keep us safe.[1]

Politicians are not stupid. They know the best way to get elected is to appeal to our sense of fear and then tell us they are the best ones to protect us from that which scares us. (Home alarm system sales companies know the same thing, which is why there are all the television ads showing shadowy intruders in ski masks, late at night, breaking into houses occupied only by sleeping mothers and their children, who are then saved by the home alarm system.) For most of us, criminals lurking in dark alleys scare the living heck out of us. Thus, in many regions of the country, the law-and-order candidate promising to "get tough on crime" is the one who wins. In today's America, no elected official can be too tough on crime. Protecting people's civil liberties—especially the rights of the criminally accused—is just not a big vote getter for your average local, state, or federal politician.

Thus, if you find yourself or a family member or a friend accused of a crime, you must take into account from the outset that the playing field is not level. The prosecutor is not looking at your case from the point of view that justice must be done and that under no circumstances should an innocent man be convicted—or that a criminal defendant, whether guilty or innocent, must be treated as an individual human being and dealt with mercifully. No, the district attorney sees you as someone who, once arrested, is in all likelihood guilty of whatever you are charged with and, therefore, worthy of being prosecuted and punished. Are the facts of the case close, meaning a jury could easily decide one way or the other? Hmm, maybe your county district attorney will order his associate trial attorney to "throw it up to the jury and see if it sticks." That way, in the event that the defendant is found not guilty at trial, the elected district attorney can turn around and blame his young and inexperienced associate or the muddle-headed jurors or—best of all— that dastardly, no good, overpaid and overdressed villain of the courtroom: the criminal defense lawyer who "got his client off."

Realize, too, that when you find yourself in the unfortunate position of walking into a criminal courtroom as "the accused" and you look at the assistant prosecutor on your case standing at the front of the courtroom, that his or her boss, the district attorney, is standing right there, too, and right behind the DA are the voters. Those voters expect the district attorney to fulfill, to the greatest extent possible, the pre-election promises to get "tough on crime" that he made over the free lemonade and blueberry pie.

The judge sitting up there looking all independent and omnipotent in his or her billowing black robe is usually in a similar situation. The judge didn't get elected by the voters or appointed by the governor by promising the local electorate to always be fair and mindful of the civil liberties and constitutional rights of your criminally accused butt. The district attorney and the judge have gotten their marching orders from their bosses, the voters—prosecute, punish, and incarcerate to the greatest extent possible under the law! And the person they are looking to do it to, oh, ye good, decent, law-abiding citizen now accused of a crime, is you. Hey, you may even have voted for each of them in the last election!

Special Interest Groups

Now let's look at the special interest groups that influence our criminal justice system. What is a "special interest group"? It is a group of citizens who use their constitutionally guaranteed right "peaceably to assemble" to join together and form a political lobbying organization with a specifically stated public policy goal. Political special interest groups work to achieve their goals by raising money to promote public awareness of their causes through the media, by donating and raising money for politicians who promise to promote their public policy goals, and by voting for those politicians on Election Day. Then, once their chosen politicians are elected to public office, the political special interest groups keep tabs on these officials by checking up on how they are performing their jobs.

The National Rifle Association (NRA), for example, works hard to get representatives who will not pass restrictive gun control legislation elected at both the state and national levels, as the NRA's stated public policy goal is to fully maintain the Second Amendment right of all Americans to bear arms. The Sierra Club, which wants to see wind and solar energy replace coal and petroleum as the main energy sources in the United States, works hard to elect public officials who will vote to promote the development of wind and solar energy.

For now, let's focus on what I call law-and-order special interest groups. The general public policy message and mission statement of law-and-order special interest groups is that the criminal justice system is too lenient on criminals and that local, state, and federal officials must vigorously prosecute criminals by passing tougher and broader criminal laws and enforcing these laws with stiffer penalties. Law-and-order special interest groups want more police, more jails, and longer prison terms. Their ultimate goal is what they call "zero tolerance" for particular types of crime or for crimes in general. Law-and-order special interest groups work hard to influence voters in local, state, and federal elections to choose judges and prosecutors who will "not let criminals off the hook." They work to elect state and federal legislators who will pass more and tougher criminal laws and enforce zero-tolerance policies.

Law-and-order special interest groups tend to fall into two broad categories. The first is made up of groups of people who work in the criminal justice industrial complex, such as police officers or prison guards and operators. The second category is full of those groups that have an axe to grind about a particular type of crime. Many times the groups in this second category are started and run by victims (or parents, spouses, or other loved ones of victims) of the type of crime that their special interest groups are fighting against.

In their public service messages and in their websites and media materials, the leaders and organizers of the groups in this second category of law-and-order special interest groups emphasize their victimhood. They talk about how they have "made it their mission to rid the world" of this type of criminal and to make sure "tougher laws are passed." They express the determination to be "absolutely merciless" toward any perpetrator of that particular type of crime so that no one else in the future will have to suffer the pain and anguish they have experienced as victims. These special interest groups wear the "mantle of victimhood" to promote their law-and-order public policy agenda of more government limitations on civil liberties of accused persons and zero tolerance for all offenders.

Sounds great, right? I mean, come on, how can you *not* support a group with a message like that? Most of us, including myself, have been victims of crime, and some of us, including myself, have lost family members or close friends to perpetrators of crime. The messages of these law-and-order special interest groups are very compelling, and the people who run these organizations are usually hardworking, dedicated to their cause, and determined to make the world a safer place.[2]

So what's the problem? The problem is that these groups exert a tremendous amount of political pressure on America's criminal justice system, and their stated public policy goals are, at times, in opposition to the fundamental *constitutional* principles of our criminal justice system. These special interest groups have helped make America's criminal justice system biased, harsh, overly broad, and merciless. Why? Because the stated public policy goals of law-and-order special interest groups are outcome-determinative—in other words, for them, the ends justify the means.

Law-and-order special interest groups are not focused on protecting the constitutional rights of the accused, nor are they focused on maintaining civil liberties, or on restricting police and the prosecutorial power of big government. They are not interested in fair and balanced punishment for those convicted of crimes or in maintaining or expanding judicial and prosecutorial discretion when it comes to sentencing and punishment. When law-and-order special interest groups raise money in local and state elections and vote for "tough judges" and "tough prosecutors," what they truly want is judges and prosecutors who never use their judicial or prosecutorial discretion and knowledge of the law to give any person accused of a crime a break or a second chance. They are not particularly concerned with the constitutional rights of the criminally accused to a fair trial. They are certainly not concerned about the impact of a criminal conviction on that individual's future life or the terrible, inhumane fate that awaits someone who is locked up in an American jail or prison.

When a person accused of a crime is found guilty by a jury or admits guilt in court, these groups want that person to receive the exact same sentence as everyone else convicted of the same crime, and they want that sentence to be the harshest one possible. The special interest groups are not concerned about the background or character of the individual who committed the crime or about mitigating evidence concerning the convicted person's actions. Law-and-order special interest groups despise judicial and prosecutorial discretion and want zero tolerance and "one-size-fits-all" justice for everyone accused and/or convicted of a crime. They don't want impartial judges carefully and objectively weighing the facts and evidence in each and every individual case—even though that is the judges' *constitutional* responsibility. They don't want police officers or prosecutors who use their professional discretion to not make arrests or to dismiss cases they feel don't warrant criminal prosecution. No, these groups want judges and prosecutors who march in tune with the stated political agenda of law and order and zero tolerance. Many state and local judges and prosecutors have their elections heavily financed by these law-and-order special interest groups, who then expect "their judges" and "their prosecutors" and "their police forces" to lock everybody up and throw away the key no matter what the cost to individual human lives, civil liberties, personal privacy, and constitutional due process.

I'll say it again: to law-and-order special interest groups, the ends justify the means. These groups are not interested in how they achieve their goals, only that their goals are achieved. The problem is that this runs completely against the fundamental legal principle of America's criminal justice system—the basic idea of balance. As I described in Chapter Two, our system is an adversarial one, set up with the defendant and defense lawyer on one side of the courtroom and the prosecutor's team on the other side of the courtroom, each side striving to win within the ethical rules of the law. The judge's constitutional role is to be fair and impartial to both sides—the prosecution and the defense. As we've discussed, the judge is like the referee at a tennis match who makes sure each of the opponents has a fair shot. And on those occasions where the prosecution wins the contest, the judge's job is to punish the defendant found guilty of the crime by taking into account all of the information and evidence in the individual case—as presented by both sides—and meting out a fair and balanced punishment.

Under the Constitution, the prosecutor's primary role in America's criminal justice system is to "make sure that justice is done in each and every individual case."[3] The prosecutor's role as the "adversary to the defense" should actually be a secondary role. The prosecutor's primary job is to review each case independently, to receive and listen to not only evidence presented by his or her own investigators (and the police) but also any evidence presented by the defense, and then to make sure that no innocent person is prosecuted for a crime when there is not enough evidence to support formally accusing that individual. Thus, only after an objective and cold reading of all of the evidence in a particular case is a prosecutor legally authorized to formally accuse and prosecute a citizen in this country. After which, it is up to a jury (or judge, depending on the type of case) to determine whether there is evidence "beyond a reasonable doubt" that warrants a criminal conviction. Jurors are supposed to make this decision only after balancing and weighing all the evidence, guided by an impartial judge who is fair and balanced to both sides.

The problem with the agendas of law-and-order special interest groups is that they are not focused on creating and maintaining a fair and balanced criminal justice system that impartially weighs civil liberties against police and prosecutorial power, or on maintaining impartial judges, or on balancing justice with mercy. That's not why these groups have assembled and organized themselves (as it is their right to do under the First Amendment) into highly funded and well-organized political pressure groups. No, their purpose is to eliminate crime—or a particular type of crime—by prosecuting and arresting as many people as possible for that crime and then throwing them in jail or prison. They also want to add other types of burdens (such as fines, community service work, or the loss of voting rights, the right to own a gun, or the ability to legally drive a car) on the criminal defendants as part of their sentences.

These special interest groups also frequently push for more, and more complex, computer monitoring devices and other technological ways to disrupt or eliminate the privacy and civil liberties of persons accused, or convicted, of crimes. In the most extreme cases, they want to banish certain criminal defendants or make it virtually impossible for them to legally live in their community or state. The members of these groups are not objective or impartial. Indeed, they are passionately *partial* toward their stated law-and-order public policy goals. And they may be more than happy to trample and destroy the civil liberties and constitutionally protected rights of their fellow citizens in order to achieve their ends.

The members of these special interest groups, especially their founders and leaders, hold views that are extreme and on the fringes of those views held by the general population. Thus, they are naturally biased, and their extremist views are out of touch with those of a fair and impartial person objectively weighing the facts and evidence on both sides of the issue. In the next section of this book, we will see how the stated political objective of these groups became "zero tolerance"—an evil, dangerous, and malignant political notion that is nothing less than a cancer threatening to destroy our nation's most cherished civil liberties and our free and open society.

Plaintiff's Lawyers

What is a "plaintiff's lawyer"? A plaintiff's lawyer is a lawyer who sues people or organizations for money on behalf of other people or organizations. For instance, when a person is injured in a car accident, the lawyer for the injured person (the plaintiff's lawyer) sues the other driver's insurance company in order to collect money for the injured person (the plaintiff). The plaintiff's lawyer is paid by receiving a percentage of whatever money he or she collects from the person or organization that was sued.

Lawsuits are nothing new. Lawyers have been suing people on behalf of other people since the ancient times of the Greeks and the Romans. What has changed in the past few decades in our country, however, is that people and organizations are being successfully sued in new ways and for actions for which they never would have been sued in the past. These lawsuits have had a major impact on America's criminal justice system in the past generation as government and business alike have found themselves under siege by a creative and aggressive body of plaintiff's lawyers and their clients, who are using the law of torts to sue them in new and untraditional ways. (A "tort" is a civil wrong, as opposed to a violation of a criminal law.) How can a lawsuit possibly have an impact on America's criminal justice system? Lawsuits and the threat of lawsuits have spawned zero-tolerance arrest policies in our schools, businesses, and public institutions, "criminalizing" conduct that a generation ago would not have led to a person being arrested. Let's take a look at two examples.

Start with what's happening in our schools. Let's take a journey back in time to when I was growing up and going to school in the 1960s and 1970s. Assume for a minute that you and your friends are having lunch in the school cafeteria. You are all sitting there with your trays of French fries laden with lots of good, old-fashioned tasty trans fats and a greasy fried hamburger loaded with cheese and ketchup and your carton of whole milk. You and your buddies are hanging out, stuffing yourself with all that great-tasting food and talking about the latest Led Zeppelin or Earth, Wind & Fire album, when a fight breaks out between two boys at the next table. They square off, and the one boy, Billy, hits the other boy, Bobby, right in the nose. Then Bobby swings and misses, and then all hell breaks loose as Billy and Bobby grab each other and roll around on the floor in one of those wrestling matches boys get into. Your friends and the other students form a circle and start cheering. French fries and ice cream start flying around, and the whole cafeteria seems completely out of control, until the principal, Mr. P., and the football coach, Mr. C., rush in and break up the fight. They yell at the kids and tell them to sit down. A couple of the kids who were watching the fight don't listen, and Mr. C. walks over and grabs these two kids by the arms and tells them to "have a seat or you're going to be in big trouble." No one is quite sure what "big trouble" means, but it sounds bad, so the two kids respectfully park their butts back in their Day-Glo orange plastic molded seats. OK, so Mr. P. and Mr. C. have regained control of the situation, and they yell at everyone to pick the fries off the floor and shut their traps, which the children all dutifully do as they calm down and order is restored by the adults in the room. Then Mr. P. and Mr. C. take Billy and Bobby by the arms and march them back to that most dreaded of places, the principal's office.

Mr. P. lectures the two boys, while Mr. C. gets some ice for their bruises. Then they call the boys' parents, who drive over to the school to pick up their children. The boys are suspended for three days and they get a week's detention cleaning blackboards after school. When the parents come to the school and pick up their sons, each dad smacks his boy on the side of his head, yells at him for causing so much trouble, and takes him home. Billy, who landed the punch, gets grounded for a week. Bobby, who got hit in the nose and missed when he tried to punch back, gets a boxing lesson from his dad so he knows how to duck next time and how to land a decent punch. End of story. Good, rational, intelligent solution. You have boys acting like, well, boys, and being disciplined by an organized, intelligent, rationally behaving group of adults who form a united front of authority, coordinating their actions to deal with two boys in need of discipline and boundaries.

OK, so . . . let's now fast-forward to the present day and take a look at how the exact same situation would be handled in the average American high school in the twenty-first century. The first thing that happens when Billy and Bobby are hauled into the principal's office is not a call to their parents. Nope, instead Mr. P. calls the police. After calling the cops, Mr. P. then calls the parents, but when they arrive, instead of being asked to take their children home to face parental discipline, they find their fourteen-year-old children in handcuffs ready to be hauled off to the local jail. Billy and Bobby's parents are summarily informed that their children violated the school's zero-tolerance policy by committing the crime of battery, and that the boys are going to be arrested, jailed, and possibly expelled from school.

The parents still chew out their kids, like in the old days, and Billy's dad still gives him a smack on the head. But now, instead of working with Mr. P., the parents are on the defensive. Furious at the principal, they start yelling and threatening to sue the school and the principal for not properly supervising the school cafeteria and for having their boys arrested by the police. Instead of taking their sons home and lecturing them on the evils of fighting, the parents run out and retain lawyers to sue the school, the principal, and the police. They also have to retain criminal defense lawyers to defend their children against criminal charges.

But wait, it gets even more ridiculous. A week after their children are arrested, a Department of Family and Children's Services (DFACS) social worker shows up at Billy's house to talk to his parents. DFACS has opened an investigation against the parents to see if Billy is being abused and to decide whether he should be placed into foster care. *Huh? How did that happen?* Well, remember when Billy's dad smacked his kid upside the head while scolding him for fighting? The school also has a written zero-tolerance policy concerning the principal's need to report child abuse. It states that the principal must report to the police and DFACS any signs of child abuse he witnesses, no matter what the facts or circumstances. The result is that Billy's parents now have government DFACS agents knocking on their door, snooping around in their private affairs, and questioning their worthiness as parents, all over a fatherly smack on the head. Oh, and wait—remember the two boys in the school cafeteria who wouldn't sit down after Mr. P. and Mr. C. broke up the fight? If you recall, Mr. C. grabbed both boys by the arms and told them to sit down or the boys would be in "big trouble." Well, in today's Looney Tunes Land of school zero-tolerance policies, police intervention, and lawsuits flying everywhere, the children run home and tell their parents that the gym coach abused and threatened them. The parents hire a lawyer who sues the coach and quotes the school's third zero-tolerance policy, which states that no teacher can touch or "verbally abuse" a child in any way.

In the end, the school has to pay out money to the families of two bratty kids, the gym coach gets fired and has his career ruined, the plaintiff's lawyer collects a tidy sum, and the criminal defense lawyers earn nice fees defending Billy and Bobby. Oh wait, I almost forgot—both Billy and Bobby must go to "anger management" classes as part of their probation and then are diagnosed by their shrinks with attention deficit disorder. The result is that both Billy and Bobby are prescribed heavy doses of Ritalin, so that when they return to school they have been transformed into heavily sedated zombies who won't cause any more trouble.

So unlike back in the good old-fashioned 1970s, where you had the school principal, the gym coach, and the parents all acting together as adults to properly discipline the children and teach them proper behavior, you have, in the twenty-first century, adults behaving irrationally, hiring lawyers, and squabbling amongst themselves like so many overgrown children. When did a fistfight between two adolescent boys in a school cafeteria go from just that—a fistfight between two boys in a school cafeteria—to a "crime scene" requiring police enforcement and resulting in lawsuits flying everywhere? Is it because of concerns over school violence? I respectfully say no. It is due to the rise of zero-tolerance policies that permeate our school systems today and are largely the result of plaintiff's lawyers and the threat of lawsuits.

The practical result of this change in policy is that two teenage boys are arrested and charged with a crime. The police are called in to intervene in a situation that would have been dealt with privately between the school authorities and the parents a generation or two ago. In today's world, the principal has no choice but to call the police because the school has a written zero-tolerance policy against fighting that says if children engage in normal adolescent behavior, the result is that they get arrested. Why such a drastic change in school policy? Let's take a look behind the scenes and see what really is going on here.

Sometime in the past generation, plaintiff's lawyers came up with creative new reasons to sue schools and teachers and principals for stuff that they never would have been sued for in the past. They came up with the bright idea of suing schools under several "theories of negligence." What are these theories? The first one says that if the school fails to "properly and adequately supervise" Billy and Bobby and a fight breaks out, it is the school's fault, not the fault of the children. That's right, ladies and gentlemen, it's not Billy and Bobby's fault they got into a fight, today it is the school's fault. In this legal fantasyland of responsibility and blame-shifting, schools are to blame for normal teenage-boy behavior. But wait, it gets even more ludicrous. Teachers and principals can be sued for disciplining a child too harshly: they can't touch a child in any way, and any action to discipline their students has the potential to result in a lawsuit. *Wait a minute,* you may be asking, *I thought they could be sued for not adequately supervising children and preventing fights?* Yep—that's right! The school can be sued either way: for not disciplining enough *or* for disciplining too harshly. Plaintiff's lawyers have put our schools, teachers, and principals between a legal "rock and a hard place." So what is the only solution for the school?

The solution is for the school to institute a written zero-tolerance policy concerning violence involving students at school. The school officials will, of course, have asked their lawyers what is the best way to protect the school from being sued, and their defense lawyers will have advised them to institute a zero-tolerance policy toward fighting in school—and to put it in writing. The zero-tolerance policy clearly states that any child punching another child in school will be dealt with by having that child arrested. No exceptions are allowed. The school then institutes policies that criminalize normal adolescent behavior while tying the hands of the principal so that he or she cannot use adult professional experience and common sense to make a judgment call as to whether a fight between two students in his or her school is best dealt with privately or by calling the police.

It's not as if the police were never called in the 1960s and 1970s. The problem stems from the fact that the principals, the adults in the room who have been given the responsibility and training to make decisions regarding student behavior, have had their hands tied and their professional discretion taken away by zero-tolerance policies. What is the reason why principals and professionals are now forced to call the police in situations that common sense would dictate could be better handled privately at the school with the parents? It is so that the school board can wave this written policy in the face of the trial lawyer when he or she tries to sue them and say, "See? We did everything we could to protect Billy and Bobby. We have a zero-tolerance policy in place, which criminalizes fighting between students—no exceptions." The plaintiff's lawyer is thwarted! The zero-tolerance policy is the "silver bullet" used by the schools to kill lawsuits filed by plaintiff's lawyers against them.

So the school board is happy (zero-tolerance policies are self-serving, by the way, as we shall explore in Part II of this book), but the result is that Billy and Bobby pay a terrible price: they get arrested and prosecuted for behavior that would have landed them a stint clapping erasers a generation or two ago.[4]

This kind of thing is not just limited to schools, either. Private businesses now have policies designed to protect them against a glut of plaintiff's lawsuits. These policies have led to a rise in arrests in the last generation. Let's take another example.

Suppose a teenage girl, let's call her Sarah, works for a franchise doughnut shop. Sarah is in high school, and she gets stuck working the Saturday night late shift. She has worked for the store for over a year and the franchise owner is very fond of her, as she is a great employee. One Saturday night after a big football game, Sarah's friends descend on the store, ravenous for doughnuts. Not all of her friends have money, however, and they want Sarah to give them some free doughnuts "just for fun." They pressure Sarah, demanding free doughnuts. Sarah refuses at first, but she doesn't want to upset her friends, so she gives out some free food. She's caught by one of the security cameras, and the next day her boss finds out.

When her boss confronts her, Sarah tearfully confesses and asks to have a second chance. She offers to work for free to pay back the value of the doughnuts—about twenty-five dollars. She asks to be forgiven and for her boss to take into account her dedicated service. Sadly, her boss explains that he can't do this. He tells her that he would give her a second chance if he could, but he has to call the police and have her arrested because Corporate—the big conglomerate headquartered in Dallas that owns the franchise—has, upon the advice of its own lawyers, instituted a zero-tolerance policy concerning employee theft.

No matter what the surrounding circumstances, corporate policy states that the employee must be arrested and criminally prosecuted to the fullest extent of the law. Now, is this policy in place because corporations fear theft by employees? Sure. But the other basis for the policy is the fear that Corporate will be sued by plaintiff's lawyers seeking monetary damages for selective, discriminatory firings. Plaintiff's lawyers who sue under "selective prosecution" claims seek patterns of firings based upon race, gender, disability, religion, body mass index, or a variety of other "group" categories. They then claim that an employer or corporation selectively prosecutes only individuals from the allegedly aggrieved group. Or, looking at it another way, they claim that the employer only lets its employees off the hook by choosing *not* to prosecute them if they fit a certain profile. So what did Corporate do when facing a claim of selective prosecution? Enact a zero-tolerance policy, of course, requiring all of its franchise owners to call the police whenever an employee takes *anything*—including a few dollars worth of doughnuts. The result of the zero-tolerance policy, thus, is that it has robbed the franchise owner of his discretion when it comes to making a decision about how to discipline his own employees.

You might ask, "Can't the doughnut shop owner just fire Sarah?" No, because Corporate's defense lawyers have counseled their client in a way that makes it impossible for franchise owners to choose whether or not to prosecute *anyone* for *anything*—such as an employee embezzling lots of money. This is based on the same reason as above: the embezzler could then go hire a lawyer and claim he/she was selectively prosecuted and sue Corporate on those grounds. So once again you have one-size-fits-all justice with the adult in charge, the doughnut store manager, unable to use his common sense and rational discretion to make a judgment call as to how best to handle Sarah's "great doughnut heist." Sarah is hauled off to jail, all for the fear that not to do so will get Corporate sued down the road by a plaintiff's lawyer claiming selective prosecution.

Thanks to plaintiff's lawyers, many private businesses and government institutions now have some type of zero-tolerance policy in place to protect themselves from lawsuits. The plaintiff's lawyers get rich, while the adults entrusted to manage our private and public institutions are not allowed the discretion to make the day-to-day decisions essential to good leadership. Instead, they are turned into robots repeating the inane and dangerous slogan "zero tolerance, zero tolerance." The result: persons who interact with these organizations—be they employees, students, teachers, customers, or anyone else—are frequently arrested and treated like criminals for violating zero-tolerance policies put into place to combat lawsuits from plaintiff's lawyers. (In Part II, we'll take a closer look at zero-tolerance policies and where they came from.)

The Prison and Corrections Industry

We have all heard about the decline of good, solid, "blue-collar" jobs in our nation. But what is a "good, solid, blue-collar job"? Essentially, a blue-collar job can be defined as a job that can be performed competently by a high school graduate who has received, perhaps, technical training of some type. A good one comes with a middle-class salary, overtime, health insurance, retirement benefits, and, perhaps, the protection of an organized union. Historically, we think of persons such as autoworkers as having jobs of this type. Politicians from a variety of backgrounds bemoan the loss of such jobs as they move from the heartland of America to places like China, India, and Mexico.

There is one industry in our country, though, where the number of good, solid, middle-class jobs is growing: the industry that operates the prisons, jails, and detention centers in our country—and that provides the corresponding pretrial supervision and probation services. The men and women who work as prison guards in this country have some of the more coveted and better-paying jobs in their communities, with excellent health and retirement benefits and union protection, all at the expense of the taxpayer. In fact, American taxpayers seem willing to pay ever more of their hard-earned money for these services. While some traditional blue-collar jobs in manufacturing and industry are disappearing, similar well-paying jobs in the prison and corrections industry are strongly funded and increasing.

Of course, the only way the prison and corrections industry can continue to prosper and expand is—like any other industry—it must grow! This means that the prison and corrections industry of the United States needs more and more people to arrest, throw into its prisons, or place on probation in order to thrive economically and to provide more better-paying jobs to its employees. Hence, the politically motivated law-and-order and zero-tolerance policies we have just looked at are promoted and supported by those who depend upon those policies to remain employed in good middle-class jobs.

I realize it may be difficult at first to see those government workers who are employed as prison and jail guards (or the people who own or control the prisons) as part of a huge industry like the automobile or steel industries. Yet, that is exactly what they have become. Thus, they and their leaders—the people who own and/or control the jails, detentions centers, and state and federal prisons—have a very clear and obvious vested interest in seeing the number of persons arrested and criminally prosecuted in this country expand—and to see that number keep expanding as much as possible. Beyond these basic organizations are even broader "secondary beneficiaries," including a wide range of private companies and services designed to profit from the arrest and criminal prosecution of persons in our country. These include private probation, pretrial supervision, and detention services, community service providers, counseling services (think DUI schools or "anger management" counseling centers), private detective services, and of course the manufacturers of all of the products used by the police and by prison operators. Then, of course, you have private detectives, psychologists and psychiatrists, jury experts, and, last but certainly not least, criminal defense attorneys. All of these folks, yes, including yours truly, profit and benefit from the ever-increasing numbers of persons arrested and prosecuted criminally in America.

So, the next time you are in court, realize that any jail or prison time you serve is supporting the economic livelihood of a vast array of people and organizations, all of whom are counting on your arrest, prosecution, punishment, and incarceration to put food on their tables. This industry is a huge lobbying force. The public and private organizations that benefit economically from your criminal arrest and prosecution all exert their influence on the judge and prosecutor in every case. This is especially true in areas of the country where the local factory that used to produce toasters or car parts has moved to China, India, or Mexico, leaving the prison guard or probation officer job as the "only game in town" (besides working at the local big-box retail store at seven dollars an hour with zero benefits). With such economic realities, you better believe that tremendous pressure is on the local court system to maintain a fresh and always increasing supply of prisoners for the local jail, prison, and probation system. This economic pressure will usually override any more idealistic and thoughtful concerns about the constitutional right to a fair trial.[5]

The Media

One other group heavily influencing America's criminal justice system from outside the courtroom is the news media. The media has always been heavily entangled with America's criminal justice system because, let's face it, all of us are fascinated with criminal law. I was recently doing some legal research in the law library of the New York City Bar Association. On display in the library were old books and magazine articles about infamous crimes from the mid-nineteenth century—long-forgotten stories of human tragedy involving the commission of deadly crimes and their subsequent punishments. The stories were no different than they are today.

Defense lawyers need to be adept at handling the media—especially media inquiries into their clients' cases. In the twenty-first century, this includes two types of media. The first type is the traditional media, which I define as newspapers, television, and magazines. The second type is the Internet, which can include everything from news gathered on websites, to blogs, to social media like Facebook, Twitter, Instagram, and whatever comes next. Whenever possible, defense lawyers must make sure their clients are not "tried and convicted" in the media, while also doing their best to protect their clients from the glare and embarrassment of media attention.

Today, we are also seeing lawyers (be they prosecutors or defense lawyers) step out of their traditional roles as advocates and into the roles of media commentators and personalities. This happens whenever they discuss or comment on a criminal case in the media—whether traditional or new media. I, myself, have appeared on various national and local television and radio shows to discuss aspects of various criminal cases that have been in the news. As citizens, it is our right to be informed about newsworthy criminal cases, and the press has the constitutional right to follow these stories; and lawyers, such as myself, hopefully help to provide thoughtful commentary about newsworthy cases.

As a practicing criminal defense lawyer representing a person accused of a crime who is in the news, on the other hand, I find making sure my client is treated fairly in the press—and not "tarred and feathered" on television before the case ever goes to trial—to be one of my most important jobs, especially in today's nonstop, twenty-four-hour news cycle. When the accused people in the news are my clients, my job is to be an advocate for their causes and to be the protector of their privacy as much as possible. A courtroom is the only place for guilt or innocence to be decided. In high-profile, media-frenzied cases, it is vitally important for all of us to remember that lady justice is holding a set of scales and a sword, not a microphone and a television camera.

PART II: BREEDING A MEANER BEAST—

THE IMPACT OF ZERO TOLERANCE ON AMERICA'S CRIMINAL JUSTICE SYSTEM

In today's America, zero tolerance is everywhere. Police departments have zero-tolerance arrest polices. Judges and politicians run for elected office on a platform of zero tolerance for crime and criminals. Victim's rights groups, criminal watchdog groups, and neighborhood action committees all demand zero tolerance for crime. In schools, principals and educators all espouse their faith in, and support for, zero tolerance toward student misbehavior and juvenile delinquency. In corporations and government, employers all now practice and enforce zero tolerance toward employee indiscretions or "inappropriate" behavior. Indeed, in all sectors of our society, zero tolerance has not only become the norm, it has become a mantra—chanted and preached, practiced, and enforced in every type of private and public institution throughout the United States.

Zero Tolerance Is Everywhere

Nowhere has the idea of zero tolerance been more embraced and enforced than by those involved in America's criminal justice system. Walk into any police precinct and you will see signs with stern-looking police officers and members of "task forces" staring down at you and declaring that their sworn duty is to enforce zero tolerance against crime.

Judges and prosecutors also declare that they will "get tough on crime" by enforcing zero tolerance.

As we saw in Part I, in our criminal justice system zero-tolerance policies are fueled by law-and-order special interest groups that heavily influence the outcomes of local, state, and federal elections. Politicians, be they judges, prosecutors, sheriffs, police chiefs, or state or federal representatives, oppose the zero-tolerance policies of law-and-order special interest groups at their own peril. Organizations such as Mothers Against Drunk Driving (MADD), the National Center on Sexual and Domestic Violence, the Jane Adams Hull House Association, the National Center for Victims of Crime, and the Crime Victims Action Alliance carry tremendous heft in terms of both money and votes, and they will attack any elected official foolish enough to challenge their no-holds-barred political agendas of zero tolerance.

But political groups on the left also push zero tolerance as a means of achieving equal protection under the law and equal treatment for all offenders. Civil liberties watchdog groups see zero tolerance as a way to eliminate "loopholes" in the system for privileged elites so that all persons are both treated equally and *punished* equally under the law regardless of race, ethnicity, religion, gender, sexual orientation, age, physical ability, or economic class. They demand zero tolerance toward police, prosecutorial, and judicial misconduct.

Interest groups on both the left and the right also demand zero tolerance in schools, corporations, government, and other public and private institutions to promote their specific political agendas. One of the reasons for the great proliferation of zero-tolerance policies throughout American society is that, in many respects, it is not a left-wing or right-wing issue. A law-and-order special interest group may demand zero tolerance in workplaces because they want to punish white-collar criminals and get tough on crime. At the same time, a feminist group may demand zero-tolerance policies against telling off-color jokes about women because they want to eliminate sexual discrimination or sexual harassment in the workplace. A group against drug use may scream for mandatory drug testing for all employees and zero tolerance against marijuana use. Corporations, meanwhile, react to threats from lawsuits by plaintiff's lawyers or negative media attention by enacting zero-tolerance policies against almost everything in an attempt to avoid liability or public relations problems.

The police are stuck in the same boat. If they use too much discretion and don't arrest everyone they suspect of committing some type of crime, then they can be disciplined for not following the police department's zero-tolerance policy. On the other hand, if they rigidly enforce the law in every case, or use excessive force in a questionable way under tough circumstances—especially in high-crime areas with high minority populations—members of the police force can come under fire the police agency's zero-tolerance policies toward police misconduct or using excessive force, even in cases where it's not clear they actually used excessive force. Or they can end up in the media spotlight and get fired simply for bringing media heat down on the local precinct.

In short, American special interest groups of all stripes have embraced the concept of zero tolerance as the optimal tool for achieving their specific political, social, or moral agendas. The term "zero tolerance" as it is currently used is about two decades old. People my age can remember a time when the term did not exist in our everyday lives. But it's everywhere now, and it seems that everyone with an axe to grind wants to claim it as his or her own. Is this a virtue? My opinion is no.

Why Should You Care?

Zero tolerance has personally impacted the lives of countless Americans over the past generation. As police have enforced zero-tolerance arrest policies and courts have enforced zero-tolerance sentencing policies, ordinary people are being arrested, prosecuted, and jailed for acts and indiscretions that they would not have been arrested or prosecuted or incarcerated for a generation ago. Beyond the criminal justice system, ordinary people are also having their lives upended by zero-tolerance policies at school, in the workplace, and within their communities in ways that were unheard of before the widespread enactment of zero-tolerance policies. In today's America, when good people do bad things, zero tolerance makes sure that very bad things can happen to those good people. Whether these bad things constitute justice is a matter of opinion, but whether they are happening is not—they are happening all the time and to lots of people. And in our land of zero tolerance, if bad things are happening to other law-abiding citizens, then they can happen to us.

Let us begin Part II of this book with a general history of zero tolerance—where the concept came from and how it has developed over the past thirty years. I will then explain how zero tolerance has influenced the modern American criminal justice system. Next, I will look at some of the frightening consequences zero-tolerance policies could have for the safety of our country and ourselves in the future, if we continue our blind devotion to zero tolerance. At the same time, not all is doom and gloom. In the final chapter of this section, I will discuss how some public policy experts, politicians, judges, prosecutors, defense lawyers, and community leaders across America are working to develop ways to improve America's criminal justice system. These people are using and promoting methods of alternative punishment and rehabilitative sentencing that allow those convicted of crimes the opportunity to pay their debt to society while preserving their freedom and civil liberties.

CHAPTER FOUR

A BOOK, A MOVIE, AND A MAGAZINE ARTICLE LEAD TO ZERO TOLERANCE

Where did the idea of zero tolerance originate? How did a concept that has come to permeate our legal and political landscape today first find its way into our minds and imaginations? Technically speaking, zero tolerance can be traced back to a term first used in the mid-1990s, but the modern American form of the concept goes back to that golden age of my youth, the 1970s.

As defined by the *American Heritage Dictionary of the English Language*, "zero tolerance" is a policy of very strict, uncompromising enforcement of rules or laws and a policy that imposes automatic punishment for infractions of a stated rule, with the intention of eliminating undesirable conduct.[6] Wikipedia describes zero tolerance as a set of policies that "forbid persons in positions of authority from exercising discretion or changing punishments subjectively to circumstances: they are required to impose a predetermined punishment regardless of individual culpability, extenuating circumstances, or past history. This predetermined punishment need not be severe, but it is always meted out."[7]

One does not have to use the term "zero tolerance" to practice it. Regardless of whether they actually use the term in their mission statements, many organizations—police departments, courts, legislatures, law-and-order special interest groups, victim's rights advocates, schools, and workplaces—advocate and practice methods steeped in the concept of zero tolerance.

The origins of the modern-day concept of zero tolerance can be traced back to a single book and a single movie, both of which came out in the mid-1970s, when I was growing up as a teenager in suburban Maryland. The book was *Thinking About Crime*, by UCLA professor James Q. Wilson, published in 1975.[8] The book blasted onto the academic and political scene immediately after it was published. In its arguments, police departments, prosecutors, judges, and elected officials found a basis for developing and enforcing zero-tolerance criminal justice policies. Professor Wilson never used the term "zero tolerance." (The term came into being in the 1990s, as explained later in this chapter.) But Wilson laid out all of the arguments and justifications for creating and enforcing zero tolerance. I will get back to Wilson's book a little later, but first I want to talk about the movie that I believe established, in popular culture, the idea of zero tolerance.

The Movie *Death Wish* Plants the Seeds of Zero Tolerance

The idea for enforcing zero tolerance in American society as a response to escalating crime sprang into the popular imagination by way of the blockbuster movie *Death Wish*, starring tough-as-nails actor Charles Bronson. Now a cult classic, *Death Wish* burst onto the American scene with the energy and violence of a shotgun blast. It's the story of an upper-middle-class architect who turns vigilante in response to the inability of an inept and uncaring police department to track down and arrest the men who raped, brutalized, and murdered his wife and daughter.

The movie felt like a punch in the guts to every American who watched it on the big screen in the long, hot summer of 1974. The movie crashed into the imagination of Americans who were fed up with crime and urban decay and sensed that America was culturally and morally in decline. This was still a time when people went to movies in droves, before videos and DVDs, and when a popular movie like *Death Wish* would remain at the local neighborhood movie house for weeks or even months over the course of the summer. *Death Wish* also spawned several sequels over the next decade, including *Death Wish II, III, IV,* and *V.*

To understand the true impact of *Death Wish* and how it helped to bring about the idea of zero tolerance, you must first understand what America was like in the 1970s. In the mid-1970s, Americans were recovering from more than a decade of turmoil and social change. The 1960s had witnessed the Cold War, the Vietnam War, violent war protests, the establishment of civil rights for minorities and women, and the assassinations of President John F. Kennedy, his brother Bobby Kennedy, Martin Luther King Jr., and Malcolm X. The 1960s also witnessed revolutions in sexual freedom, music, and the arts, and the culture of youth and drugs.

Then, in the early 1970s, Americans watched their nation lose the Vietnam War and President Nixon resign office under threat of impeachment. Gasoline supplies dried up, so people sat in their cars in mile-long lines to get fuel from the local gas station. Americans witnessed the massive loss of well-paying, union-protected, blue-collar jobs in industry, the flight of whites and the middle class from cities to the suburbs, and the lethal combination of rising prices and economic recession. In the once-great American cities, urban decay set in and crime rose to new record levels. Whole communities collapsed. Along with the rise of urban crime came a string of grisly serial killers and other madmen such as Charles Manson, Ted Bundy, the Zodiac Killer, and the Son of Sam, who filled the nightly news with horror stories of ordinary people being abducted, shot, stabbed, strangled, and mutilated.

Not all was grim, of course. Ironically enough, in some ways the 1970s are now seen as the last decade of true innocence for Americans. As a child and teenager growing up in suburban Maryland, I lived in a world where kids in my neighborhood all played sports together at the local park and playground without parental supervision or leagues or coaches. My parents, who never heard the terms "play group" or "play date," simply let me, my sister, and our friends roam the entire community freely on our ten-speed bikes. The only parental admonishment I ever received was to be home by sundown or on time for dinner. On the radio, disco, rhythm and blues, British rock, California rock, soft rock, and Southern rock filled the airwaves with a wonderful kaleidoscope of harmony and rhythm. We had no cable TV, computers, cell phones, Internet, or other electronic wizardry. People could still smoke cigarettes, drink alcohol, eat fatty foods, drive without seatbelts or child restraints, throw away their trash, not exercise, tell off-color jokes about whomever, and just sit on their butts on their front porches or back decks and enjoy themselves, all without fear of criticism or social condemnation.

There was no twenty-four-hour news cycle; the news only lasted about an hour each night before the three TV networks switched over to a steady diet of detective shows, comedies, and family sitcoms. Many of the popular expressions of the time captured the idea that everyone needed to chill out after the tumultuous events of the 1960s and early '70s; expressions such as "just hang loose," "have a nice day," "don't worry, be happy," and "keep on truckin'" captured the average American's desire for retreat and escape from the social problems and economic woes of 1970s America.

But, underneath it all, lay a very real and justified fear of crime, which had been rising steadily in America since the early 1960s. By the 1970s, people were terrified of being mugged or robbed or criminally victimized. Nowhere was this truer than in American cities. In many cities, people never walked through the parks at night (or sometimes even during the day) or went out for a stroll after dark. Many areas suffered from urban blight and neglect as the more well-to-do people moved out of neighborhoods, stores and shops closed, and sidewalks and parks became neglected and run down.

Nowhere was this truer than in New York City. The "Big Apple"—once the urban envy of the world—had, by the late 1970s, fallen onto hard times. Urban decay, flight to the suburbs by the middle class, and financial woes had left New York City literally on the verge of bankruptcy by 1975, requiring the federal government to bail New York City out to avoid completely falling apart. Whole neighborhoods were filled with abandoned and burned-out buildings and vacant lots, while graffiti-strewn subway cars, broken and cracked sidewalks, and general urban malaise were everywhere.

Throughout New York's neighborhoods, petty and violent criminals lurked in alleyways and the shadows, dealt drugs on street corners, prostituted themselves, and engaged in general predation of the ordinary citizen. Public spaces like Times Square, Central Park, and Grand Central Station were filled with ne'er-do-wells, drug dealers, homeless people, the mentally ill, and petty criminals. Indeed, at times, all of New York City seemed out of control and unsafe for ordinary citizens to live in.

This was the New York City where the movie *Death Wish* was filmed. Shot in New York City during the winter by director Michael Winner, the film captured the stark, grim feel of 1970s New York. Ultimately, the movie came to symbolize the urban problems facing all American cities, especially the worsening fear of being victimized by crime. I can still remember being a teenager, sitting in the darkened cinema packed with people, munching on buttered popcorn and drinking Coke, and being absolutely enthralled as Bronson gunned down one no-good criminal after another in bloody, brutal revenge for the crimes committed against his innocent family.

The plot of *Death Wish* is simple enough. Charles Bronson plays a craggy, middle-aged architect who is married to Hope Lange as his beautiful, sophisticated wife. They have a beautiful twenty-something daughter, who is married to a nice, all-American guy. Bronson and his wife live in a respectable upper-middle-class apartment on Manhattan's Upper West Side.

The movie opens on a typical afternoon when Bronson is still at work in his midtown Manhattan office. He and his wife have just returned from a pleasant Hawaiian vacation. Bronson enjoys his work as a talented architect and he is busy finishing up his duties at the office before heading home to have dinner with his wife and daughter. The next scene shows Bronson's wife and daughter at the local grocery store, picking up supplies for dinner. They pay for their groceries and leave the store with their groceries bagged and set aside by the clerk for delivery to the apartment by one of the grocery store's delivery boys. The movie then quickly turns dark and tragic when the two women are noticed in the store by three thugs. The three thugs, all young criminal scumbag types, grab the groceries from the delivery area and follow the two women back to their apartment. They lurk for a while until they are able to slip past the security door and into the building. They then make their way to the Bronson family apartment, where one of them poses as the delivery boy while the other two thugs wait out of sight. When Lange opens the door to collect the groceries, the scumbag thugs break in, and mayhem, rape, and murder ensue. Bronson's wife is savagely murdered and his daughter sexually assaulted, beaten, and left in an apparently permanent vegetative state from the trauma of the violent assault.

Like a good citizen, Bronson talks to the police and assists them with their investigation. He is heartbroken and devastated beyond words, but also determined to help the police track down the no-good, violent criminals who assaulted and destroyed his innocent family. The problem is, the police don't do much to help. They ask around, see if anybody saw anything, and then shrug their shoulders at Bronson when he asks that they do more to investigate the crime. (This, of course, is long before pervasive video surveillance, sophisticated communications, or crime-scene technology.) The police—overworked, understaffed, and overwhelmed in a city that is close to fiscally bankrupt and overwhelmed by violent crime—are able to do nothing to help Bronson in his quest for justice. When the police close the case after a brief and fruitless investigation, Bronson's family seems destined to become just another statistical victim in a 1970s America torn apart by escalating crime, urban decay, and moral degeneracy. Bronson is left alone in his once-happy apartment, bereft, with seemingly no way of obtaining justice.

But, of course, this is Charles Bronson, not just any old hapless victim but one of the toughest, roughest actors of his generation. And, with typical Charles Bronson gusto, he silently declares his revenge on his family's attackers. He first gets the idea of how to deal with the criminals when, as fortune would have it, he visits a client who is a real estate developer in Tucson, Arizona. Bronson goes out to the "great wide-open West" where he meets his new client, Aimes Jainchill, who is building a new housing development outside of Tucson. Bronson and Aimes hit it off and he takes Bronson to see an old-fashioned "Wild West" show in "old Tucson" near the construction site. The actors playing cowboys from Arizona's Wild West days act out the time-honored skit of the bad guys riding into town to rape, rob, and pillage the local townsfolk. The no-good bad guys plot to rob the local bank and beat up the town's marshal. The robbery is thwarted when the marshal's deputy takes on the bad guys. He confronts the bad guys with pistol and shotgun, and when the bad guys try to resist, the deputy blasts away until every last bad guy is dead and lying in the dust of Main Street. The audience goes wild while the public address announcer explains to the crowd that "the outlaw life seemed a shortcut to easy money that could buy liquor, women, or a turn at the gambling table, but there were honest men with dreams who would fight to protect their businesses and homes and that would plant the roots that would grow into a nation."

Bronson and his new friend, Aimes, wonder aloud what has happened to the backbone of America. How is it that the America of the 1970s was so pussyfooted about dealing with thugs and criminals, when, less than a hundred years before, an earlier generation was so able to set things right and enforce law and order through the use of deadly force when necessary? Why had the backbone and moral fiber of America seemingly vanished?

Aimes asks Bronson if he owns a gun. "No," Bronson tells him. The developer explains to Bronson that a gun is just a tool like any other piece of hardware, or at least this is how nineteenth-century Americans considered guns. At the end of the project, Bronson gets ready to board a plane for home. Aimes walks him to the airport gate and hands him a gift-wrapped package. In it is a semi-automatic pistol, chrome-plated and ready for use. "Let me slip a little going-away present in [your luggage] there for you," the real estate developer tells Bronson, and with a knowing nod he bids Bronson farewell and good luck. Since this takes place in the 1970s, and the airport has no metal detectors, baggage checks, or other twenty-first-century security screenings, Bronson easily boards the plane with his new gift tucked away in his luggage and heads for home.

Back in New York, Bronson quickly gets to work. He does not know the identities of the thugs who attacked his family, so instead he goes on a one-man law-and-order vigilante spree. Bronson takes his revenge on any and all thugs he encounters in the dark streets of New York. This pre–Rudy Giuliani 1970s New York is a dark and desolate urban landscape, teeming with petty criminals, muggers, and assorted urban misfits. Bronson has no trouble finding crime. By simply walking through a city park at night or flashing a wallet full of cash in a greasy diner, he is able to attract potential attackers bent on mugging him—or worse. When confronted by thugs who demand his wallet, he pulls out his gun and blasts away, gunning down each criminal in his tracks. Night after night, Bronson lights up the New York City night with gun blast after gun blast into the hearts and bellies of would-be muggers and murderers.

In the New York newspapers and press, word quickly spreads that there is a vigilante loose in the city. The police embark upon a massive manhunt. Seemingly inept and uncaring when they were summoned to investigate the attack on Bronson's innocent family, they are somehow able to muster the manpower and official police resources to track down a vigilante whose only crime has been to rid the city of a bunch of no-good criminal deadbeats. The even bigger irony is revealed when the crime rate starts to precipitously decline. At a socialite cocktail party Bronson attends, the party is all abuzz about the exploits of the unidentified "New York Vigilante."

At the end of the movie, a rumpled veteran police detective, played wonderfully by Vincent Gardenia, tracks down Bronson, who is shot while attacking three would-be robbers. At the hospital where Bronson is recuperating, the detective confronts Bronson and tells him to get out of town or face police arrest and prosecution. (The police don't want to arrest and prosecute Bronson, because it will create too much of a media circus. Earlier in the movie, the mayor and district attorney tell the detective that they want no part in arresting and prosecuting Bronson, fearing it would only turn him into a modern-day Robin Hood.)

The detective tells Bronson he is going to throw the gun in the river and orders him to leave town or else.

"By sundown?" Bronson replies, linking his actions with the values of the Wild West in a way that is abundantly clear to the entire movie audience.

In the final scene of the movie, Bronson has traveled by train to relocate to Chicago. He is seen standing in the Chicago rail station, a scene of urban decay and neglect. Standing in the middle of the train terminal, he witnesses a young woman being harassed by a gang of young punks. Smiling, he helps the lady, who has dropped her packages in the melee, and then turns to her attackers, who are running away howling and laughing at Bronson and the lady. He forms a gun with his thumb and index finger, closes one eye, and aims at the fleeing assailants and smiles. The message is clear: Bronson will be back with his brutal form of justice.

The movie *Death Wish* never used the term "zero tolerance," but Charles Bronson practiced true zero tolerance when it came to dealing with criminals. Faced with a would-be mugger attempting to rob him, Bronson simply pulled out a pistol and blew the mugger away. Talk about zero tolerance! No arrest, no jury, no judge, just point-blank execution for the would-be thug.

Thus, although not one viewer in the movie audience walked out of the cinema that summer of 1974 uttering the term "zero tolerance," we had all seen it firsthand. Here was an ordinary man not putting up with any crap from society's criminals. Nope, he just blew them away. For a teenage boy, this was pretty cool stuff. But, for America as a whole, it was a turning point. *Death Wish* drew a proverbial line in the sand for all politicians, police officers, and social theorists. The threat was clear and simple: unless American leaders got ahold of America's crime problem and quick, the end result could be real-life versions of Bronson's character in the movie taking the law into their own hands. Zero tolerance was going to happen somehow, either through the actions of ordinary, law-abiding citizens blasting away or by the leaders of America's criminal justice system figuring out how to effectively combat crime, especially in American cities.

A Book Establishes the Social Arguments for Zero Tolerance

The author of the book *Thinking About Crime* was about as different from Charles Bronson's character in *Death Wish* as you can get. Author James Q. Wilson was a professor of government at Harvard University when he first published *Thinking About Crime* in the summer of 1975, one year after *Death Wish* hit the screens. Wilson's book set off a firestorm of debate and angered ideologues on both the political left and the right.

Writing in a scholarly, analytical style, Wilson laid out his argument that the commission of a crime is a rational choice made by people who logically weigh the risks and benefits of committing the crime before acting. He argued that the rising crime rate could not be directly linked to increasing poverty or declines in equal opportunity or social services. Using statistical analysis, Wilson showed that while crime had been rising since the early 1960s in America, so had the economy, equality of opportunity, and government spending on social services and antipoverty programs. He pointed out that police departments had been focusing their resources on investigating and combating major crimes at the expense of policing petty criminal behavior and juvenile delinquency.

He argued that middle-class people—regardless of race and regardless of whether they were living in the cities, suburbs, or countryside—all wanted the police in their communities to protect them from the criminal class. Ultimately, he argued for a more rational and predictable criminal justice system that enforces the laws against minor transgressions and misdemeanors as the best way to keep major crimes from happening. He then argued for a rational, predictable range of punishments for persons convicted of crimes. He asserted that these punishments should not be overly harsh, but just harsh enough to make the commission of the crime less beneficial to the would-be lawbreaker than not committing the crime would be.

Wilson infuriated the political left by arguing that simply putting more money into government antipoverty and equal rights programs would not end urban crime. He also angered the right because he argued for punishments to be relatively mild and not vengeful in nature. He believed that short periods of incarceration were probably most effective for most crimes, because they would make committing crime less beneficial but not turn offenders into hardened, lifelong criminals who would then choose to commit more crimes. Long prison sentences should be left for those persons committing very serious crimes, Wilson argued, and for those career criminals who needed to be taken off the streets for long periods for the protection of society.

When *Thinking About Crime* was published, its impact on America's politicians and social theorists was immediate. Marvin A. Wolfgang of the *New York Times Book Review* wrote, "I recommend this book to the president, Attorney General, Congress, police, judges, correctional administrators and the general public for a succinct review of what our major crime problems are and what the potential solutions may be for deterrence, prevention, law enforcement and sentencing."[10]

Wilson never used the term "zero tolerance." What he did do was advocate for a criminal justice system that did not tolerate persons committing crimes, whether petty or serious, against the American populace. He argued that American society neglected the punishment of criminals at its peril, and that both petty and serious crimes had to be prosecuted or else people would be emboldened to commit more and more crime. Although Wilson did not coin the term "zero tolerance," he laid out the argument that a society that tolerated crime could expect more of it, and that the only way to stop crime was to not tolerate it.

By the time the 1970s came to a close, American society was ripe for social change and the establishment of zero tolerance as the new crime-prevention policy. Wilson had laid out all of the academic arguments for it, and *Death Wish* had brutally portrayed what the result could be if America's leaders did not adopt it. The term "zero tolerance" did not yet exist, but all the urgency of its importance as a tool for combating crime had been stamped deep into the minds of the politicians, the police, the social theorists, and the population at large.

The only thing still missing was a blueprint, a practical nuts-and-bolts explanation of how to establish a criminal justice system based upon the principle of zero tolerance. It would take another eight years for this blueprint to be worked out and explained to the general public.

A Magazine Article Establishes Zero Tolerance as the Key to Crime Prevention and Urban Renewal

The blueprint for zero tolerance finally arrived in the form of a magazine article called "Broken Windows," published in the March 1982 issue of *The Atlantic Monthly* (now called *The Atlantic*), a national magazine covering social and cultural issues. In their article, James Wilson and coauthor George L. Kelling, an American Criminologist and Professor at Rutgers University, initially laid out a practical method for establishing zero tolerance as the official crime prevention policy for America.[11]

"Broken Windows" also appeared as one of the essays in Wilson's 1983, revised edition of *Thinking About Crime*.[12] But, by being published in the widely read *Atlantic Monthly*, the essay gained a much broader readership than it ever would have had as one of thirteen chapters of Wilson's academic book. Reprinted in the popular monthly news magazine, "Broken Windows" became a stand-alone explanation of how best to curb crime and social disorder in American cities.

Kelling and Wilson began their article by describing the Safe and Clean Neighborhoods Program, a policing experiment conducted in the mid-1970s in Newark, New Jersey. The program involved taking officers out of their patrol cars and reorganizing them into foot patrols. Many people were unenthusiastic about the idea—especially the police.

As Kelling and Wilson explained, "Many police chiefs were skeptical. Foot patrols, in their eyes, had been pretty much discredited. It reduced the mobility of the police who thus had difficulty responding to citizen calls for service, and it weakened headquarters control over patrol officers."[13]

"Police officers," Kelling and Wilson noted, "also disliked foot patrol for different reasons: it was hard work, it kept them out on cold, rainy nights, and it reduced their chances of making a 'good pinch.' In some departments, assigning officers to foot patrol had been used as a form of punishment."[14]

When the results of the Safe and Clean Neighborhoods Program were published five years later, they proved the skeptics' claims that the program "had not reduced crime rates."[15] This led some to proclaim the program an abject failure and a waste of time and money. But Kelling and Wilson noted that an unexpected phenomenon occurred, not one predicted or anticipated by either the program's original supporters or its detractors:

> Five years after the program started ... foot patrol had not reduced crime rates. But residents of the foot-patrolled neighborhoods seemed to feel more secure than people in other areas, tended to believe crime had been reduced, and tended to take fewer steps to protect themselves from crime (staying at home with the doors locked, for example). Moreover, citizens had a more favorable opinion of the police than did those living elsewhere. And officers had a higher morale, greater job satisfaction, and a more favorable attitude toward citizens in their neighborhoods than did officers assigned to patrol cars.[16]

So, if the crime rate did not go down, why did the citizens of Newark feel safer and the police more satisfied with their jobs? Kelling and Wilson explained:

> [F]irst we must understand what most frightens people in public places. Many citizens, of course are primarily frightened by crime. . . . But we tend to overlook or forget another source of fear—the fear of being bothered by disorderly people (not violent people, nor, necessarily, criminals, but disreputable or obstreperous or unpredictable people: panhandlers, drunks, addicts, rowdy teenagers, prostitutes, loiterers, the mentally disturbed).[17]

Kelling and Wilson concluded that, although the actual crime rate in the foot-patrolled neighborhoods did not go down, the overall *sense* of safety was increased for the average citizen of the neighborhood by the increase in public order.

> What foot patrol officers did was to elevate, to the extent they could, the level of public order in these neighborhoods. Though the neighborhoods were predominantly black, and the foot patrolmen were mostly white, this order-maintenance function of the police was performed to the satisfaction of both parties.[18]

To defenders of civil liberties, the means used by the police in Newark to enforce civil order could be seen as disturbing. Kelling and Wilson pointed out that many of the methods employed by the police to maintain public order would probably not pass constitutional scrutiny, and the rights of some of the neighborhood's citizens were probably violated in the pursuit of order and a sense of public safety for all. Despite this, Kelling and Wilson concluded that "the people of Newark, to judge from their behaviors and remarks to interviewers, apparently assign a high value to public order, and feel relieved and reassured when the police help to maintain that order."[19]

In "Broken Windows," Kelling and Wilson reintroduced and emphasized the traditional police officer's duty of maintaining public order. This was not to say that investigating and solving crimes and responding to 911 emergency calls for service were not equally important. But, as a nation, Americans had become so focused on these relatively new police responsibilities that they had forgotten the all-important role of the police as the ultimate maintainer of "good public order" within American communities. Kelling and Wilson argued that any community that ignored this traditional police function of maintaining order did so at its own peril. Using the analogy of a broken window in a vacant building, the authors explained why not maintaining public order led to urban decay, community blight, and an increased fear of crime.

At the community level, disorder and crime are usually inextricably linked, in a kind of developmental sequence. Social scientists and police officers tend to agree that if a window in a building is broken *and is left unrepaired*, all the rest of the windows will soon be broken. This is as true in nice neighborhoods as run down ones. Window breaking does not necessarily occur on a large-scale basis, because some areas are inhabited by determined window-breakers whereas others are populated by window-lovers; rather, one unrepaired broken window is a signal that no one cares, and so breaking more windows costs nothing. (It has always been fun.)[20]

Kelling and Wilson went on to describe different examples of how the police had been able to assist communities to prevent their neighborhoods from spiraling over the "tipping point" and out of control. The solution was determined police intervention at the community level—with acknowledgment and encouragement by the residents of the community that whatever steps the police took to maintain public order were methods acceptable to the majority of the residents of the community, and especially to those persons with the greatest stake in the community: homeowners, long-term residents, and business owners. Only through the concerted actions of the good, solid citizens of a community and the police working together could good order and the perception of public safety be achieved. Failure to do this would ultimately result in the destruction of the neighborhood. Wilson concluded:

> I suggest that "untended behavior" leads to a breakdown of community controls. A stable neighborhood of families who care for their homes, mind each other's children, and confidently frown on unwanted intruders can change, in a few years or even a few months, to an inhospitable and frightening jungle. A piece of property

is abandoned, weeds grow up, and a window is smashed. Adults stop scolding rowdy children; the children, emboldened, become more rowdy. Families move out, unattached adults move in. Teenagers gather in front of the corner store. The merchant asks them to move; they refuse. Fights occur. Litter accumulates. People start drinking in front of the grocery; in time an inebriate slumps to the sidewalk and is allowed to sleep it off. Pedestrians are approached by panhandlers.[21]

This passage is particularly poignant to me as an illustration of the breakdown of social controls and public order that can occur, especially in urban settings. Reading those words, penned more than a quarter of a century ago, conjures up a still-vivid memory from my experience living in New York City as a young man, recently graduated from college, in the late 1980s.

On a weekend evening sometime around 1987, I was having dinner on Columbus Avenue on the Upper West Side. My girlfriend and I were seated in the outdoor sidewalk café section of a restaurant. It was one of those beautiful blue-sky early summer evenings when New York City takes on all of the magic that has captivated visitors and residents alike for so many generations. There my girlfriend and I sat with our well-dressed fellow diners, enjoying the food and the weather and the weekend break from the regular toil of our busy, career-driven work lives. As we sat in the open-air café, my girlfriend and I watched the endless throng of passers-by, fellow citizens carrying packages or herding children, everyone moving this way and that to their next destination. We were lost in some now long-forgotten discussion about the day's events when, all of a sudden, our peaceful evening repast was shattered by a bedraggled, obviously intoxicated homeless man. He seemed to appear out of nowhere and started to curse and scream and bellow at the people sitting a couple of tables down from us. Dressed in "typical" homeless garb—layer upon layer of filthy coats and rags—he stood there staring menacingly and screaming profanities at the dining couple as he wobbled drunkenly ever closer to their table. The couple was clearly shocked and scared. Everyone stopped eating while nearby pedestrians stopped in their tracks, not sure whether to be afraid, amused, or angry. Suddenly, the homeless man grabbed the food off of the couple's table and stuffed a piece of meat into his mouth. He then flung the plate into the street, knocked over a couple of empty chairs, almost fell over a table, and finally righted himself enough to stumble drunkenly on his way down the sidewalk cursing, screaming, and flailing his arms at the people standing on the street watching him.

Everybody sitting in the café watched in stunned silence. Then, as the man wandered away and the threat of physical danger receded, nervous laughter broke out among the diners.

"Gee, I guess he was hungry," someone joked.

"Yes, but what awful table manners," another diner quipped.

"He's hungry. Someone should be providing these poor people with food. It's ridiculous that that poor man should go hungry," another café patron sympathetically chimed in.

"He should be arrested and tossed in jail," an angry voice piped up.

"No, better yet, ship him to New Jersey!" another diner hollered out, and the whole café shook with laughter. There is nothing more restorative to a New Yorker's good humor than a joke at New Jersey's expense. At least it worked that evening as a kind of a tonic after the disturbing event.

In the New York City of the 1980s, such "civil disturbances" were commonplace. So was the very real fear of crime—many of my friends were robbed at some point or another, some at gunpoint. When I went to a sketchy neighborhood, I always carried "street rental," a ten- or twenty-dollar bill in the bottom of my shoe. The hope was that if I got mugged, the mugger would just take my wallet and leave my shoes unexplored, and I would still have cab or subway fare to get back home.

On a far graver scale were the horror stories of the mid- and late-1980s. A female jogger was brutally attacked and raped in Central Park. (A gang of five youths, called a "wolf pack" in the local press, was arrested and convicted of the crime. Only later did it come to light that the attack was most likely committed by a single assailant.) A man who felt threatened by three teenagers gunned them down on a subway car. Other young men were beaten or killed when they went into the "wrong neighborhood," i.e., one ethnically or racially different than their own. A young woman was strangled to death during an episode of "rough sex" in Central Park, leading to the yearlong "Preppy Murder Trial."

There were other signs of social disintegration and disorder as well: riding the subway cars, which were strewn with trash and covered in graffiti; walking through Times Square when it was filled with porn films, drug addicts, and prostitutes; and having to constantly worry about your general safety when walking around the city. One night, a thug wielding a razor attacked me, and on another night, a mugger with a gun robbed a friend in the East Village. Thus, for me—and many of my fellow 1980s New Yorkers—Kelling and Wilson's linking of social decay and social disorder to crime certainly rang true.

At the same time, in the article "Broken Windows," Wilson and Kelling concluded by voicing the fears that all of us dining at that Upper West Side café felt on that warm summer night when public order and decorum were interrupted:

> Above all, we must return to our long abandoned view that the police ought to protect communities and not just individuals. Our crime statistics and victimization surveys measure individual losses, but they do not measure communal losses. Just as physicians now recognize the importance of fostering health rather than simply treating illness, so the police—and the rest of us—ought to recognize the importance of maintaining intact communities without broken windows.[22]

As in Wilson's original 1975 book, *Thinking About Crime*, Kelling and Wilson never used the term "zero tolerance" in "Broken Windows." What Kelling and Wilson did make clear is that the citizens of a community must not tolerate leaving one broken window unrepaired or they will surely all be broken. Kelling and Wilson argued that social order must be maintained by the police as the ultimate community goal, even, when necessary, at the expense of individuals' rights and liberties. To do otherwise, they warned, was to invite social disorder, urban decay, and violent crime into the community.

In my opinion, the really important message of "Broken Windows" has been lost in present-day America. Zero tolerance has come to be seen as a public policy cure-all, not just for crime but also for our social problems in general. But the modern-day approach to zero tolerance is not at all what Kelling and Wilson were advocating for in "Broken Windows."

In the Safe and Clean Neighborhoods Program in Newark, the Newark police on foot patrol were hardly enforcing a stringent, zero-tolerance arrest and criminal prosecution policy to keep the streets of Newark safe and social order intact. In fact, it was just the opposite. The policing method utilized by the Newark police on foot patrol was one of wide restraint and enforcing the strict letter of the criminal law only in limited instances, at their own discretion, and as a matter of last resort. Newark's Safe and Clean Neighborhoods Program was effective because it allowed the police on foot patrol a large amount of discretion over how and when—and against whom—to enforce criminal laws and make arrests. The Newark experiment showed that it was through maintaining close ties with the community's civic leaders, enforcing unwritten local neighborhood customs, and using extra-constitutional restrictions on certain individuals' civil liberties, that public order and a sense of community safety could best be achieved—not through strictly enforced, government-mandated zero-tolerance arrest and prosecution policies. As Kelling and Wilson explained:

> The people on the street were primarily black; the officer who walked the street was white. The people were made up of "regulars" and "strangers." Regulars included both "decent folk" and some drunks and derelicts who were always there but "knew their place." Strangers were, well, strangers, and viewed suspiciously, sometimes

apprehensively. The officer—call him Kelly—knew who the regulars were, and they knew him. As he saw his job it was to keep an eye on strangers, and make sure that the disreputable regulars observed some informal but widely understood rules. Drunks and addicts could sit on the stoops, but not lie down. People could drink on the side streets, but not on the main intersection. Bottles had to be in paper bags. Talking to, or bothering, or begging from people waiting at the bus stop was strictly forbidden. If a dispute erupted between a businessman and a customer, the businessman was assumed to be right, especially if the customer was a stranger. If a stranger loitered, Kelly would ask him if he had a means of support and what his business was; if he gave unsatisfactory answers, he was sent on his way. Persons who broke the informal rules, especially those who bothered people at the bus stop, were arrested for vagrancy. Noisy teenagers were told to keep quiet.

The rules were defined and enforced in collaboration with the "regulars" on the street. Another neighborhood might have different rules, but these, everybody understood, were the rules for this neighborhood. If someone violated them then the regulars not only turned to Kelly for help but also ridiculed the violator. Sometimes what Kelly did could be described as "enforcing the law," but just as often it involved taking informal or extralegal steps to help protect what the neighborhood had decided was the appropriate level of public order. Some of the things he did probably would not withstand legal challenge.[23]

The authors of "Broken Windows" acknowledged the inherent friction between encroaching on individual civil liberties and effectively maintaining law and order by giving the police wide latitude and extra-constitutional authority to decide when and how to make an arrest or otherwise enforce the criminal laws. They readily admitted they really didn't have an answer that would satisfy those critical of the practice of giving the local police so much discretion in how best to maintain neighborhood order.[24]

Kelling and Wilson gave another example of what today could be called "community policing," describing a housing project in Chicago, home to 20,000 people, where both the residents and the police were black. The police there successfully utilized methods similar to those used in Newark for maintaining order and combating crime.[25] The authors also showed how, in the upscale white neighborhood of Palo Alto (near San Francisco), an abandoned car ultimately led to vandalism, crime, and a loss of public order when police and neighborhood controls were not in place.[26] Based on these various examples, Kelling and Wilson concluded:

> The essence of the police role in maintaining order is to reinforce the informal control mechanisms of the community itself. The police cannot, without expending extraordinary resources, provide a substitute for that informal control. On the other hand, to reinforce those natural (communal) controls the police must accommodate them. And therein lies the problem. *Should police activity on the street be shaped, in important ways, by the standards of the neighborhood, rather than the rules of the state?*"[27] (Emphasis added)

Later, Kelling and Wilson ask the even more pointed question, "How do we ensure, in short, that the police do not become agents of neighborhood bigotry?"[28]

To these two all-important rhetorical questions, Kelling and Wilson's response is, for me, wonderfully obtuse—while at the same time fair, balanced, and utterly reasonable. Their response, therefore, is also intolerable and unacceptable to those activists on both sides of America's political divide over the past generation who have labored zealously for the enactment and enforcement of zero-tolerance policies throughout America's criminal justice system and in other spheres of American society. Kelling and Wilson answered their own rhetorical questions thusly:

> We can offer no wholly satisfactory answer to this important question. We are not confident that there is a satisfactory answer, except to hope that by their selection, training, and supervision, the police will be inculcated with a clear sense of the outer limit of their discretionary authority. That limit, roughly, is this—the police exist to help regulate behavior, not to maintain the racial or ethnic purity of a neighborhood.[29]

This well-reasoned answer to the all-important question of how to best balance individual civil liberties while still allowing the police the tools necessary to maintain public order in American communities has proven, over the past twenty-five-plus years since Kelling and Wilson wrote it, to satisfy no one standing on the left or right side of the political aisle. For law-and-order types, the police need to enforce zero-tolerance policies by arresting anyone and everyone who breaks even the slightest criminal law. Otherwise, the result will be social disorder, spiraling crime rates, and moral degeneracy. For "get tough on crime" types, providing the local foot patrolmen with such wide discretion to choose when, and when not, to arrest a lawbreaker is intolerable and a flagrant violation of the basic principle of strict enforcement of the criminal laws.

At the same time, for many left-wingers, providing the police with such wide discretion as to when and whom to arrest is to allow the police to "take the law into their own hands" and to enforce the criminal law against only those citizens who are vulnerable to police brutality: minorities, teenagers, homeless people and the dispossessed, the citizen dedicated to individual self-expression, and anyone else whose behavior, ethnicity, social or sexual orientation, class, or dress is at odds with "community standards." To those concerned with curbing police misconduct or selective arrest and prosecution policies aimed at minorities or the poor, zero-tolerance policies are the means for ensuring all citizens enjoy equal protection under the law. Thus, Kelling and Wilson's recommendation satisfies no one. Be it law and order's desire for equal and ruthless enforcement of the criminal law, or the left's quest for equal and ruthless enforcement of equal protection under the criminal law, both sides have ended up with the same prescriptive solution to what they perceive as the inequities in American society: zero tolerance.

Looking back more than three decades, Kelling and Wilson's suggestion that any fears about police officers being either too lenient or too forceful when maintaining civil order may be assuaged by ascribing to the police "a clear sense of the outer limit of their discretionary authority" seems almost quaint. Today, in America's land of zero tolerance, in a world of screaming bloggers, haranguing twenty-four-hour news channels, social action committees, civil rights groups, law-and-order political activists, the Internet, and "concerned citizens" groups, to many people the idea that the police can be trusted simply to use their discretion seems almost laughable.

Kelling and Wilson's moderate reply to their own suggestion, stating that the best way to balance civil liberty with maintaining public order is by allowing the local police wide discretionary authority over the neighborhood populace, reminds me of a scene from another great crime movie—*The Untouchables*, from 1987. *The Untouchables* focused on the young Elliot Ness and Jimmy Malone, a police officer. We first meet Malone as he walks his beat late one night in Prohibition-era Chicago. Federal agent Ness throws a balled-up piece of paper into the river out of frustration with his job, which is to arrest and destroy Al Capone. Malone, a streetwise Irish cop, sees Ness throw the piece of trash into the river, in violation of a municipal ordinance, and chastises Ness for doing so, telling him to throw his garbage in the trash basket and not in the river. Ness then starts to reach inside his breast coat pocket to get a match to light a cigarette. In response, Malone pulls out his nightstick, taps Ness on the chest and demands to know why he is packing a gun. Ness responds that he is a treasury officer. Satisfied, Malone tells Ness that he can go about his business. Baffled by Malone's trust in his response, Ness replies, "Wait a minute, what the hell kind of police do you have in this goddamned city? What do they teach you? You just turned your back on an armed man." The street-smart Malone doesn't miss a beat as he replies, "You're a treasury officer." Ness then pushes further, asking, "How did you know that? I just told you I was." Malone replies confidently, "Who would claim to be that, who was not?" Ness is so impressed with Malone's police smarts he invites him to join him in bringing the fight to Al Capone. And thus, the organized crime-fighting team of the Untouchables is born as the street-smart Irish cop joins the idealistic government bureaucrat in his battle to stop the violent gangster overlord, Al Capone.

Fast-forward and play out this same scene in any city street in America today, and it probably comes out quite differently, thanks to zero tolerance. Malone is forced to arrest Ness for littering, because if he doesn't he will face condemnation by his superiors for not enforcing the department's zero-tolerance policy against minor infractions such as littering. Compounding Malone's problems will be the near-certain fact that his actions will have been caught on video by the city's video street surveillance system. A blogger will air the footage, criticizing Malone because he gave a fellow law enforcement officer a break he might not have given another citizen, and will demand Malone's dismissal from the police department. Of course, the fact that Malone pulled out his nightstick and tapped Ness on the shoulder to get Ness's attention may also land Malone in hot water with some other activist group, upset at Malone's violation of the department's zero-tolerance policy against police misconduct in the use of nonprescribed force when detaining a suspect. Any way you slice it, Malone never gets to join Ness's crime-fighting team of Untouchables, even though Malone had clearly displayed and used his "clear sense of the outer limits" of his "discretionary authority" as a police officer.

The Road to Zero Tolerance—From 1982 to Today

Since Kelling and Wilson published "Broken Windows" in *The Atlantic Monthly* in 1982, it has been argued that the authors were advocating zero-tolerance police tactics.[30] There is logic behind this argument, especially because, as explained below, Kelling is credited with first using the term in 1994. I do not agree, however, that Kelling and Wilson intended to advocate for zero-tolerance policies—I see it as quite the opposite, in fact. Looking back at the way Kelling and Wilson describe "Officer Kelly" handling his job as a neighborhood cop in Newark and maintaining public order, he was hardly practicing zero tolerance. He certainly was not strictly enforcing New Jersey's criminal code or Newark's municipal ordinances when he was patrolling under Newark's Safe and Clean Neighborhoods Program. What he *was* doing was enforcing unwritten neighborhood norms for civil conduct and good manners, while using his professional discretion to enforce the criminal and municipal codes as one of many ways of maintaining public order— usually as a last resort when other, less severe, methods had failed to resolve a situation of potential conflict. People were allowed to drink alcohol unmolested in public; panhandling could occur, but not at the bus stops; strangers were stopped and questioned but not ultimately frisked or arrested for simply giving vague or questionable answers. Drunks were not arrested for public insobriety, addicts apparently were not frisked and seized even though they were obviously on one illegal substance or another, and the "regulars" probably got cut more "slack" than strangers to the neighborhood if they did break the law in some way. Officer Kelly's method of operation was to keep order by utilizing his full quiver of law enforcement weapons in order to maintain public order and keep the peace. His ability to balance maintaining public order while also maintaining good and cordial public relations with those he protected and served—including all members of the community of all races, classes, and walks of life—depended upon his good common sense and professional training and not a robot-like, knee-jerk adherence to government-mandated "tough on crime" zero-tolerance policies.

So why is it that Kelling and Wilson's work has led American society down the road to zero tolerance—not only as the governing mandate for America's criminal justice system but as a guiding principle for many other of its public and private institutions? How could that come about when those sources never used the words "zero tolerance" and when the authors never argued in favor of zero-tolerance policing, prosecutions, or sentencing policies, let alone zero-tolerance policies in workplaces or schools?

My discussion in this chapter of the three sources—the movie, the book, and the "Broken Windows" article—is, of course, my way of illustrating that the idea of zero tolerance sprang into the popular imagination during the 1970s and early 1980s through a combination of academic writing, public policy discourse, popular culture, law-and-order initiatives, and other forms of public policy debate. The basic argument—if not the actual name—for zero tolerance can be extrapolated from the three sources I have highlighted.

In *Thinking About Crime,* Wilson clearly argues that American society is under assault by ever-increasing crime and labels as dangerous fallacy the basic liberal notion that an increasing equality of opportunity and personal wealth will deter crime. Bronson's character in *Death Wish* demonstrates that individual citizens will ultimately take the law into their own hands and invoke their own brands of zero tolerance if America's criminal justice system is too weak or inept to combat crime. And, most assuredly, in "Broken Windows," Kelling and Wilson—despite all of their attempts at explaining the need for, and ways to implement, a fair and balanced criminal justice system—have, at their core, a clear invocation of a form of zero tolerance when it comes to fixing society's problem of decreasing civil disorder, which it warns may lead to increasing crime. Their take-away message is that if a *single* "window in a building is broken *and is left unrepaired* all of the rest of the windows will soon be broken" (emphasis added). As a prescription for restoring American communities and preventing crime, this cautionary tale of that single broken window can be—and has been—interpreted as a call for zero tolerance as the solution for fixing both America's criminal justice system and society's ills in general.

The insistence by Kelling and Wilson that each and every broken window must be fixed each and every time, or the result can lead to social disorder, urban decline, and increased crime, can arguably lead to only one logical conclusion: that society must practice zero tolerance when it comes to fixing its proverbial "broken windows," because to do anything less is to invite neighborhood disorder and never-ending increases in social destabilization and crime. Kelling and Wilson's discussion about fixing broken windows, so that an urban area does not look neglected by its residents, which, in turn, may lead to more broken windows—and ultimately to increased neighborhood disorder and, finally, to more crime—is a long way from demanding zero-tolerance arrest, criminal prosecution, and sentencing policies. A community can be vigilant over fixing broken windows, or public graffiti, or litter in the streets, or other signs of community neglect and malaise without arresting *anyone*. These are called "municipal improvements," and they have been shown to do a great deal in establishing a renaissance in urban, suburban, and rural communities all over the United States. They are exactly the type of prescriptive for which Kelling and Wilson were advocating. Police, as described so ably by Kelling and Wilson, can utilize many tools as sworn and uniformed police officers to improve community relations, maintain clean and orderly public streets, improve a neighborhood's morale, and lessen residents' fear of crime—both real and imagined.

Regardless, the urging for moderation and tolerance in Wilson's 1975 book, and in Kelling and Wilson's 1982 article, have been lost to us as politicians, political activists, and the like have seized upon the simplistic concept of zero tolerance by taking a very limited "ends justify the means" argument concerning fixing a neighborhood's "broken windows," in both the actual and the figurative sense, and extrapolating from this reasonable idea the radical and pervasive argument that zero tolerance must be adopted to solve all of society's problems.

Can we pinpoint when zero tolerance came to the fore? If Kelling and Wilson were not using the term in the 1980s, when did it come into being? The first use of the term is said to have appeared in a 1994 report coauthored by Kelling.[31] He was discussing how to deal with the public nuisance of the "squeegee men," who were running out into the intersections of New York City with buckets of soapy water and squeegees and cleaning the windshields of motorists stopped at red lights.

I had this happen to me in New York on a couple of occasions. A man would scurry out into waiting traffic with a plastic bucket of dirty, soapy water and without asking permission start "washing" your windshield. Then, before the light changed, he would run to your window and demand payment for this "service." If you said no and refused to pay or tried to wave him away, he might go peacefully, but he might also get mad and bang on your hood or stare menacingly at you or start yelling and screaming. The whole tactic was intimidating to me as a driver, because I had not asked for these men to touch my car—they just took it upon themselves to do so, and then they sort of held me hostage. Like most people, I value my car as one of my most important possessions, and a person bold enough to just start washing your windshield without first asking might do some type of damage to your car if you made him unhappy by refusing to pay.

In his 1994 article, Kelling explained that the New York City police had created a "task force" to establish a "no-tolerance" policy toward allowing squeegee men to operate on the streets of New York. If a man (or woman) attempted to squeegee the windshield of a motorist, he was arrested and charged with petty harassment. By focusing police resources on the squeegee men and instituting a zero-tolerance arrest policy toward the behavior, Kelling explained, New York City was able to stamp out the squeegee problem and thus eliminate the fear and intimidation by New York City motorists that resulted from the behavior.

Much has been written about how the use of zero-tolerance arrest policies, first used against the squeegee men, were ultimately used throughout the New York City police force during Rudy Giuliani's tenure as mayor. The concept of creating police task forces to focus on a particular community or a particular type of unwanted illegal behavior, and then practicing zero tolerance by arresting anyone and everyone who stepped outside the bounds, has been well documented in books and articles over the years.

For someone who remembers the "bad old days" of 1980s New York City, the impact that Rudy Giuliani's policies, as put into effect by Kelling and Police Commissioner William Bratton, has been truly awe inspiring. The New York City of today seems radically safer and less chaotic than in the days when you literally lived in regular fear of being harassed or mugged by a wide variety of sketchy people stalking the streets. But there has also been a huge backlash against many of the policies that Giuliani's administration used, as civil liberties watchdog groups and others have asserted those policies went too far, infringed upon civil liberties, or were racist because they targeted minorities.

As someone who considers himself a champion of civil liberties, I certainly believe that some of the criticism of the policing practices of the Giuliani era has merit. At the same time, I am glad to see New York City doing well again, with safer streets and once-abandoned neighborhoods now home to thriving communities.

One great example of how radical the shift has been over the past twenty-five years is Tompkins Square Park on the Lower East Side in Manhattan. Shortly after I moved to New York in 1985, I volunteered at a boy's club located at 10th Street and Avenue A, bordering Tompkins Square Park. I would arrive at the boy's club after work in the early evening to help coach basketball. I never once walked into the park the entire year I volunteered at the boys club. In the evening hours while I was at the club, the park was overwhelmed with homeless people, drunks, drug dealers, and petty thieves. The benches, sidewalks, and lawn were a mess. I knew that to walk into the park dressed in my suit and tie was to foolishly invite being harassed—or much worse.

Fast-forward to today, and the difference is unbelievable. The park is beautiful, and the grounds, benches, and flowerbeds are all well maintained. The drinking fountain in the center of the park actually works! The children of residents who live all around the park play in safe, updated playgrounds. Gone are the drug dealers, drunks, and addicts, as well as most of the homeless people. Well into the evening, pedestrians stroll the park, joggers run through it, and restaurants and cafés around the park do a brisk business. Tompkins Square Park is once again what it originally was back when it was created in 1878: a leafy haven for neighborhood residents and visitors.

Ask most New Yorkers and they would never choose to go back to the New York of the 1980s. Controversial though they may have been, Giuliani's policies have created civic improvements deeply cherished by New York residents. These policies have been modified during Mayor Bloomberg's administration, which during his tenure pushed for better community relations with the police by emphasizing "community policing." (These updated policies come much closer to what Wilson and Kelling were advocating in their 1982 article.) In any event, few would wish to see Tompkins Square Park return to the demoralized and dangerous condition it was in, circa 1985.

With the success of zero-tolerance policing in New York City in the 1990s, the concept rapidly spread throughout America to its cities, suburbs, and rural communities. The result has been a renaissance in many urban communities as middle- and upper-class people stopped fleeing America's cities and started moving back in. As someone who is a true lover of city life, I am grateful that America's mayors, police departments, and civic leaders have figured out ways to once again make America's cities safe, enjoyable places to live and work.

So about now you might reasonably be asking, "Wait a minute, Mr. Conaway, I thought you were opposed to zero tolerance and that you believed that it is an evil concept threatening our civil liberties. Why are you now hailing zero-tolerance arrest policies as good public policy?" My response has three parts.

First, provided the police are allowed to use their professional discretion as to when and when not to make an arrest, I am comfortable with the police doing their job, which is to arrest someone whom they have probable cause to believe has broken the law. Second, zero-tolerance policing has been modified and improved, to some extent, by the influence of community policing concepts that have been developed by civic leaders to combat the excesses of zero-tolerance policies. Third, and most controversially, I am a middle-aged, white, professional man, and thus not a typical target for zero-tolerance policing. In fact, not only am I not the target, I am one of the types of people most likely to be protected by, and to benefit from, the results of zero-tolerance policing.

This is not true across the board; as we shall see, there are now zero-tolerance policies that can impact middle-aged professional people, but the policies that impact city streets generally do not. If I were a teenager or young man, or a person of color, or poor and homeless, or a mental health patient, I might very well feel very differently about zero-tolerance arrest policies.

A few years ago, I represented a teenage boy who was in high school. We were in my office discussing his case, which involved a basic breach of the law. His dad was sitting in the office with us. My client was suburban, relatively affluent, and white, yet his opinion of the police was radically different from mine. When I asked the boy how he felt about the police, he angrily declared he was sick of the "goddamned pigs" because they were constantly harassing him and his friends. If they tried to hang out in a public park or drink a few beers, score a little weed, or drive around town in their cars and just hang out with their girlfriends, they were—according to him—continuously harassed, stopped, questioned, and threatened with arrest by the local municipal police, who targeted them as troublemakers. My client was not from some tough inner-city neighborhood, nor were he and his friends persons of color. Yet his feelings were similar to the complaints voiced by young people in many minority neighborhoods who find themselves the targets, and not the beneficiaries, of zero-tolerance policing policies. The behavior for which he and his friends were targeted by the police was certainly not unusual for teenagers. At least, it certainly did not sound any different from the type of behavior my friends and I practiced when we were teenagers hanging out in a similar suburban neighborhood in the late-1970s pre-zero-tolerance days. I am glad I grew up in the America of the 1970s, when the police were more tolerant. Thus, when it comes to zero-tolerance and community-policing policies, your viewpoint may very well depend on whether you are the target of these policies or one of the beneficiaries. Regardless, as American citizens, zero-tolerance policing policies are a dangerous threat to the civil liberties of all Americans, black and white, rich and poor, and young and old. In an America that values its civil liberties, the police need to be able to use their professional training and expertise to decide whether to arrest a person or not within reasonable boundaries of common sense. No American benefits from a system of strict zero-tolerance policing tactics, as we are all put at risk as potential targets. The criminal laws in our country need to be enforced by thinking, well-trained law enforcement officers utilizing their street smarts and common sense to create a safe and tolerant society for all Americans. Our civil liberties and our safety are most gravely imperiled if we as American citizens insist that our streets and communities be patrolled by law enforcement officers transformed into mindless, intolerant arresting machines, hamstrung and made brain-dead by the soulless manifesto of zero tolerance. We have the power to create the kind of criminal justice system we want, but before you decide what you want, take a long look in the mirror and realize that in a land of zero tolerance policing tactics, you may just be the next victim.

CHAPTER FIVE

HOW ZERO TOLERANCE IMPACTS POLICE INVESTIGATIONS IN AMERICA

In Chapter Four, we saw how the idea of zero tolerance developed from the idea that a community could not afford to allow a single broken window to be left unrepaired. As I explained, it is my belief that Kelling and Wilson's "broken windows" argument has been misinterpreted ever since. They were talking about maintaining an orderly community by making sure civic improvements were maintained; by providing regular police presence and reassurance by reinstating regular foot patrols; and by allowing neighborhood police officers the authority to be *tolerant* by using their professional discretion to determine when and under what circumstances to make an arrest. Kelling and Wilson were thus advocating for a system of tolerance practiced by community police officers that should be given wide latitude in choosing when and whom to arrest. Indeed, Kelling and Wilson never used the term "zero tolerance." And yet, as we have seen, in the past twenty-five years zero tolerance has taken America by storm.

The Role of the Task Force

In America today, zero-tolerance arrest policies are truly everywhere. Each one is enforced using similar methods to those first worked out in New York City during the Giuliani administration. The first step usually involves community and law-and-order activists uniting politically at the national, state, and local levels to implement zero-tolerance arrest policies targeting specific illegal behavior that they find intolerable and view as a menace to community safety. Next, the local police department may form a "task force."

The website WiseGEEK provides a detailed description of how these police task forces are organized:

> A task force is a group of people who are temporarily assigned to work together to achieve a very specific and clearly defined objective. For example, a drug task force works independently of a police force to address issues relating to the manufacture, sale, and use of illegal drugs. Although the concept of a task force is military in origin, task forces today are often found beyond the boundaries of the military, appearing in the business world, law enforcement, and charitable organizations.[32]

The first step to creating a law enforcement task force is for the police department to organize a group of patrol officers, detectives, and other personnel and assign them to specifically focus on arresting anyone and everyone allegedly committing a specific illegal activity. The police cars used in these operations many times have the name of the task force painted on the side, such as "Drug Task Force" or "DUI Task Force." The cars dedicated to a specific task force often have special equipment useful to the police for arresting and charging people with the violation of the specific offenses they are searching out (such as drug testing equipment for a drug task force). Most of the police officers assigned to these units will have received special training in spotting the type of criminal behavior they are instructed to target.

Task forces are designed to promote the aggressive investigation of the types of crimes on which they are focusing. Any personal property seized from arrested persons and viewed as being part of the commission of the crime, such as a car or cash used in a drug deal, will be confiscated by the police, and any goods may be sold to buy more and newer equipment, more police cruisers, more officers, and the like for the task force. Many times, a division of the state or federal prosecutor's office will cooperate closely with the police task force in the arrest and prosecution of those persons charged with violating whatever set of laws the task force is responsible for handling. These police task forces are watched carefully by law-and-order political interest groups and graded on their effectiveness, which is generally defined as the number of arrests and prosecutions they have achieved.

The concept of zero tolerance permeates these organizations. Go into any police precinct and you will see public relations posters with the members of a police department task force all standing in a group with stern looks on their faces declaring that their task force practices "zero tolerance." Even if the term "zero tolerance" is not actually used, it is implied by the way the officers are presented in the photograph. Grouped together, they often appear as a quasi-military unit, dressed in military-style uniforms, armed, and staring unsmiling into the camera. "Officer Kelly," Wilson and Kelling's neighborhood cop with the discretion to use common sense and apply community norms, is conspicuously absent from police task force public relations photos. The message of these photos is clear: the task force is designed to not tolerate illegal behavior of the specified type, and if you are caught doing—or suspected of doing—that particular illegal behavior, there will be no warning given. You will go to jail and you will be prosecuted.

Every police department has its own list of task forces. Here are some of the task forces now in operation across America:

- Anti-Terrorism
- Burglary
- Citywide Vandals Task Force to Attack Graffiti on Subways
- Crimes Against Women and Children
- DUI
- High Crime Area Prevention
- Illegal Narcotics Prevention

- Marijuana Prevention
- Organized Crime
- School Safety
- Sexual Assaults
- Stopping Drivers From Using Hand-Held Cell Phones and Texting While Driving
- Suicide Prevention
- Violent Crimes

One of the reasons why zero tolerance and the use of task forces go hand in hand is the very military nature of the concept. In fact, the term "task force" originates from the military. The task force concept was first created by the United States Navy:

> A task force (TF) is a unit or formation established to work on a single defined task or activity. Originally introduced by the United States Navy, the term has now caught on for general usage and is a standard part of NATO terminology. Many non-military organizations now create "task forces" or task groups for temporary activities that might have once been performed by ad hoc committees.[33]

The connection between zero-tolerance policing policies and the creation of task forces to combat particular types of illegal behavior can even be seen in the routine use of the term *war* to describe the purpose of establishing the task forces to begin with, namely to fight a "war on crime" or against a particular type of crime. Zero-tolerance policing policies are established under the philosophy that the police, allied with civic organizations and law-and-order political action groups, are "at war" with a particular group of American citizens who are committing, or suspected of committing, a particular type of illegal activity. In order to effectively fight this war, the police must organize themselves into task forces, just as the U.S. military does to engage in warfare against the enemies of the United States. Indeed, today many police departments are led by former military officers who bring their military experience with them and use military methods to "combat" crime.

Hence, we now have an American culture that popularly uses the terms "war," "combat," and "task force" to describe routine policing methods. Today even local police departments promote themselves as waging a "war on drugs," a "war on terrorism," a "war on sex crimes," a "war on cybercrimes," and/or a "war on domestic violence."

The concept of zero tolerance is utterly imbedded within these military terms. Why? The answer is simple logic. The primary purpose of our military forces is our national defense, and, from time to time, that requires them to fight and win wars. In combat, zero tolerance is not just part of the equation; it is the all-consuming goal. If the police say they are fighting a war against crime, the implication is simple: they are going to use all of the weapons at their disposal to win that war. It is hardly an atmosphere for tolerance.

Zero tolerance is echoed in the use of the term to describe the development of newly gentrified city neighborhoods, as well. Once-downtrodden neighborhoods have been "reclaimed" for good, decent citizens. Who exactly have these neighborhoods been reclaimed from? I mean, in order to reclaim a territory or neighborhood, you have to take it away from someone who controlled and was using the territory before you. The enemy, of course, is a vaguely defined group of what are called "sketchy types," which can include everyone from poor people to criminal types, homeless people to other "undesirables" who create fear and a sense of civic disorder. In the neighborhoods where gentrification has taken hold, it is due in part to the "defeat" of these types through zero-tolerance policing policies.

Police departments imbued with the mission of zero tolerance use a variety of tactics to fight their wars on crime. Zero-tolerance arrest policies are certainly part of the program, but the task force concept reaches far beyond simply putting police officers onto the streets of a targeted neighborhood and telling them to arrest anyone and everyone they suspect is committing a crime or a particular type of crime. The zero-tolerance policing philosophy involves a whole range of practices, many of which are implemented through task forces.

Community outreach is one important mission for any police task force. This is made successful by having task force leaders meet with community associations and business groups and explain their mission to members of the community. Like-minded law-and-order political support groups then support the task force, working to get funding for it from local, state, and federal legislatures. The task force employs public relations tools such as press releases on their activities, promotional websites, and printed literature such as brochures. Local newspapers provide coverage for events where the task force leaders speak about their mission. As the arrest numbers mount, the public relations machine heralds those statistics on the websites and in the press releases—all in the name of community outreach.

Some of the most powerful tools for effective task force crime fighting are data-mining techniques and the collection of information regarding people suspected of committing the particular type of criminal activity the task force is designed to fight. In the age of computers, masses of information about people who have previously committed crimes similar to the activity the task force is targeting are stored in huge databases. The reason for doing this is to gather as much data on suspected perpetrators as possible, including DNA evidence, arrest records, spending patterns, computer Internet Protocol (IP) addresses, criminal profiles, police reports, fingerprints, and so on.

Police task forces have a large intelligence-gathering and sharing component to them that is very similar to the way our military is supported by intelligence gathered by organizations such as the CIA and FBI. For example, antiterrorism task forces—some created after the events of 9/11—use data mining to create dossiers on suspected terrorists and keep tabs on their activities. Police task forces engage in similar types of activities in fighting all types of targeted domestic crime, be it crimes against children, drug crimes, organized crime, or DUI.

Task forces purposely use military tactics developed for fighting a foreign enemy and put them instead to use against *us*—American citizens—in order to fight domestic crime. The more serious the crime is, the more it is to be *hoped* by many in society that these tactics will be employed. The problem, of course, is "how far is too far?" When do the techniques utilized by the police simply go too far and encroach upon or destroy our ability to live in a free and open society, unfettered by unwanted snooping and harassment by the police. Under the stated and implied goal of zero tolerance—that being "tough on crime" means that the end justifies the means—the police can, in theory, never go too far and do whatever they want, provided they can demonstrate some tenuous reasoning behind moving from thwarting crime to infringing on American citizens' privacy and right to be left alone.

Granted, any attempt to destroy our civil liberties would be met by a huge fight from the civil liberties groups. But as you look at more serious types of crimes and you consider the ever-more-rapid development of technological weaponry and technological advances, the threat of all-knowing, all-seeing, ever-more-aggressive police task forces encroaching upon our simple right to be left alone becomes a genuine threat when police forces are operating under the principle of zero tolerance.

At the Dawn of our Information Age—The Potential for a Terrifyingly Absolute Zero-Tolerance Police State

One of the most terrifying aspects of the idea of zero tolerance is that we are literally at the dawn of a new technological age. In her 1978 book *A Distant Mirror*, narrative historian Barbara Tuchman laid out the argument that the fourteenth century in Europe was a lot like the twentieth century. The fourteenth century was the last century of the Middle Ages, she argued, and a time of massive, often violent, social change. The next century brought about the beginning of the Renaissance in Europe, which led to the rise of the Industrial Revolution and rapid social change. Tuchman argued that the twentieth century was similar to the fourteenth century because it was the end of its own long historical period.[34]

Just as the fourteenth century was the last century of the Middle Ages, the twentieth century was the last century of the industrial era that began with the Renaissance and ended with the rise of the Information Age, which is what we are living in now at the dawn of the twenty-first century. Today, we live in a society dominated by computers, digital information, the Internet, and all of the rapidly expanding technological wonders. If we accept Tuchman's argument, then the Information Age—if it lasts as long as the Industrial Age as defined by Tuchman—will go on for another 600 years, until approximately the year 2600. Use your imagination and think about how much has changed technologically in the last generation. I am probably from the last college graduating class that wrote term papers on typewriters. I tell this fact to the twenty-something paralegals in my office and they giggle at me, clearly seeing me as a true technological Neanderthal. What powers of communication and data tracking will be available in the next ten or twenty-five years, let alone the next 500 years? The idea staggers the imagination. We are much like someone living in the early 1400s, whom could never have imagined the miracles that industrialization would one day create—cars, trains, airplanes, spaceships, and so forth. We can't really know what types of digital and computerized power will exist in the next few decades, let alone the next several hundred years.

Now take the awesome power of our new technological age and just try to imagine how the police soon may be able to monitor and track our every movement, even read our minds or peer into our very souls, in support of the "ends justify the means" philosophy of having zero tolerance toward crime. If we allow the police to fight a war against private citizens, utilizing all of the wonders of our technological age to stamp out crime, how soon can it be before we live in a police state so complete that it would make Hitler, Stalin, or Mao Zedong blink in amazement? In our technological age, mindless devotion to zero-tolerance police tactics, matched with endless improvements in technological wizardry, can only lead to a very dark and ruthless police state where no one will be safe from police intrusion, state-sanctioned violence, and "tough on crime" ruthlessness on a scale never seen before in human history.

In the 2002 movie *Minority Report*, the police arrest persons involved in "thought crimes." At the beginning of the movie, a jealous husband suspects his wife is having an affair. He pretends to leave home in the morning for work but then lingers outside his house hiding in the bushes. He soon discovers his wife is indeed having an affair as a male stranger arrives and she ushers him into the house. The husband has a gun, and he starts up the stairs to the bedroom, where he hears cries of passion from behind the closed door. As he nears the bedroom, perhaps to shoot the man and the cheating wife, the police break into the house and arrest the husband. The police, who monitor everyone's thoughts through a high-powered computer system, have read his mind. Public safety is restored, but at what price? In a world that, in the past ten years, has seen many technological advances, one has to wonder how far away we are from seeing a Hollywood fantasy about an all-knowing, mindreading police state made real.

In another thriller, *The Island of Dr. Moreau*, the evil doctor breeds a race of half-human, half-animal beings and then controls them by inserting a computer chip under the skin that sends a painful electric shock through the body of any creature who becomes unruly or violent. The doctor controls the administration of the electric shock with a hand-held remote control device that he can turn on or off at will. In a gripping scene, one of the creatures discovers the chip in the corpse of a fellow creature and claws open its own chest to tear out the controlling computer chip. The creature is then free to destroy the evil doctor, who can no longer control—through electric shock—his half-animal, half-human creation.

In a land of true zero tolerance, how soon would it be before some nut-bag, vote-seeking politician demands that anyone ever arrested—or perhaps just suspected of any type of criminal behavior—has to submit to the installation of such a device into his or her body for purposes of public order and safety? We already allow the police to tase an individual suspected of criminal behavior, even though this is an act that can reduce that individual to a mass of writhing, contorted jelly by means of electric shock. In our love affair with zero tolerance, we could easily take the next step and require even more powerful torture devices to be used against the citizenry for the sake of public safety.

When I stand in a grocery line today and see all of the products I am purchasing, each tagged with a computerized barcode, I can't help but reflect upon Hitler's concentration camp victims, each of whom was tagged with a serial code for identification. If the Gestapo had had access to our barcoding system, they surely would have utilized this technology to track their concentration camp victims by barcoding each one of them. Infatuated as we are with tough-on-crime, zero-tolerance policies, what is to stop us from deciding that our need for public order and safety is so great that each of us should be barcoded at birth, so the police can track our every move from the cradle to the grave?

In our constitutional system, our right to privacy—our right to be kept free from police and government snooping and interference—is always balanced against the perceived need for police and government protection from civil disorder and threats to public safety. If we fall too deeply in love with zero tolerance, it is only a matter of time before we submit to having all of our thoughts, ideas, and movements controlled by the police through any technological means available. The technology is either already here or will soon be here. How we restrict its use so that the "land of the free and the home of the brave" does not become "the land of the tracked and the home of the slave" is up to us. Tossing our love affair with zero tolerance into the ashcan of history is a good start.

Is Officer Friendly Dead? Why Zero Tolerance Has Put Him on Life Support

Who is Officer Friendly? He's a lot like Wilson's Officer Kelly. If you recall from Chapter Four, Wilson described how "Officer Kelly" in Newark handled the community in which he patrolled the streets. Kelly's job was to maintain order not just by enforcing the strict letter of the law, but also by maintaining the neighborhood's generally accepted rules as laid down by the community leaders of the neighborhood: business owners, homeowners, and long-term residents.

A policeman who sees some kind of crime being committed has traditionally had a variety of ways of dealing with the situation. Suppose, for example, while he is in his patrol car, Officer Friendly sees a bunch of teenagers drinking beer in the parking lot of a suburban shopping mall. Let's assume the teenagers are all between the ages of seventeen and nineteen. They are clearly breaking the law: any person under the age of twenty-one who is consuming alcohol in our country is guilty of underage consumption of alcohol, which is normally a misdemeanor.

When Officer Friendly spots three teenagers drinking beer, he has several choices of action. One, he can ignore the situation and leave them alone. Two, he can approach the teenagers, lecture them about the dangers of drinking alcohol, make them pour the beer out and throw away the bottles, and send them home with a warning. Three, he can issue them a citation for underage possession of alcohol, which will require the teenagers to appear in court at a later date, and then call the teens' parents and tell them to come down and pick up their kids. Four, he can arrest them and take them to jail. He can also ask the teenagers where they bought the alcohol, confiscate any fake IDs they have on them, and go have a talk with the store owner who sold them the alcohol.

Imagine for a minute it was your child hanging out in this group. Which choice would you want Officer Friendly to make? My guess is that if you asked a hundred different parents, you would get a variety of answers. There is no clearly "right" answer, but I do know that I firmly support Officer Friendly having the authority to make a decision based upon his professional judgment. Does he know the teenagers? Are they from the same neighborhood in which they are drinking the beers, or are they from the other side of town? When he approaches the teenagers, are they respectful of his authority or do they give him a hard time? Are the teenagers drunk or just tipsy? Have there been complaints from local residents about this issue, or problems with vandalism in the area that could be linked to the kids hanging out drinking beer? How are the kids dressed? Are they members of a local gang known for committing much more serious crimes, or are they just local kids out for a good time? Does Officer Friendly know the parents of any of the kids? Are they well-established residents of the community, perhaps heavily involved in school and civic affairs? Should any of these things matter to Officer Friendly?

Now let's make the above situation more serious. What if the teenagers have marijuana, instead of beer? What if they have beer and a small amount of cocaine or methamphetamine on them? What if they are throwing rocks and breaking the windows of a local business? What if the teenagers are caught drinking and driving, as opposed to just standing around a mall parking lot? What if they are not drinking beer at all, but breaking into a store and stealing merchandise? What if they have handguns and are holding up the late-night convenience store clerk?

As the seriousness of the crime goes up, of course, the more important it seems that Officer Friendly actually arrest the teenagers. The last example—armed robbery—is a serious felony, and few people would not want him to arrest the teenagers for that crime. The other examples are either misdemeanors or some level of felony, depending upon the state in which the above scenario takes place. At what point do you say, "Hey, professional discretion be damned, Officer Friendly needs to arrest these kids"?

Our knee-jerk reaction, politically, over the past generation has been to simply have Officer Friendly arrest everyone for everything. This is why task forces, with their mandates of zero tolerance, are so popular. For proponents of pure zero-tolerance policies, who want all criminal behavior targeted in their communities by military-style police tactics, none of the above considerations matter. They don't want Officer Friendly to use his traditional discretionary powers to make a decision based upon all of the extralegal facts and circumstances surrounding the situation. They just want him to arrest the teenagers, period—end of story.

This is why Officer Friendly is an endangered species in America today. Political interest groups on both the left and the right want their police officers to be like robots who see a crime being committed and make an arrest.

On the political left, civil rights groups are fearful of selective enforcement of the laws by the police. They fear that Officer Friendly may only arrest the poor kid, or the teenager of color, or the teenager known in the community to be gay. They fear that the rich kid whose father is in the local country club will get cut more slack than the working-class kid with baggy pants, so they want the rich kid punished just like the poor kid.

On the political right, law-and-order "tough on crime" political interest groups want all suspicious kids locked up, because they want to see the law strictly enforced. They fear the neighborhood task force will "go soft" on crime if Officer Friendly cuts the teenagers drinking beer any slack by letting them off with a warning. To them, giving Officer Friendly discretion is like allowing a single window in their community to remain broken.

Hence, Officer Friendly's professional discretion is hamstrung by both sides of the political aisle, because the left wants "one size fits all" justice to ensure equal enforcement of the law, and the right wants him to be "tough on crime." This unholy alliance of political left and right has left Officer Friendly with little choice but to simply become an arresting machine, mindlessly collaring anyone he sees breaking any law—even committing minor infractions of the law that were probably treated more mildly in previous generations.

So is this a good thing? Has our society made progress by mandating zero tolerance for even the most minor offenses? Or have we created more problems for ourselves and restricted our liberties to a point of ridiculousness? One of the things that I find matters most to people considering this question is whether it was their teenager who was approached by Officer Friendly. Ask almost anyone who has had a teenage child arrested for a minor offense. They will insist they wish the police officer had used the discretion not to make an arrest and had gone lighter on their child. Is this hypocrisy, or is it simply someone experiencing the rude awakening of life in America today under the brutish policies of zero tolerance? For my part, I am for allowing Officer Friendly wide discretion when confronted by a relatively minor crime. On the other hand, as a criminal defense attorney, I can tell you that business has never been better. Zero tolerance clearly has been good for my livelihood: whether it's good for you and your family and your community is another question.

In the next chapter, we first look at zero-tolerance prosecution policies, or what happens after you're arrested. We then move on to the part of America's criminal justice system where zero tolerance has had its greatest impact—punishment for persons convicted of crimes. It is through changes in punishments and sentencing structures over the past quarter century that our desire for zero tolerance has taken us furthest down the road of intolerance.

CHAPTER SIX

THE IMPACT OF ZERO TOLERANCE ON PROSECUTION, PUNISHMENT, AND SENTENCING

It is in the courtroom that our nation's "get tough on crime," zero-tolerance policies have had the greatest impact. Much has been written about the vast number of American citizens now locked up in our jails and prisons or under some type of long-term parole or probation supervision. In comparison with other nations, the numbers are indeed enormous.[35] This expansion of our prison system is largely due to zero-tolerance, tough-on-crime laws that, over the past generation, have been passed by federal and state legislators and enforced by law-and-order judges and prosecutors. Many of these public officials were elected to office on platforms promising to not "pander to" criminals. Many of them were elected by only a tiny fraction of the electorate, and their elections were funded by law-and-order public interest groups who finance the campaigns of zero tolerance judges and prosecutors and then actually vote in their municipal, county, and state elections. Thus, judges and prosecutors with impressive statistics on prosecutions, convictions, and sentencing are more likely to get elected.

For my part, I want to go beyond the statistics and give a micro-level, from-the-trenches view of what I see in the courtroom every day as a criminal defense lawyer representing not statistics but real flesh-and-blood human beings. To do so, I will first discuss prosecutors and then move on to judges, sentencing, and other forms of punishment.

Prosecutors and Judges

In some ways, the most powerful person in the courtroom today is the prosecutor. He or she has wide discretion in deciding whether to charge someone with a particular crime, whether to reduce the charge to a lesser offense, and whether to allow some type of alternative treatment (other than prosecution and conviction). In many ways, this system works fairly well. Prosecutors look at the matters before them on a case-by-case basis and decide which ones require the most severe punishments and which cry out for some type of lesser, more merciful treatment. As mandatory minimum sentences have become the norm in many states for particularly harsh crimes, the prosecutor is often the only one who may be able to help a defendant avoid a long sentence by taking a deal and pleading to a lesser charge. The most important thing to understand is that prosecutors hold enormous power over whether to bring charges against an individual in the first place.

And yet the prosecutor's power is not absolute: district attorneys must answer to the electorate. As we have discussed, in many places these days, the people most likely to show up and vote in local elections are members of well-organized, well-funded, law-and-order special interest groups. Hence, the pressure on prosecutors to be ruthless and merciless toward people accused of crimes is very real. In order to get elected, they have to preach zero tolerance, and then they have to deliver on their promises once they get elected if they wish to keep their jobs.

Yet, the traditional role of a prosecutor is more nuanced than this, especially before a case gets to the courtroom. The prosecutor's job is ultimately to make sure justice is served. Now, if you believe that justice is best served by locking everyone up who is prosecuted for a crime for as long as is possible under the law, then you have no need to read on. My guess is that you want all the teenagers in the United States who are caught drinking beer to be arrested and thrown in jail, too. Hey, it's a free country, and you certainly are entitled to your opinion. But, in my view, prosecutors are given both so much power and so much discretion because they sit at the crossroads of each individual defendant's life. When a prosecutor gets hold of a case file, he or she is literally holding the fate of an individual human being in that file. That prosecutor may very well determine how that individual will spend the rest of his or her natural life. Prosecutors play God in some very real sense, deciding who may be damned to a lifetime of hardship and disability, and who will receive some level of grace and mercy, based upon the totality of the circumstances surrounding the acts of the individual involved in the case.

In today's America, law-and-order special interest groups hold such sway over district attorneys that they affect the delicate balancing act that is the prosecutor's job. These groups have limited prosecutors' ability to do their jobs fairly and properly by tempering punishment with mercy. At the same time, I must say that I fully support the election of district attorneys to their positions. We are fortunate to live in a democratic republic where the local prosecutor is not the appointed crony of the king or some other tin-pot, third-world despot. However, at some point the pressure to be elected can become a problem.

> If you believe law-and-order public interest groups preaching zero tolerance for prosecutors have gone too far, then get involved! What's the easiest way to get motivated? Imagine for just a minute that you are accused of some type of a crime, even a minor one. Or even worse, a family member or loved one has been arrested and is facing criminal prosecution. How do you want your local prosecutor to review the case? Do you want a knee-jerk lackey of the lock-'em-up-and-throw-away-the-key crowd deciding your, or your loved one's, future? Or would you prefer someone who takes all the facts and circumstances of the situation into account? As we have already seen, in today's America there is a fair chance you or a loved one will be arrested for some infraction of the law, be it major or minor. If you want to make a difference, it's as easy as getting involved in the next election for your local prosecutor.

Judges have probably lost the most courtroom power over the past few decades. In 1984, the U.S. Congress passed into law the federal sentencing guidelines for all crimes that are prosecuted in the federal courts of the United States, which essentially turned federal judges into human calculators, dutifully adding up points like so many jots on a scrap of paper to determine the "proper" sentence in each case. When the guidelines were passed, they caused a huge uproar, and many longstanding federal judges quit the bench in protest. Yet the guidelines, adored by some U.S. prosecutors, stayed firmly in place for over twenty years. In the past decade, some level of balance has been restored to the system as a series of U.S. Supreme Court rulings have made the guidelines now "merely advisory," so that federal judges have regained their traditional right to render punishments on a case-by-case basis.[36] But the guidelines still retain tremendous power and heavily influence sentencing decisions by judges in federal courts, as well as in some state court systems that have sentencing guidelines.

In both state and federal courts, judges are hamstrung by mandatory minimum sentences that don't allow them to sentence a person below the mandatory amount of jail or prison time put in place by the state legislature or U.S. Congress.[37] Mandatory minimum sentences are not the same thing as sentencing guidelines. Sentencing guidelines exist to help advise a judge on what may be a generally just sentence in a particular type of case but leave the final decision to the judge as to what the convicted person's punishment will actually be. Mandatory minimum sentences, on the other hand, are passed by state legislatures and the U.S. Congress to tie judges' hands so that they cannot sentence a person convicted of a particular crime to less than a specified minimum amount of jail or prison time, literally taking the power to "judge" out of judges' hands.

To me, this is the biggest problem in our system today. Such rules don't allow judges to make exceptions or to have the flexibility to enact fair sentences on a case-by-case basis. Many times the mandatory sentencing rules do not take into account whether a convicted person is a first-time offender, is remorseful, has undertaken counseling, or has worked to mitigate the harm done by committing the crime. Mandatory minimum sentences also cast a huge shadow over the American population by guaranteeing that certain types of behavior will put people in prison for part, most, or all of the rest of their lives. In recent years, these mandatory minimums have applied especially to sex and drug crimes, and to crimes of violence.

When I have spoken off the record with my colleagues, I have found that many judges and prosecutors hate mandatory minimum sentencing. The laws reduce their autonomy and flexibility in working out truly just resolutions on cases. They do not like their prosecutorial and judicial independence to be obstructed by politicians whose only true interest is getting reelected and who are largely influenced and financed by victims' rights and law-and-order special interest groups.

In his 1975 book *Thinking About Crime*, Professor Wilson wrote a series of balanced, well-reasoned, nuanced, and—yes—*tolerant* suggestions for how America's criminal justice system should operate when prosecuting the accused and sentencing the convicted. Today, his scholarly sense of balance and fair play seems rather quaint, even downright naive, in a law-and-order world that has become so hyper-politicized, imbalanced, and intolerant. Wilson argued for a system of largely moderate penalties to be meted out swiftly and fairly by judges interested in both protecting the public *and* promoting the ultimate moral reformation of the accused. Nowhere in his book did Wilson jump up and down, ranting and raving for zero tolerance for all crimes, merciless treatment of all criminals, and never-ending retribution in the name of the outraged victims and the state. Nor, on the other hand, did he advocate letting all criminals off the hook. Instead, he landed squarely in the middle when it comes to prosecuting and punishing America's criminal offenders—a policy position that, like his position on police arrests, today seems to please no one.

In Wilson's vision:

> Well-staffed prosecutorial and public defender's offices would be prepared for an early trial (or plea bargain) in . . . priority cases; judges would be loath to grant continuances for convenience of counsel. Sentencing would be shaped, though not rigidly determined by,

sentencing guidelines that take into account not only the gravity of the offense and the prior conviction record of the accused, but also the full criminal history including the juvenile record and the involvement, if any, of the accused with drug abuse. The outer bounds of judicial discretion would be shaped by society's judgment as to what constitutes a fair and just penalty for a given offense; within those bounds, sentences would be designed to reduce crime by giving longer sentences to high rate offenders (even when convicted of a less serious offense) and shorter sentences to low rate offenders (even if the offense is somewhat serious).

Persons convicted of committing minor offenses, who have little or no prior record, would be dealt with by community-based corrections: in particular by supervised community service and victim restitution. Probation officers would make sure these obligations are, in fact, met. Individuals failing to meet them would promptly be given short jail sentences.

Offenders sentenced to some period of incarceration would be carefully screened so that young and old, violent and non-violent, neurotic and psychotic offenders would be assigned to separate facilities, and, within those facilities to educational and treatment programs appropriate to their personalities and needs.[38]

To be fair to many of the judges, prosecutors, defense lawyers, correctional personnel, counselors, probation officers, and others laboring in America's criminal justice system in the first decades of the twenty-first century, many of Wilson's prescriptions for effectively prosecuting, sentencing, and rehabilitating criminal offenders are either in use or at least being promoted to some extent. Many who work in the field recognize the practices he urged as the ideal no matter how short actual current practices fall. The problem is that all officials working in America's criminal justice system today are faced with the constant and never-ending political drumbeat of zero tolerance. Any attempt to maintain the type of balanced and tolerant treatment for criminal offenders described by Wilson is sure to be met by political outcry from political interest groups on both the left and the right, groups whose members see any attempt to balance justice and mercy, deterrence and rehabilitation, as being either too hard or too soft on crime.

Wilson spoke of his desire to balance the need to "shame" the criminal, on the one hand, with the need to not destroy his or her chance at rehabilitating and going on to live a satisfying and productive life as a law-abiding citizen, on the other. Perhaps more than in any other passage of Wilson's book, he hit the nail on the head when he invoked the need to temper retribution and deterrence with mercy and rehabilitation in order to maintain the human dignity of the person arrested, convicted, and incarcerated for a crime. Speaking more than thirty-five years ago, Wilson expressed a sense of fairness and tolerance that stands in stark contrast to today's shrill and pervasive advocacy for zero tolerance.

> Much is made today of the fact that the criminal justice system "stigmatizes" those caught up in it, and thus unfairly marks such persons and perhaps even furthers their criminal careers by "labeling" them as criminals. Whether the labeling process operates in this is yet unproved, but it would indeed be unfortunate if society treated a convicted offender in such a way that he had no reasonable alternative but to make crime a career. *To prevent this, society should ensure that one can "pay one's debt" without suffering permanent loss of civil rights, the continuing and pointless indignity of parole supervision, and the frustration of being unable to find a job.* (Emphasis added) But doing these things is very different from eliminating the "stigma" from crime. To de-stigmatize crime would be to lift the moral judgment of crime and to make it a particular occupation or avocation which society has chosen to reward less (or perhaps more!) than other pursuits.[39]

Wilson's approach does not square with the concept of mandatory minimum sentences, which have come into being over the past generation, in some instances many years after he published *Thinking About Crime*. Yet today, for the most part, mandatory minimum sentences are wildly popular with much of the public, law-and-order special interest groups, and the politicians. When these sentences are criticized in the press, the criticism usually comes because the sentences are causing too much prison overcrowding or are too expensive to maintain. The criticism is almost always from the point of view of the cost the punishment has on the taxpayers or on overworked prison personnel.[40] Almost never are the sentences criticized for simply being barbaric and unjust.

> From the trenches of the courtroom floor, you can see that the "statistics" batted around by politicians and the media are all actual human beings. I urge you to take a day and go down to your local courthouse on criminal docket day and sit in "the pews," the rows of benches everyone is required to sit on behind "the bar" that separates the accused and their families from the lawyers and the judge.
>
> Walk into your local courtroom and one of the first things you will probably notice is that the vast majority of the people accused of crimes are poor or working class. In a county with a mixed population of whites and minorities, the vast majority of the accused are almost always minorities. Beyond those persons accused of crimes sitting in the pews, many others have been held in jail without bond for months or years before their cases go to trial. When their cases are called, the accused persons are led out in chains and jumpsuits for their brief moment in the courtroom.
>
> The list of court cases presented on any given day is endless. People often sit for hours waiting for their names to be called. Often, people's cases take months or years to be resolved. Some people's cases get lost; some others do not receive proper notice to attend. People who are the least able to miss a day of work

> or afford a babysitter or miss school are left helpless, forced to attend court month after month, year after year, until their cases are finally dealt with by overwhelmed prosecutors and judges.
>
> People sentenced to jail or prison are literally at risk for their lives. American prisons, although better than those in many parts of the world, are still terrible, cruel, and inhumane places. If someone is facing a mandatory minimum prison term, he or she may face decades or the rest of his or her life in a hellhole unimaginable to anyone who has not suffered this fate. Prison inmates can suffer beating or torture; they may be sodomized, raped, or murdered. They may have medical or dietary needs that are not properly handled, or suffer from malnutrition and disease. Inmates may have to join a particular gang based upon race or ethnic affiliation just to survive. I have had clients emerge from the county lockup after just a few hours or days in jail who have told me they will never forget the sheer terror they felt every moment they were behind bars. As a criminal defense attorney, I have been in many, many county jails and state and federal prisons, and even though I am treated as a privileged guest—escorted by guards to my client and then allowed to leave when my meeting is finished—the places still leave me with a deep sense that we are still living in a time of barbarism when it comes to our prison system.

Do I have a better solution? As far as a way of eliminating prisons altogether, no, I do not. Perhaps in the distant future, human beings will come up with something better. But should we be throwing so many of our citizens into prison at a rate that is close to the highest in the world?[41] No, I think not. I'd like to think we can do better than choose to treat our fellow human beings so cruelly, regardless of what they have done to end up in prison.

That being said, what is vitally important is that judges be given wide latitude and discretion when it comes to the type of sentence they impose in a given case. Likewise, prosecutors need to be given the same discretion as to what cases they choose to prosecute and which ones they feel merit alternative forms of treatment. The professional discretion of judges and prosecutors has been taken away in many instances through zero tolerance policies put in place by politicians and political interest groups. One-size-fits-all justice is ultimately not justice at all, and zero tolerance prosecution and sentencing policies, which tie the hands of our prosecutors and judges leads more often than not to injustice.

A Review of Punishments in America's Criminal Justice System

Prison is just the tip of the iceberg when it comes to punishing people accused or convicted of crimes in the Unites States today. The ways and means of government-sponsored punishment and harassment established over the past generation are breathtaking to behold. Each new politician, urged on by law-and-order zero tolerance groups, comes up with new forms of state-sponsored cruelty to inflict upon those hapless folks who end up in the clutches of the Beast. Let's take a look at some different scenarios to see how people accused of crimes today can end up being punished by the powerful machinery of America's criminal justice system.

Not too long ago, I was sitting with a client in my office, discussing his case. We'll call him Joe, although that is not his real name. Joe was a young man charged with a serious criminal offense, and he and I were discussing whether we should go to trial or try to work a deal with the prosecutor. The facts in the case were not particularly good for our side, and going to trial would mean the greater chance that my client would be convicted. The assistant district attorney assigned to the case had indicated he was willing to work out a deal involving a short stint in jail followed by lengthy probation. If, on the other hand, we went to trial, my client was potentially facing many, many years in prison.

As we were talking, I dutifully explained the possible punishments in the case. Of course, as a defense attorney, I am ethically bound to explain all offers of settlement made by the prosecutor to my client. I compared what would probably happen if Joe accepted a plea deal and "cut his losses" versus going to trial, where he might win his freedom but—based upon the evidence against him—was more likely to be convicted and go to prison. As I was discussing the various punishments, Joe looked at me and, with a look of desperation and anger in his eyes, asked me: "But, Mr. Conaway, haven't I been punished enough already?"

Joe's question made me halt in my tracks, stop talking for a minute (something always difficult for lawyers to do), and simply reflect upon what he was saying. I had been looking at his case through my "lawyer's eyes"—that is, professionally assessing the risks and benefits of potential future outcomes, then advising him of such. This is part of my day-to-day job as a defense attorney. I was discussing my client's punishment the way the legal system views punishment, as something that happens *at the end of* a criminal case once a defendant is found guilty and then is sentenced by a judge. This is the view of criminal punishment taught in law schools, discussed in criminal procedure books, and held by members of the general public with no experience with our criminal justice system.

But I realized that, from Joe's standpoint, the experience was very different. Joe was absolutely correct. He had been arrested some fourteen months earlier and, in his experience, he had been getting punished ever since. He had not admitted guilt, nor had a jury found him guilty. He lived in a country where a person is innocent until proven guilty under the Constitution. So why did Joe feel punished?

When Joe was first arrested, he had been handcuffed and made to wait for hours until the police took him down to the local jailhouse, where he was put into a cell—a metal cage—where the door was locked. He had to wait several days to make bail, and during that time, he was locked up just as though he had already been convicted of a crime. Then, he had to put up something of value to get out of jail, which was an administrative nightmare as his family raced around desperately trying to raise the necessary funds and property. Joe's picture had been published in full color in a local news rag sold at gas stations and convenience stores for popular consumption by anyone buying gas or a cup of coffee.

Once out on bail, Joe had to report once a week to a pretrial services officer. In theory, he could report by phone, but when he called, no one ever answered the phone, so it was easier just to go down in person. The burden was solely on Joe to prove he had reported to his supervisor properly, so if he called and left a message that was somehow not received by the overworked and underpaid pretrial services person, Joe would be the one who would pay the price by being thrown back in jail. (Sure, he could try and dispute the fact that he had called in as directed, but it would be his word against the pretrial supervisor, so you can imagine who would win that argument in front of the judge.) If he wound up back in jail, Joe might sit there for weeks or months before he got back in front of a judge. So Joe went in person each week to his pretrial supervisor's office, where he signed in at the front window and sat patiently in a gray metal folding chair, in a shabby gray government office building, waiting until his pretrial supervisor had the time to see him. After "checking in" with the supervisor, he was allowed to leave until the next week. He followed the same routine week after week, month after month, essentially already placed on a form of reporting probation for a crime for which *he had never been convicted*. This made it incredibly difficult for him to keep a job or move from one place to another. The arrest was already part of his "public criminal background" so any time an employer ran an employee criminal background check, Joe ran the risk of being fired, if he had managed to get hired in the first place.

Joe also had to report to court each month, even though his case moved like molasses because of endless procedural delays and prosecution and defense tactics. Each month, he emotionally girded himself to appear in court, to see his name ignominiously displayed as criminal defendant number such-and-such on the docket sheets posted all around the courthouse. His name was called and he had to step up to the bar while his case was discussed and a new round of prosecution and defense issues was aired out, his case was reset, and he was released—for the moment. Each day he awoke from his bed living the nightmare of being accused of a crime and fearing what would happen to him if he were ultimately convicted. Each night he went to sleep with the dread of the unknown hanging over his head.

Joe's car had been confiscated from him at the time of his arrest. The police had taken control of it, by declaring it forfeit because it was used in the course of committing the *alleged* crime. He also had to pay for me, his attorney, and for related services such as a private investigator. He was kicked out of his apartment when his landlord discovered the accusation against him. He had to scramble to find a new place, leaving an apartment he had lived in for many years. This cost him additional time, money, and emotional trauma.

As the months wore on, Joe became increasingly depressed and anxious. He sought counseling to deal with his trauma. His mother suffered, too, along with the rest of his family, constantly wondering what was going to happen to her son, terrified of the potential horrors a prison sentence could bring.

Thus, long before he was ever convicted of anything, Joe's entire life was turned upside down, while he was also enduring the day-in, day-out trauma of wondering whether he was going to be locked away in a prison filled with dangers and degradations most of us don't even want to think about—worrying whether he would be beaten, raped, stabbed, or tortured. Would he even survive? Joe had already endured all of this, and he had *not even been punished* yet! He was supposedly still "innocent" in the eyes of the law but, if he was, he certainly wasn't being treated that way.

I can hear the law-and-order advocates saying, "So what? The guy's probably guilty so he gets whatever he deserves." My response to those people comes from my professional experience. I have represented many, many people and families who were staunch law-and-order advocates their whole lives, cluck-clucking sanctimoniously along whenever one of their politicians pounded the pulpit for a new and tougher way to punish criminals. Yet, all of that changed when it was they or one of their family members in the crosshairs of government prosecution.

Now I am going to walk you through the various forms of punishment our criminal justice system inflicts upon people and show them from the point of view you will have if it is ever you or a loved one going through a criminal prosecution. As we saw in Joe's case, your punishment begins from the very moment you are contacted by the police. You may be "innocent until proven guilty" under our legal system, but the methods of punishment even for being under criminal investigation are many, and they begin from the very moment you end up face-to-face with the criminal authorities.

The Pre-Arrest Stage
The first punishments occur at the pre-arrest stage. This stage does not occur in many criminal cases. Take an unsuccessful bank robbery, for instance. Two guys walk into a bank and hold up the teller. The teller is able to alert the police. The police arrive and capture the bank robbers—end of pre-arrest stage. But in other scenarios, especially in federal criminal investigations and some complex state investigations, the pre-arrest stage can last months or even years.

"So wait a minute, how is this a punishment stage?" you are probably asking. And it's not—in any formal sense, at least—but the emotional hell you will go through, and which your family will endure with you, will feel like a form of punishment and persecution. Let's take a federal white-collar fraud investigation as an example.

Suppose you are a small business owner and there are allegations made against you and your company concerning fraudulent activity. Two FBI agents show up at your office at three in the afternoon with a search warrant, guns drawn, right in front of your employees and customers. They take all of your computers, your files, and everything related to your business and haul it all away.

You ask what the reason for the raid is, and they sneer at you, saying, "You know what it's all about. Better start talking now while you've got the chance." You wisely do not say anything but sit quietly and wait until you are allowed to call your lawyer. The agents then leave, toting all of your computers and other business paraphernalia out the door.

They don't arrest you, but they inform you that you are under investigation and that they will get back in touch with you "later" when their investigation is complete. This could be months or years later. They have lots of time to complete their investigation. In the meantime, you hear nothing. How are you going to feel in the months and even years ahead while this investigation hangs over your head like an axe, ready to fall at any given moment? Suppose their investigation uncovers nothing? How are you going to stay in business, repair your business reputation, and remain emotionally sane while undergoing the uncertainty of an ongoing federal investigation into your business practices?

Or, let's look at a milder situation. Suppose agents just stop by your house. They have "a few questions for you" concerning a real estate transaction you were involved with a few years back. They drive up and the neighbors spot them entering your house. Everyone on the block starts to talk. The agents are very polite and let you know that it is an ongoing investigation and they will be back in touch, but they are vague as to any specifics. After they leave, you are left hanging, wondering what the hell is going to happen next. The neighbors' tongues are all wagging. What do you think your emotional state is going to be like in the weeks and months ahead?

Now, please understand, I am not trying to argue that the police and federal agents should not do their jobs. They have to do what they have to do to investigate and prosecute crime. But that does not alter the effect it has on you, as a simple private citizen, who now finds that your life has turned upside down and inside out. There is probably no greater hell than being the target or suspect of an ongoing criminal investigation. The government moves at its own pace and on its own timetable. It is not particularly interested in yours. Meanwhile, you are living with the dread of uncertainty, day in and day out, month in and month out, possibly even year in and year out.

The Arrest Stage and Pre-Indictment Stage

Now let's move to the "arrest" stage. The first thing to understand about being arrested is that it is an act of violence perpetrated against you by the government. It is state-sanctioned violence, to be sure, but it is still violence and it still harms you, sometimes irreparably. No one really thinks of getting arrested as a violent act, but consider the fact that in almost any other situation detaining someone against his or her will through the use of force—or threat of force—and then transporting that person to a location where they are forced to remain is legally defined as a crime of violence in the United States and is commonly known as "kidnapping."

To illustrate, suppose you decide to get a gun and a set of handcuffs and then drive to your local shopping mall. There, you walk up to a stranger, display your gun, and order the person to put their hands behind their back. You then handcuff that person and transport them in your car to your home, where you lock them in your basement. Did you just commit a violent crime? Of course you did. It is called kidnapping. The same basic scenario occurs whenever the police make an arrest. They are *legally* detaining someone against his or her will through the use of force or the threat of force and then transporting him or her to jail. Their actions are perfectly legal, provided the police officers have an arrest warrant or probable cause to arrest the person under certain exceptions to the warrant requirement. But it is still an act of violence perpetrated by an agent of the government against you, the private citizen. The fact that the police are legally authorized to make arrests does not change the fact that, each and every time they arrest someone, they are perpetrating an act of violence against the person they are arresting.

When you are arrested, you will be handcuffed, shackled, and locked away in the back of a squad car or paddy wagon. Your wrists and hands may go numb. You will be caged like an animal in a box. Then you will be taken to a "detention center," today's euphemism for jail, where you will be held behind bars or in a "holding area" with other inmates behind locked doors, until (and if) you "make bail." If you are lucky, the jail will have a sickeningly sweet disinfectant smell to it. If you are unlucky, it will stink like perspiration, urine, or feces (or all three).

If you have to wait several days or weeks before you are able to make bail, you will have all of your personal possessions taken away from you. You will be stripped of your clothing and forced to wear an orange, white, or blue jumpsuit. You will be given a tracking number or booking number, which you will keep throughout the time you are in jail. The food will consist of bologna or cheese sandwiches, or some other type of bare-bones food. Your time will no longer be your own. At night, you will be locked in a cell and only allowed to leave when the guards tell you that you can leave. Your loved ones may or may not be able to see you. If you can't afford a private lawyer to help you make bail in a complex case, or if you are too poor to afford to make bail, you might simply sit for weeks or months, until your case finally reaches a courtroom. Remember that you haven't yet been convicted of any crime, or in many instances even *indicted*—just arrested. Yet your life has already been altered through state-sanctioned violence in such a way that you may never be the same again.

When I was a young defense lawyer, I had a case where the judge appointed me to represent two indigent persons accused of armed robbery. They were a boyfriend and girlfriend who had allegedly robbed a Mexican migrant worker of his wristwatch by pointing a knife at him. When I went to meet them in jail, they explained that they had no money and could not make bail. They denied being involved at all and said that they had been wrongfully accused. I went to the district attorney's office to read the evidence against them. There wasn't any. No knife had been recovered, nor had the watch. The couple had not been found at the scene but had been identified later by the alleged victim. When I tried to track down the victim, it turned out he was a migrant worker who had left the state and left no forwarding information. There were no other witnesses. The police hadn't seen anything, they had simply responded to the complaint. The case, from a prosecution standpoint, was a complete joke. There was no physical evidence, no victim, no police witness or other eyewitness, no video, nothing. My clients, because they were poor and had no money, had never made bail, and they had never seen a lawyer because they couldn't afford a private one. Instead, they sat in jail for eight months, waiting desperately to get in front of a judge.

I filed a motion to dismiss the case for lack of prosecution. When my clients' day in court finally came, the judge said to the prosecutor, "You know, I wonder how many other people we've got sitting over in that jail just like these two." The prosecutor responded rather blandly, "Your honor, this case is being handled in the normal course of business." The judge shot back, "Yes, I know, that's the normal course of business as defined by the district attorney's office."

The judge did not dismiss the case that day but set a deadline for the prosecution to handle the case by. The prosecutor then offered to dismiss the armed robbery charge in exchange for a plea to disorderly conduct, a local ordinance. My clients accepted the deal and were released—after eight months in jail.

Some may say that if my clients were arrested then they probably did it, and therefore they should get whatever is coming to them, right? I disagree. Even putting to one side the fact that there was precious little evidence of my clients' guilt, if our legal system means anything, it means that you really are *innocent until proven guilty*. Whatever restraints are put on a person accused of a crime prior to the completion of the case, it is a finding of guilty or not guilty that determines whether that person should be subject to punishment. A person not yet convicted of a crime should be subject to as little state-sanctioned violence, restriction on their freedom, and government confiscation of their personal property as possible.

There are lots of other ways people are punished while their cases await trial or disposition. These punishments usually occur through one of three processes. As we saw above, one is by incarceration prior to trial for a period that can last anywhere from a few hours to several years. A second way is through the seizure of personal property as either evidence or "fruits of crime." These items may or may not ever be returned to the accused person. Some of the more egregious examples occur in federal white-collar investigations and in state and federal drug cases. In white-collar cases, the authorities usually seize anything and everything they believe might be associated with the alleged white-collar crime. This usually means they take all of the accused person's computers, DVDs, printed documents, diaries, business and personal financial records, personal letters, client files, and/or cell phones—in short, anything and everything that can even be remotely related to an alleged financial crime. The accused person's home and office are searched and, in essence, his or her entire personal and professional life is seized. The person is left with little or nothing related to his or her financial, business, and—at times—even personal life that was saved on a computer, stored digitally, or printed on paper.

In a drug case, the police will take the accused person's car, his or her computer, cash, and anything else the police declare to be drug paraphernalia (which can include all personal property). I had a client once tell me the story of a policeman laughing and jumping up and down with joy after he busted my client with cocaine in his car. My client drove a vintage corvette, and the cop gleefully opened the hood to look at the engine. He was so excited because he was going to get to seize the car—and hoped to buy it for a song later at auction.

The other way persons accused of crimes are punished before trial or disposition is through "bond conditions." Over the years, the laundry list of conditions—or, more accurately, forms of state-inflicted pretrial punishments—that state and federal courts and state legislatures and Congress have creatively come up with to impose on the person fortunate enough to finally obtain a bond and post bail has become long indeed. Accused persons out on bond and awaiting trial have been required to do such things as to move out of their homes, have no contact with their children or wives or husbands, give up their Fourth Amendment constitutional rights against search and seizure, undergo blood and alcohol screening, report to a pretrial supervisor, stay in place and not travel, wear *and pay for* a GPS monitoring device on their ankle, have a tracking chip implanted in their arm, submit to a curfew, submit to home visits from a pretrial supervisor, not use the Internet or have any computers in their home, and/or not consume alcohol. And all this may take place after the person has already posted cash or property to a bondsmen or the court in order to make bail. If the accused person does not abide by all of the conditions of his or her bond, then the person will be rearrested and thrown back in jail. All of these "conditions" are really just forms of government-sanctioned punishment inflicted upon persons who are supposedly presumed innocent and have not been found guilty or ever been convicted of any crime in a court of law.

To be clear: under our criminal justice system, not only is a person legally innocent until proven guilty, but he or she also normally has a constitutional right to bail. So there is an argument to be made that all of the above types of restrictions violate these persons' constitutional rights. The basis for imposing bond conditions is the idea that they are necessary to make sure the person shows up in court and does no harm while out on bond. But this results in the punishment of a person merely *accused* of a crime, instead of simply allowing a person to post bond and then remain free of punishment until trial, unless of course he or she actually fails to show up in court or commits a new crime.

For persons who already have a criminal record or where the alleged crime is particularly violent or egregious, exceptions can be made, of course, and bail can be denied. But what we see more and more today is a systematic methodology for state-sponsored sanction, punishment, and, ultimately, control over innocent persons *merely accused* of crimes. The government essentially treats them like criminals—deliberately and calculatingly squeezing out their freedom to live—from the moment they are arrested. This mechanistic method of control has now become more and more the norm as people merely accused of crimes are systematically robbed of their freedom, dignity, property, and privacy, by a criminal justice system intent on controlling the merely accused, through ever more restrictive and sophisticated means, while they await their day in court.

Like a giant boa constrictor, our criminal justice system slowly but surely grabs, gains control, and then squeezes the life out of merely accused citizens, so that by the time they finally get to trial, months or years later, they have already had the financial, emotional, and physical life crushed out of them by the government. So much for "innocent until proven guilty."

Many Tools to Choose From: the Myriad Ways a Convicted Person Is Now Punished Under Our Criminal Justice System

When we think of people punished for committing crimes, we tend to think that they are either sentenced to a certain length of time in prison or placed on probation or parole for a period of time. During the time those persons are incarcerated or on probation, they are "paying their debt to society." During the probationary period, they may be required to complete community service work, undergo counseling for some type of addiction or mental health issue, pay a fine, and/or pay restitution (money owed to the victim in the case). At the end of their sentence, we assume they have "done their time," so to speak, and now they have the opportunity to return to society as free citizens. Provided they do not again break the law, they can live the rest of their lives as good, upstanding citizens, having paid their debts to society for the crimes they committed.

This is the traditional idea most people have about how our criminal justice system operates. With the rise of zero tolerance law enforcement, however, tough-on-crime policies have resulted in a departure from this traditional sentencing structure. Instead of allowing persons convicted of a crime to pay their debt to society—and then move on with their lives—with more and more frequency our criminal justice system is imposing a series of lifelong sanctions that never end. All of these are put in place and justified under the standard rationale for all restrictions on individual liberties: "public safety."

As we have seen, just about all acts of government restrictions on our civil liberties are based upon the justification that they protect public safety and morals. Based upon our love affair with zero tolerance and our deep fear of crime, most Americans not only have not questioned the virtue of these lifelong restrictions and impositions on personal freedom, they have even openly supported them. After more than a generation of moving away from the philosophy of striving to rehabilitate people convicted of crimes, and, instead, figuring out new ways to rigorously punish those who are convicted, the laundry list of lifetime sanctions has grown ponderously long for more and more types of criminal offenses. We will now take a look at some of the principal ways people are being punished for the rest of their lives by our criminal justice system.

Lifetime Incarceration

Today there are many more crimes that carry long mandatory minimum sentences without the possibility of parole. There are also laws around the country under which, after two or three strikes, you spend the rest of your life in prison, even for crimes that a generation ago would have resulted in a sentence of only a few years.[42]

Lifetime Disqualification from Basic Civil Liberties and Lifetime Restrictions on Personal Freedom and Privacy

In many states, when someone is convicted of a felony, that person loses the right to vote in all elections, sit on a jury, and possess a firearm (whether for hunting, personal protection, or any other reason) for the rest of his or her life. Hence, for example, a young man (or even an adolescent child under certain circumstances) can be arrested for robbery and end up losing some of his most basic constitutional rights and civil liberties for the rest of his life.

But that's just the tip of the iceberg. If there is no provision for his arrest and conviction record to be sealed or expunged, his criminal record will remain open to the public for the rest of his life. He will forever have it appear on criminal background checks with employers. It may make it impossible for him to ever get various professional licenses or to work in a variety of fields. While this, in itself, is not a new development, the wide availability of electronic criminal records means that he will never be able to completely move on from something he did when he was young and, perhaps, stupid and reckless. For his entire life, he will be punished for a mistake that he made in his youth.

In previous centuries, the court would use a hot branding iron with an *F* on it for *felon*, or some other letter specifying conviction for some other criminal offense. The convicted person would be branded on the cheek or forehead or hand with the permanent mark of a criminal. Another punishment involved having an ear cut off.[43] In *The Scarlet Letter*, Hester Prynne, a young woman who had committed adultery, was forced to appear in public with a red letter *A* attached to her dress.[44] Such shaming methods have been commonplace for centuries in America's criminal justice system.

Today, anybody willing to pay a few dollars for a criminal background check can gain access through cyberspace to a potential employee's criminal background. In theory, the job applicant can refuse to consent to the search. In reality, he or she really has no choice, because refusal to allow the background check is an absolute guarantee of being turned away. Of course, to some extent at least, criminal background information needs to be available to employers, professional licensing boards, and the like. But at what point does a person have the right to simply move on from the damning and shaming that cyberspace allows? We no longer need branding irons or embroidered scarlet letters. We have a much more effective system today for branding people. Their criminal arrests and convictions simply stay tucked away in computer files, readily accessible by any employer, often with no regard to when the crime was committed. Today, a conviction may trail you to the end of the earth—and to the end of your days.

Traditionally, America has been the land of fresh starts and second chances for people, a place where the past can be forgotten and a person can set out for a new frontier. In the movie *Wyatt Earp*, the young Wyatt is deeply depressed after watching his wife die. He starts drinking, burns down their home, and drifts from town to town where he eventually gets in trouble in Arkansas, commits a crime, and is sent to jail. His father helps him get free, and he sets out for the Wild West, where he ends up a marshal on the right side of the law. In twenty-first-century America, Wyatt Earp would be plum out of luck. In this respect, our love affair with maintaining open public criminal records on people who have long since supposedly paid their debts to society means they never really stop paying. They are doomed to a lifetime sentence of shame, reduced opportunities, and never-ending inquiries into their pasts.

Modern data-gathering techniques contribute to the maintenance of a lifelong criminal record for persons convicted of a crime. For some offenses, a person convicted of a crime can be required to provide a DNA sample. Once taken, these samples stay on record with the government forever. To have to hand over to the government something that is unique and intimate to the individual is a grave invasion of that individual's privacy. The fact that the government keeps it forever means the person is never sure who will gain access to it, how it will be used, or for what purpose.

For some crimes today, the law requires that a convicted person's face be published in the local newspaper with a caption providing the information about the crime of which he or she was convicted. This form of shaming has become popular in many states for crimes such as drunk driving, prostitution, and the solicitation of a prostitute. Once again, thanks to the handy Internet, this information never really goes away, as digital versions of the newspaper can always be found somewhere on line. Because of this, the person convicted of such a crime can never really move on, and, because the convicted person's privacy is not valued in America today, many see no particular problem with this information hanging around in some corner of the information highway for all eternity, unless, of course, it is their picture or the photograph of a family member.

Even worse, as I mentioned earlier, in some states today, private newspapers publish all of the digital mug shots of everyone *arrested* that week in the local area. The papers are then sold at local gas stations and convenience stores for public information and entertainment, while a digital version is posed on the Web. The person hasn't been convicted of anything yet is already branded as an *implied* criminal by way of the local press and digital photography and computerization.

Sex Crimes—The "Third Rail" of Criminal Conduct

By far the most serious lifetime punishments today are reserved for what has truly become the "third rail" of criminal conduct in American society—sex crimes. (For those who have never lived near a subway or other electrified train system, the third rail is the rail that provides the electricity to power the train. While falling onto the tracks may be painful, if you fall onto the tracks and touch the "third rail," you are immediately electrocuted, usually to death.)

All states now have some version of a sex offender registry, requiring persons convicted of a variety of sex crimes to place their names on a public list at the county jail. Being convicted of any of a wide range of crimes—from sexual assault, to sexual contact with an underage person, to child pornography charges—can (depending on the state) land a person on the sex offender registry. Failure to register with the state's registry is also a crime in and of itself. Persons on a sex offender registry must register again if they move and, in many instances, whenever they simply travel from one place to another for work or vacation. And there are huge penalties if you do not comply. In Georgia, for example, the maximum penalty for failing to register a second time is thirty years in prison.[45]

I will focus on the Georgia registry for a moment, in part because I am familiar with it as I practice in Georgia, and in part because it is one of the most notorious in the country. (In fact, the Georgia registry is wildly popular with the general public, even though the federal courts have ruled that portions of it are unconstitutional.[46]) Once registered as a sex offender, many people will spend much or all of their lives on the registry. The Georgia sex offender registry law makes it illegal for a registered sex offender to live within 1,000 feet of a wide variety of public facilities. In practicality, the law forces sex offenders into a ghetto consisting of the handful of places where they can legally exist. Many people have been forced at one time or another to live under bridges or in the woods, where whole camps have been set up.[47]

Supporters of sex offender registries believe they are being tough on crime and benefitting "regular" Americans by imposing this inhumane treatment on our fellow citizens. The fact that the law is largely unenforceable and widely derided by sheriffs and probation officers as dangerous and impractical is lost on its advocates. From a public safety standpoint, having a large group of sex offenders living under a bridge or hidden away in a forest is a scary idea—I certainly don't want that encampment near my house. But what is almost never mentioned in the press is the simple injustice of treating our fellow human beings as a form of vermin best dealt with by shipping them off to a legally designated gulag, where they must exist on the fringes of society for the rest of their lives. Such action—spurred on by our love affair with zero-tolerance crime policies—is not only inhumane and unjust, but also seriously threatens the civil liberties of us all.

There is an application for the iPhone that allows the user to type in a location and see all of the sex offenders in that area, based upon data compiled from sex offender registries. The symbol on the iPhone is a man behind bars wearing a prison jumpsuit. Of course, the people on the registry are not in prison—they have "paid their debts" by serving their prison sentences and are now trying to get on with their lives. But the application symbol has it right on the money. People who are forced to register as sex offenders really are imprisoned in very real and tangible ways for the rest of their lives. Regardless of how much time goes by, they are forever branded the worst of the worst criminals, thanks to our love affair with zero tolerance and the advances of our digital information age.

At the same time, however, sex offender registries are incredibly popular with the general public. Why? For the same reason that I have mixed feelings about the creation and maintenance of sex offender registries. As a parent and father, I greatly appreciate being able to look up who is moving into my neighborhood and to know whether that person is a registered sex offender. So ask me—as a father—whether I support the sex offender registry, and I will reply, "Sure, it's great, as long as the registry is structured in such a way that the police can enforce it." On the flip side, the lawyer and civil libertarian side of me sees very real dangers in the creation and enforcement of sex offender registries. Why? The sex offender registry is a slippery slope toward government tyranny. How? I will explain.

The reason why sex offender registries are dangerous to our civil liberties as a free people lies in their justification. Supporters of a registry argue that sex offenders are so bad, that their actions are so terrible, and that they are so likely to repeat their crimes in the future, that it justifies the establishment of a sex offender registry. The most disturbing thing about this justification is you can make the same argument for any type of crime: drug crimes, domestic violence, traffic offenses, white-collar crime, shoplifting, DUI, or violent crimes, and the list could go on and on. If we are willing to strip one group of persons of their civil rights and send them literally "beyond the pale"—like the Russian czars did to the Jews of Eastern Europe—on the basis that they are simply too terrible to have living among us, then we can justify the same action for *any* group of persons. We have certainly segregated large portions of Americans in the past. When I was born in 1962, segregation of African Americans was still very much in effect in many parts of the country. In previous generations, Japanese Americans, Jewish Americans, Irish Americans, and, of course, Native Americans, have been denied basic civil liberties and forced to exist as lesser citizens on the fringes of society, restricted to particular neighborhoods, ghettos, internment camps, or reservations.

By using the sex offender registry, we are once again relegating a small, largely powerless, and detested minority of American citizens to the fringes while denying them basic civil rights. Nobody particularly cares about these citizens, because their crimes are seen as so heinous that they justify the extreme treatment, but this is how government repression always begins. It starts with a small minority that government leaders figure no one will care about, but then insidiously spreads from there. Under the justification used to establish the sex offender registry, all government leaders need to do to expand the repression is to decide that another class of people is so wicked, their actions so heinous, that they are deserving of the same fate as we are presently imposing on many sex offenders—a lifetime existence as a nonperson. Because of the popularity of the sex offender registry, especially among parents (like myself), ambitious politicians will no doubt pander to voters and their fears to support the creation of new registries for different types of crimes. This is, in fact, already happening in New York State, where a state politician has advocated for the establishment of a domestic violence offender registry in a bid to win popularity with the voters. [48]

The sex offender registry reminds me of the history concerning the persecution of the Jews by the Nazis represented in the movie *Schindler's List*. In the opening scene of the movie, a passenger train pulls into a station in a Polish city and Polish Jews from the countryside all exit with their bags and belongings. They stand in a long line that leads to a folding table, where German officials are sitting with pen and paper. As each Jewish family walks up, the German officer asks their name. We learn that, under a German law put into effect after the German army invaded and conquered Poland in the fall of 1939, all Jews must move from their homes in the country, live in the city, and register with the local government. The Nazi authorities saw the Jews as the enemy of the German people and their response was to enact a government registration program forcing all Jewish people to register. At first, the Jews simply had to give their names, so that the government could keep tabs on them. But, ultimately, they were denied all civil liberties, forced into ghettos, then moved into work camps, and eventually earmarked for extermination. But, remember, in the beginning, *there was only the registry.*

Match the current trend of establishing rigorous sex offender registries in our country with our love affair with zero tolerance law-and-order policies, and it is simple logic to see where we could end up. If we believe sex offenders are so bad that they deserve to register on a government list and then be stripped of their essential constitutional and human rights, then how much further are we willing to go? How many more groups of persons convicted of other types of crimes are we willing to force to register and, thus, turn into nonpersons by usurping their rights and liberties? This is how tyranny begins. The sex offender registry needs to be either limited to only the most heinous of violent sex crimes or dumped into the ashbin of history, along with all of the other methods we have contrived over the years to permanently strip American citizens of their constitutional rights and civil liberties.

Another reason the defense attorney in me believes we can live without the sex offender registry, or, at least, with only a very scaled-down version, is that there exists another, far simpler, solution to protecting Americans from the truly predatory, violent, sexual offender: prison. For those most serious of violent sexual offenders—serial rapists, for example—who have demonstrated, through their crimes, that they cannot live in American society, this is a place where they can be sentenced to life without parole (or in states with the death penalty, potentially even to death). Under these circumstances, we would not need any registry. We simply need to use our existing laws to keep these violent and predatory criminals locked away from American society.

When we look at the criminal law landscape, we see that it has shifted dramatically over the past thirty years. Few sociologists would have predicted, thirty years ago, that America's criminal justice system would behave and look the way it does today.[49] To those in love with zero tolerance and law and order, I say, "Congratulations—you have gotten your wish." But to lovers of our constitutional rights and civil liberties, and to those who simply believe we can do better toward our fellow human beings, I say, "It is time to take up the call to action." We cannot solve all of our problems by establishing an ever more brutish, ruthless, and utterly intolerant criminal justice system. It is time to consider the costs—both real and potential—not only to those human beings now in the clutches of the Beast, but to every one of us, our friends, and our families.

CHAPTER SEVEN

SIGNS OF HOPE—THE MOVEMENT TOWARD ALTERNATIVE SENTENCING AND PUNISHMENT POLICIES

By nature, I am an optimist. With that in mind, in this final chapter of Part II, I would like to discuss some of the more positive trends in America's criminal justice system. Some of the most recent promising trends have been the establishment of alternative sentencing programs, pretrial intervention programs, counseling programs, and other types of programs that have allowed persons arrested for breaking the law to avoid traditional criminal prosecution, while still requiring them to address the reasons they broke the law to begin with and to take responsibility for their actions.

An arrest can, in some cases, be a good thing to happen to a person. It can be a wake-up call. In my experience as a former prosecutor and a criminal defense attorney—having spoken to, met, or represented literally hundreds of people who have been arrested over nearly two decades—I have seen a number of similarities that apply to most people who have been arrested.

Most arrested people with whom I have come into contact got to that point because some aspect of their lives had spun out of control. In other words, some element of their lives was filled with chaos. The chaos was the result of some underlying problem, usually related to one, or several, of the following:

- problems with alcohol or drug use,
- gambling addictions,
- financial problems,
- problems with pornography or other sexual addictions,
- problems with compulsive behavior, and/or
- mental or psychological health disorders.

Usually the arrest was just the last of a long string of problems tipping over like so many dominos in the person's life when a particular addiction or behavior had gotten out of control. The individual's personal chaos had finally gotten so bad that he or she tripped on and then stumbled over the line of acceptable behavior and ended up being arrested for breaking the law.

One example of this is a person forging prescriptions for painkillers. He most likely doesn't start out planning to become a forger. He starts by simply taking a drug that his doctor prescribed for a medically necessary reason, perhaps due to chronic pain from an injury of some type. He becomes hooked on the drug, though, and starts wanting larger doses of the prescription painkiller—more than any doctor is willing to prescribe. Desperate, he starts borrowing pills from friends or family members. When this no longer works, he turns to the Internet to find drugs online, forging prescriptions to send to the Internet suppliers. He is arrested for forgery, but the real problem is his underlying addiction.

Another common example could be shoplifting. A young woman takes a few clothing items from a local department store as a high school prank. She gets away with it. Emboldened by her "success," she does it again. Psychological studies have shown that the adrenaline rush the average person gets from stealing a few items from a store is very similar to the adrenaline rush a person gets from winning at gambling. The adrenaline rush, over time, becomes a tremendous high that our shoplifter begins to seek out again and again. Ultimately, she is caught and arrested. Once again, the arrest is the final domino falling in a long line of socially destructive acts and self-defeating behaviors.

A person is working as a stockbroker for a high-pressure company. He is the company's top performer. He works harder and harder, striving to keep "winning." Eventually he begins to burn out, but "failure is not an option," so he starts using cocaine to stay awake and "on" more and more of the time. He turns to methamphetamine when the cocaine is no longer strong enough. As his addiction spirals out of control, eventually he loses his job. He is finally arrested for felony possession of illegal drugs when he is busted in an undercover sting operation.

A young man from a broken home finds solace in a local gang. He starts hanging out, takes to drinking, and drops out of school. One night, three gang members rob the local convenience store. The young man is actually not at the scene, but he is later arrested when the store clerk mistakenly identifies the young man in a photo lineup along with several other members of the gang. He almost goes to prison, but his family hires a lawyer and he is acquitted at trial. He was innocent of the crime and rightfully acquitted, but he never would have been in the situation in the first place if he hadn't gotten involved with the gang. Even so, he is responsible for creating his own bad luck and costing his family thousands of dollars in attorney fees.

Now, please understand, I am not a psychologist or a psychiatrist, nor am I trying to be one. But my experience as a defense lawyer has been that many people who get arrested did not plan to wind up breaking the law. Their arrests are simply the last of a long line of missteps and bad choices that ultimately led them to illegal behavior. These missteps usually began with a personal crisis of some sort.

Let's face it—life can be tough, brutal, and messy. To err is definitely human—at least that's what you see as a criminal defense lawyer. To the sanctimonious, law-and-order, lock-'em-up-and-throw-away-the-key, zero tolerance types, I caution you: "Look at yourself and your family and friends before you judge too harshly. Be careful throwing stones, because the next glass house you break may be your own."

What separates the people in the examples above from other people committing crimes is that they don't fall into the first two categories I described in Part I of this book: the unsuccessful criminal and the successful criminal. They are not career criminals at all. They are people who have spent the vast majority of their lives dutifully obeying the law. It was personal chaos that led them to make very bad decisions and to ultimately break the law. Are they responsible for their actions? Absolutely. Should they be held accountable? Yes. The question is: *how* should they be held accountable? Should they be given the opportunity to repair their mistakes and go back to living law-abiding, successful lives? Or should they be ground into dust and turned into noncitizens by an uncaring, unforgiving, and merciless criminal justice system?

Is there a "criminal type"? Do some people simply have an evil, criminal mind that makes them truly predatory toward ordinary society? I personally believe that, yes, there are such types. Psychologists call such people "sociopaths," and in my work as a criminal defense lawyer, I do run into them from time to time. They are the type who would steal grandma's shawl off her back if they had the chance.

I don't run convoluted tests to figure out whom I'm dealing with—I judge by their eyes. The true criminals I have met over the years all have what I think of as "shark's eyes." They can be blue or hazel or brown or black, but they all have the same lifeless, unemotional, ruthlessly calculating quality to them. The person may be smiling at you, laughing, crying, or even joking, but his or her eyes don't really change expression. There is a cruel, predatory, deadness to the person's eyes that seems to reach down to the deepest recesses of their souls. It is chilling to behold. And, because I know that you are about to ask, yes, I still do my job and represent these people when they retain me. But they scare the hell out of me.

In his book, *Inside the Criminal Mind*, Stanton Samenow describes this type of sociopathic personality:

> The criminal values people only insofar as they bend to his will or can be coerced or manipulated into doing what he wants. He has been this way since childhood, and by the time he is an adult he has a worldview in

which he believes he is entitled to whatever he wants. Consequently he is sizing up his prospects for exploiting people and situations. To him the world is a chessboard, with other people serving as pawns to gratify his desires. His actions express this view of life, and it also pervades his fantasies.[50]

Fortunately, true criminal types are few and far between, at least in my experience. Now, I am neither a sociologist nor a statistician, and I am not going to throw a lot of facts and figures at you to try and prove my argument. I am simply relating to you what my own personal experience has been as a criminal defense lawyer. The vast majority of the people I have met who ended up in trouble with the law are decent, ordinary people whose lives spiraled out of control. They are not truly "criminals," just ordinary, fallible human beings.

Fortunately, the programs set up over the past generation to address the situations of people like those described above are very helpful and mark a major step in the right direction, away from zero tolerance. Such programs take what could be the end of a person's life—being arrested for breaking the law—and, instead, make the arrest the beginning of getting real help and getting that person's life back on track. The arrest may be followed by a short period of incarceration, which can actually be a good thing. For the average person, a short stint in jail—even as little as a few days or weeks—is so terrifying that he will do whatever it takes to avoid going back. Repairing the damage he has done to the community by way of community service work, undergoing mandatory or voluntary counseling, getting medical treatment, and paying restitution to any victims are all ways that a person arrested for a crime can take responsibility for what he did and get on the road to redemption. As a criminal defense lawyer, I find that one of the most rewarding things about my job is seeing the true resilience of the human spirit. Most people arrested and/or convicted for committing crimes can be saved through their own hard work and acceptance of responsibility, if they are given the chance.

Returning to what we were discussing at the beginning of Part II, thirty years ago the academic criminologist James Wilson argued in *Thinking About Crime* that the ideal criminal justice system would operate based upon the same redemptive ideals. Wilson wrote, "Society should ensure that one can 'pay one's debt' (for committing a crime) without suffering permanent loss of civil rights, the continuous and pointless indignity of parole supervision, and the frustration of not being able to find a job."[51]

The best of today's rehabilitative programs allow the person charged with a crime the chance to leave the supervision of the criminal justice system with a clean slate. The person's arrest record is sealed or expunged, allowing her to seek profitable employment. Her civil and constitutional rights and responsibilities are restored. *She does not become an "un-citizen" but is able to, having paid her debt to society in a personally responsible manner, once again pursue her God-given rights to life, liberty, and the pursuit of happiness.* To their credit, there are many legislators, judges, prosecutors, police officers, probation officers, and criminal defense lawyers working arduously to make sure average American citizens arrested for committing crimes really can earn a second chance.

In Part III of this book, we look at what to do if you or a family member or friend is ever arrested for breaking the law. This is not intended as legal advice. It is simply my effort to provide a basic road map in case you ever come face-to-face with the Beast, America's criminal justice system.

PART III: BATTLING THE BEAST—

YOUR CONSTITUTIONAL RIGHTS, BASIC PRINCIPLES OF CRIMINAL DEFENSE, AND SEVEN CASE STUDIES

Every time someone is either investigated by the police or arrested for committing a crime, a human drama unfolds. It ultimately impacts not only the person investigated or arrested, but also all of that person's family members, friends, and coworkers. Like a stone tossed into the middle of a pond, the investigation or arrest causes a ripple effect of human tragedy that spreads outward. A human life has been threatened, and the threat keeps spreading until everyone surrounding the accused is pulled into the maw of the Beast.

In Part I of this book, we looked at *how* America's criminal justice system operates. In Part II, we examined zero tolerance and some of the political, philosophical, and sociological reasons *why* America's criminal justice system operates the way it does. In Part III, we will first examine our rights as American citizens under the Constitution of the United States as they pertain to the criminal law, then we will review some of the tools and methods regularly used by criminal defense lawyers to defend their clients who have been accused of, or are being investigated for, committing a crime. Finally, we will focus on seven different fact-based scenarios concerning seven different areas of criminal law to get a feel for the true "nuts and bolts"—or, if you prefer, "blood and guts"—of criminal defense work.

What will you do if the Beast ever sets its red-rimmed eyes, snarling fangs, and razor-sharp claws on you or a friend or a family member? What do you do when you go from the good, decent, law-abiding citizen who has always been protected by the police and prosecutors to one of their prey?[52] In the following chapters, we will take a look at many of the legal and investigational tools available to you and your lawyer as you do battle with the Beast.

CHAPTER EIGHT

YOUR CONSTITUTIONAL RIGHTS—THE BEDROCK OF AMERICA'S CRIMINAL JUSTICE SYSTEM

In order to understand how America's criminal justice system works, it is necessary to have a basic understanding of your constitutional rights as an American citizen. Our criminal justice system is based upon the principle that we are a nation of laws and not of men (and women). Simply stated, this means that no one—no police officer, prosecutor, judge, legislator, executive, government official, or regular citizen—is above the law. Our founding fathers wanted to make sure that our nation was built upon this basic principle, and to do so they provided all Americans with fundamental constitutional rights that protect our liberties. Let's look at the constitutional rights that create the fundamental framework of America's criminal justice system.

Our Founding Fathers and the Creation of the U.S. Constitution
In the summer of 1787, our young nation's founding fathers met in Philadelphia to produce a document that could form the basis of government for the young American republic. They wanted to create a legal blueprint, a written constitution, for a federal government strong enough to effectively govern the fledgling nation. Our freedom as a newly minted nation had been won through the blood, sweat, and treasure of American citizens after seven grueling years, from our declaration of independence from Great Britain in 1776 until the signing of the Treaty of Paris in 1783, when Great Britain legally recognized America's independence.

Between 1783 and 1787, however, things had not gone smoothly for the new republic. The only written legal framework for keeping the nation together was the Articles of Confederation. Drafted in 1777, the Articles had not proven strong enough to allow the federal government to properly and effectively govern the nation.

Many of the founding fathers who met to draft the Constitution in 1787 were the same individuals who had come, in 1776, to debate, draft, and sign the Declaration of Independence. Now older and more experienced, men such as Benjamin Franklin, John Adams, George Washington, and Thomas Jefferson journeyed once again to Philadelphia to draft a new United States Constitution.

Throughout the summer of 1787, the founding fathers labored over the legal framework for a strong federal government that could effectively govern the nation. Once the core document was completed and signed, it had to be ratified (accepted) by the states as legally binding, but many citizens were fearful of the amount of power the new federal government would have over not only individual American citizens, but also the thirteen individual states. James Madison became the primary champion of amending the Constitution by adding ten additional provisions, collectively known as the Bill of Rights. Adding the Bill of Rights to the Constitution helped to ease the fears of America's citizens concerned that their individual rights would be trampled under the new, stronger federal government. The government came into being once the final state ratified the Constitution early in 1789. The first ten amendments to the U.S. Constitution, collectively called the Bill of Rights, were enacted into law in 1791.[53]

In our country, we enjoy some of the best and most established civil rights on the planet. Even so, we often take them for granted in our day-to-day lives, while we are busy with work, family, and friends. Indeed, the rights that our founding fathers sat and sweated over during the long, hot Philadelphia summer of 1787 (and into the fall and winter, as they debated the Bill of Rights) often seem largely irrelevant as we move through our twenty-first-century lives.

All it takes, however, is a police officer or federal agent knocking on the door to remind us very quickly just how precious these hard-won rights are to our lives and liberties. The Bill of Rights, more than 220 years old, still stands as the first line of defense for anyone accused of a crime. Don't think so? Just ask yourself this question: if you or a loved one were to be arrested for a crime, is there any other country on earth in which you would rather be arrested? My guess is your answer is "No." Your reason for responding so quickly begins with the rights laid out by a bunch of guys wearing wigs and knickers who, weary of their own experiences with alternative justice systems in Europe, took the time to make sure that any American citizen accused of a crime was protected with certain fundamental rights.

The Bill of Rights: Your Constitutional Rights Under America's Criminal Justice System

Let us now turn to the Bill of Rights and look at its immense impact on how you or your loved one will be treated in the event you are accused of a crime. For this, let us focus on the constitutional rights that are most directly related to criminal law. These rights are laid out in the First, Second, Fourth, Fifth, Sixth, and Eighth Amendments to the Constitution. Beyond these is the right to privacy, which has been established by the United States Supreme Court as an inherent right implied within the Constitution.[54]

Restraining Tyranny—the First Amendment

> *Congress shall make no law respecting an establishment of religion, or prohibiting the free exercise thereof; or abridging the freedom of speech, or of the press; or the right of the people peaceably to assemble, and to petition the Government for a redress of grievances.*

Any discussion of your constitutional rights as they relate to criminal law in America has to begin with the first amendment to the U.S. Constitution. You may be asking, "What does the First Amendment have to do with criminal law or the rights of someone arrested and accused of a crime?" My main reason for discussing the First Amendment is to point out all of the things you *cannot* be arrested for in the United States. This may seem trivial or may seem like I am stating the obvious, but just reflect upon some basic historical and contemporary examples and you will see my point.

A family gathers in their chapel, installed in the basement of their home behind a hidden entrance. The priest lights the candles at the altar and begins to say Mass and serve Communion. Armed guards break down the door and arrest the priest and all the family members and haul them off to prison. They are Catholics trying to worship in late-sixteenth-century England.

A man peacefully assembles with his students in a public square, demanding redress from the one-party rule of his country. He is sentenced to eleven years in prison and declared a criminal by his government. He continues to write from jail, arguing against his nation's one-party system and demanding basic humanitarian reforms. He is Liu Xiaobo, subject of the Communist People's Republic of China and winner of the 2010 Nobel Peace Prize.

A Jewish family assembles to go to their synagogue only to find it has been burned to the ground, and the government is doing nothing about it. Instead, their business is confiscated and they are thrown out of their home. They are living in Nazi-occupied Europe in the mid-1930s. Of course, much worse happens to them in a few years' time as the Nazis attempt to erase Judaism from all of Europe.

Students gather to protest the occupation of their country. Some are thrown into jail, while others are gunned down in the streets or run over by tanks. They are protesters in Communist-ruled Hungary in 1956, Communist-ruled Czechoslovakia in 1968, and Communist-ruled China in 1989.

The list goes on and on and on. In the United States, however, we are free to speak, write, assemble, worship, and petition the government as we choose without fear of being arrested and convicted as criminals. These fundamental human rights, activities that we engage in throughout our lives, remain illegal in many parts of the world. Hence, I begin our discussion with the First Amendment. It protects many aspects of basic human behavior, which are fundamental to human life and liberty, and that many nations throughout history—and up to the present day—have punished as crimes.

An Armed People Are a Free People—The Second Amendment

> *A well regulated Militia being necessary to the security of a free State, the right of the people to keep and bear Arms shall not be infringed.*

The precise meaning of the Second Amendment has been debated in the courts repeatedly over the past generation. In 2008, the United States Supreme Court made it clear that no federal, state, or local government authority can prevent people from owning and keeping handguns and other basic firearms within their homes for the purposes of self-protection.[55]

Beyond this, in my opinion, the Second Amendment has a much wider importance than self-protection from burglars and so forth. The civil liberties of all United States citizens are preserved by the fact that all of us have the constitutional right to keep and bear arms. The founding fathers knew that the best way for a free nation to remain free was by having its citizens armed. If any ruler were to declare himself or herself monarch or dictator, the people of the states could rise up against such an act, while also ensuring that they were always ready and able to form into militias in the event of foreign invasion.

As 9/11 showed, we are not immune, despite all our military might, to foreign attack. And as any history book or any cable news network covering the political affairs of modern-day nations will tell you, our liberties can be destroyed by dictatorial takeover from within—or by foreign invasion from without—at any time. It is to be hoped that the need will not arise in our lifetime to appear in the public parks and squares of our towns and cities to form local militias against a president who decides he is going to stay in power even though a new president has been elected, or to combat a foreign enemy that finally has enough military power to launch an invasion against our shores—we are lucky to live in peaceful times. But, if history is any guide at all, the time will come when the practical and utter importance of the Second Amendment will become all too obvious to a future generation of Americans, just as it was to the first generation of Americans who drafted and ratified the Second Amendment. They made sure that our government could not criminalize gun ownership except under very limited exceptions.

Limiting Government Search, Seizure, and Warrants—Your Fourth Amendment Rights

> *The right of the people to be secure in their persons, houses, papers, and effects, against unreasonable searches and seizures, shall not be violated, and no Warrants shall issue, but upon probable cause, supported by Oath or affirmation, and particularly describing the place to be searched, and the persons or things to be seized.*

The fourth amendment to the Constitution is one of the most familiar to American citizens. Not only is it argued over in the courts and discussed countless times in television shows and movies, but also it involves the privacy and sanctity of our homes. The Fourth Amendment places strict limitations on when, and under what circumstances, a state or federal government official may enter our homes to search for things in relation to a criminal investigation (or for any other reason, for that matter). It also restricts when, and under what circumstances, a police officer may search our persons. The Fourth Amendment has also been extended to other areas of our private lives, including our cars, places of work, and telephone and online conversations.

The basic understanding that our homes and persons are private and should be free from arbitrary government searches, invasions, and other meddling is not a new concept, but one deeply rooted in English common law dating back centuries. In 1604, in *Semayne's Case*, Sir Edward Coke famously stated, "The house of every one is to him as his castle and fortress, as well for his defence against injury and violence as for his repose."[56] In *Semayne's Case*, the English court acknowledged that the king did not have unbridled authority to intrude on his subjects' dwellings, but ruled that government agents were permitted to conduct searches and seizures under certain conditions when their purpose was lawful and a warrant had been obtained.

Even so, in modern times—and in societies around the globe—arbitrary arrests and criminal prosecutions have routinely occurred. Saddam Hussein, the former Iraqi dictator, was famous for issuing arbitrary arrest orders. His private police would simply show up at the home of a political rival in the middle of the night and arrest the person, who would then be tried and executed before dawn.[57] During the military junta in the 1980s in Argentina, the military police routinely showed up at the homes of political adversaries and took them away, never to be heard from again. Known in Argentina as "the disappeared," many of those arrested have never been accounted for, their bodies perhaps tossed into the Rio Plata, the river that runs through Buenos Aires.[58] The illegal activities of the Argentinian military government are condemned today as one of the darkest moments in Argentine history.

The Fourth Amendment helps protect Americans from scenarios like these. It provides broad guidelines establishing our right to not be arrested or harassed by the state without probable cause. United States courts, throughout the years, have used the Fourth Amendment to create the basic rules which the police must follow when they are investigating someone for committing a crime. These rules even govern when a government official such as a police officer or federal agent can obtain a warrant to enter and search your home or person. The officer has to apply to a judge with a written statement under oath, called an affidavit, explaining in sufficient detail the facts that support the officer's belief that the search should be conducted. The judge cannot issue the warrant unless he or she determines that the facts in the affidavit show that "probable cause" exists that the search will reveal evidence of some type of illegal activity. (The need for probable cause means that there must be logical factual support for the police officer to believe illegal activity is taking place within the home to be searched, and that a warrant can't be based upon a mere hunch or the police officer trusting his or her gut instincts.) The affidavit also must specifically identify the home or other location to be searched and describe the item(s) the officer intends to search for and/or seize.

The rules that have been established for the police getting a search warrant also apply to arrest warrants. Generally, a person can be arrested only after an arrest warrant has been issued. The warrant may be based upon the results of a previous legal search or on some other information gained from a criminal investigation that establishes probable cause for an arrest. There are exceptions, of course, such as when a bank robber is arrested fleeing a bank, in which case the police will arrest the person immediately since the evidence is in plain sight and there is no time for the police to get a warrant.

"You Have the Right to Remain Silent"—The Fifth Amendment

> *No person shall be held to answer for a capital, or otherwise infamous crime, unless on a presentment or indictment of a Grand Jury*, except in cases arising in the land or naval forces, or in the Militia, when in actual service in time of War or public danger; nor shall any person be subject for the same offence to be twice put in jeopardy of life or limb; *nor shall be compelled in any criminal case to be a witness against himself, nor be deprived of life, liberty, or property, without due process of law;* nor shall private property be taken for public use, without just compensation. (Emphasis added)

The fifth amendment to the U.S. Constitution is the longest and most detailed of the ten constitutional amendments that make up the Bill of Rights. For purposes of this discussion, I will focus on four parts of the Fifth Amendment crucial to criminal prosecutions: the right to a grand jury, the protection against self-incrimination at trial, the right to remain silent in the face of police questioning, and the overall right to due process of law.

Right to a Grand Jury. The first phrase of the Fifth Amendment concerns the right of any person accused of a serious crime to be formally charged only by a grand jury. Today, this provision is interpreted to apply to crimes punishable by time in prison, commonly referred to as *felonies*.

So, what is a grand jury? It is a group of citizens sitting at the courthouse who have been sworn under oath to hear and deliberate on testimony concerning whether probable cause exists to issue a formal criminal charge against a person suspected of committing a crime. The grand jury members usually sit in an enclosed room where a prosecutor presents witnesses—usually the investigating or arresting officers and other witnesses—who testify as to what they believe are the facts of the case. In some jurisdictions, the defendant also may testify if he or she wishes, but defense lawyers are generally not allowed to participate. The important thing to remember is that a grand jury indictment (the determination that the accused should go to trial) is in no way a determination of *guilt*. It is simply a declaration by the grand jury that enough evidence exists for the case to go forward to trial. The grand jury is also important because the indictment describes specifically what crime the person is accused of committing and the general facts alleged as to how the accused committed the crime. A sample indictment might look something like this:

> We, the grand jury sitting this 1st day of August in the County of Freedom, do hereby charge and accuse Mr. William Smith with the crime of Burglary. For the said accused, on the 10th day of July 2010, did enter the dwelling house of another, located at 123 Main Street in our county, with the intent to commit a felony therein by stealing electronic equipment, including a

computer and flat screen television, valued at greater than 500 dollars.

By requiring that a grand jury be the entity to legally accuse someone of committing a crime, the Fifth Amendment provides several safeguards. First, no government official—be he a prosecutor, police officer, or federal agent—can accuse someone on his own. He has to present testimony and other objective evidence to citizens from the community, who then decide for themselves whether probable cause exists to formally accuse their fellow citizen of a crime. The founding fathers wanted to avoid the practice—common in eighteenth-century Europe—where kings could simply charge persons with crimes without any other authority but their "royal prerogative."

Second, the indictment must spell out in detail what crime(s) the person is actually accused of doing and how he or she is alleged to have done it. Referring to the sample indictment example above, to convict the person the prosecutor must be able to show that the accused person actually committed the specific act (burglary) by entering a specific house belonging to someone else (123 Main Street) on a specific date (July 10, 2010), with the intent to commit a felony while in the house (by stealing valuable electronic equipment). The indictment allows the accused to know what he or she is charged with doing, and it allows the accused and his or her lawyers to create a defense against the charge.

Another important aspect of the grand jury is the respect and responsibility it gives to ordinary members of the community. In many countries, the elite consider the average citizens too stupid, uneducated, or irresponsible to have the enormous power of hearing evidence and then voting whether to indict someone for a crime. The respect our founding fathers had for the "common man"—now the common *citizen*—to be able to handle this critical element of maintaining order and the rule of law is reflected in their decision to leave the final responsibility for formally charging someone with a serious crime up to ordinary members of the community.

I was sitting with a European lawyer at a conference of the International Bar Association (IBA) recently, where we were discussing the grand jury system in America. (I am the former co-chair of the Criminal Law Committee of the IBA, and we had just held a discussion on American juries.) After the conference, the lawyer sniffed in a dismissive tone and summed up his archaic opinion, saying, "The law is best left to the professionals to decide."

In America, our founding fathers believed it was best to let the *people* decide. They understood that the strength of the American republic lay with the involvement of America's citizens with the legal processes, especially when it came to decisions concerning life and liberty. Nowhere is this more clearly demonstrated than in the fact that a prosecutor, no matter how zealous, and no matter how committed he or she may be to the prosecution of a particular individual, must first present the case to members of the accused person's community and let them decide for themselves whether enough evidence exists to force the accused citizen to stand trial for allegedly committing a serious crime.

<u>You Cannot Be Forced to Testify Against Yourself.</u> Two basic rights of the criminally accused come from a single important phrase in the Fifth Amendment: "nor shall [any person] be compelled in any criminal case to be a witness against himself . . . ." From this provision comes the right of an accused person not to be forced to give testimony at his or her own trial, as well as the "right to remain silent" when questioned by the police, made famous in the giving of "*Miranda*" warnings in countless television police dramas.

No defendant at trial can be forced to testify. Equally important, the jury is not permitted to infer that the defendant is guilty simply because he or she chooses to remain silent, nor may the prosecutor argue to the jury that the defendant's silence is evidence of guilt. The idea goes hand in glove with the prosecution's responsibility to prove the defendant's guilt beyond a reasonable doubt at trial with evidence *other than* any statement or confession from the defendant.

Out of all of our constitutional rights, this is perhaps the toughest one for people to accept when they sit as jurors. They want to hear the defendant's side of the story and naturally wonder why any defendant does not take the stand. The answer lies in the fact that, under our constitutional system, the defendant *does not have to prove anything*. The government prosecutor has the burden of proving, through objective evidence, the accused person's guilt **beyond all reasonable doubt**. The burden never shifts to the accused. This right preserves the sacred principle in our legal system that a person accused of a crime is **presumed innocent** until the prosecutor can prove otherwise beyond a reasonable doubt.

In many foreign courts, and in centuries past, accused persons would be commanded by the judge to confess. If they did not confess, they were considered guilty. So accused persons were caught in a trap: if they confessed at trial, they were declared guilty by reason of their confession, but if they refused to confess, they were declared guilty by reason of their silence. The Fifth Amendment declares that this type of illogical and inhumane "justice" cannot be meted out against any United States citizen.

Your Rights Under Miranda. As mentioned above, the Fifth Amendment provision against self-incrimination also keeps the prosecution honest, because they have to prove their case with actual evidence that does not involve forcing the accused person to confess. The famous *Miranda* warnings are what most people understand about this constitutional right. In the case of *Miranda v. Arizona*, the United States Supreme Court declared:

> The person in custody must, prior to interrogation, be clearly informed that he or she has the right to remain silent, and that anything the person says will be used against that person in court; the person must be clearly informed that he or she has the right to consult with an attorney and to have that attorney present during questioning, and that, if he or she is indigent, an attorney will be provided at no cost to represent her or him.[59]

These essential rights—the "right to remain silent" when in police custody, and to have an attorney present during questioning—are the most important things to remember if a police officer, federal agent, or any other government official ever questions you.

Easy to remember, right? But wait! The police only need to give you your *Miranda* warning once you are in "police custody." But what exactly does that mean? If you have been formally arrested—that is, the police have handcuffed you and said you are under arrest—then you are in police custody. You can also arguably be in police custody if the police have put you in a position where a reasonable person would not feel free to leave. But the courts in recent years have allowed for more latitude for police questioning *before* a person is considered in custody (and, therefore, legally entitled to be read their *Miranda* warnings).

For example, suppose the police and FBI show up at your house at six in the morning in two unmarked vehicles and three squad cars with blue lights flashing. They pound on the door and wake you, your wife, and your two children. When you sleepily open the door, the police rush in with a battering ram in hand. They have flak jackets, helmets, and drawn guns. They pull you, your wife, and your children outside while they ransack your house. You and your wife and children stand outside under police guard in your pajamas (hopefully you had time to put them on). The neighbors all come out, staring and wondering what all the commotion is about. The officers show you and your wife their search warrant. Your son gets upset and starts yelling at the cops, and the police handcuff you and your son. When you protest, they tell you it is simply for your and your son's safety. They may say you are not under arrest and that you and your family are free to leave, even as the police continue rummaging through your house. Then, the police start questioning you or your wife or son. Or maybe you ask "What is this is all about?" and the police start asking you questions in response.

Hmm . . . are you under arrest? Are you or your wife or children entitled to *Miranda* warnings if you start answering questions or talking to the police? Are any of you in police custody? The answer to all these questions is "Maybe, but probably not." And yet, suppose the police do uncuff you and your son and tell you that you are not in custody—do you really feel free to leave? Gun-toting police are in your home, your yard, and your driveway; do you think *anyone* would feel *not* under arrest? Surprise! The law says you may not be in custody at all. You are simply having your house searched. The police don't have a warrant for your arrest and they have not told you that you are under arrest. Even if they handcuff you for "safety" reasons, you are still not necessarily under arrest.

Suppose you get a call to come talk to a policeman down at the station. You go down and the police officer leads you into an interview room and closes the door. He stands there menacingly over you, demanding that you start talking and telling him whatever he wants to hear. He has a gun and a badge and you are in police headquarters, but he doesn't say you are under arrest. Do you feel like you're in police custody? Do you really feel free to leave? Well, guess what? The law says you may very well *not* be in custody. The police are allowed to use a variety of intimidation tactics to get you to talk. Only after you have talked with them will they decide whether to arrest you, and *Miranda* protects none of your statements up to that point. So remember, if a police officer ever questions you, no matter how cordial or how threatening the officer is being and no matter what he or she promises you, do not say a word. Simply keep quiet and ask for a lawyer.

As I discussed in Part I, your lawyer can always make arrangements for you to give the police a statement later, if you and your lawyer decide (after meeting privately) that it is in your best interest to talk to the police. But without a lawyer present, you are playing Russian roulette with your life. The police can lie, deceive, bully, cajole, threaten, and make hollow promises to get you to talk. So forget about waiting for your *Miranda* warning. Just keep your mouth shut until you are able to talk to a lawyer. Let them arrest you if need be. You are not going to help yourself by talking to the police until properly instructed by your own attorney. Also never, ever sign a *Miranda* waiver form or verbally waive your *Miranda* rights. Preserve your rights! There are no exceptions to this rule—none, ever!

Your Rights to Due Process Under the Law. The Fifth Amendment also contains language that actually encompasses all of the other constitutional protections concerning the rights of a person accused of a crime: "nor [shall any person] be deprived of life, liberty, or property, without due process of law."

The basic concept of the right to "due process" encompasses all of the rights we enjoy as citizens of the United States. What it means, in essence, is that no government official can arbitrarily act against you, and all their actions must be in accordance with the rule of law. The idea in English common law goes back to the Magna Carta, signed by King John in 1215: Even the king was not above the law. He could not deprive his subjects (limited to English noblemen in the original document) of their lives, liberty, or property arbitrarily or on a whim. Even he, the king, had to follow the rule of law. This basic concept means that no one, no matter how powerful, can take the law into his or her own hands.

In the television drama *CSI: Miami*, there is a scene in which the tough-as-nails redheaded detective played by David Caruso gets a man to confess to killing the murderer of one of his own family members. The detective is sympathetic, but explains he has to arrest the man for murder. In doing so, he explains, "I understand why you killed, but that's not your right to do." In his own blunt terms, the detective was stating the simple fact that no man has the right to deprive another of life, liberty, or property without due process of law.

In the Middle East, where many disputes are still resolved by tribal law, the tribal elders will sit with the fathers of the two families involved in any crimes. Let's say that the son of one father killed the son of the other father. The elders will negotiate a settlement, such as the loss of a limb or the transfer of wealth from one father to the other as compensation for the death of the other father's son. We may or may not agree with the result, but either way the tribal elders are following—in their own customary way—the basic concept of due process of law.

The idea of legal due process is ancient and is perhaps best illustrated by the famous Roman trial lawyer and statesman Cicero, who lived in the final years of the Roman Republic, in the years 106–43 BC. The Romans had public jury trials at the time that would, if we were to travel back in time, seem to us not unlike a criminal or civil trial going on in any local county courthouse in the United States today. Cicero was known as a great orator and fiery advocate for his clients, sort of an ancient Roman version of Johnny Cochran or F. Lee Bailey.[60]

Many of our founding fathers had read Cicero in school and they, like many educated men of the eighteenth century, could read him in the original Latin. Some carried pocket versions of Cicero's famous writings with them when they traveled, and much of their thinking can be traced back to the lessons they learned from this famous Roman lawyer.[61] Cicero summed up the concept of our rights as citizens to legal due process in this way: "We enslave ourselves to the law so that we may be free."[62] What was good enough for Cicero was good enough for our founding fathers, and it remains so to this day.

Liberty's Beating Heart: The Sixth Amendment

> In all criminal prosecutions, the accused shall enjoy the right to a speedy and public trial, by an impartial jury of the State and district wherein the crime shall have been committed, which district shall have been previously ascertained by law, and to be informed of the nature and cause of the accusation; to be confronted with the witnesses against him; to have compulsory process for obtaining witnesses in his favor, and to have the Assistance of Counsel for his defence.

From my perspective as a practicing criminal defense lawyer, the Sixth Amendment is the beating heart of our liberty as a free people. Review history and you will see that every time a dictator takes power, the first thing the new ruler does is to take control of the criminal justice system. In countries with a jury trial system in place, the tyrant immediately destroys it. A dictator knows that as long as there are juries in place, he cannot force the people to their knees by arresting, prosecuting, and convicting people as he pleases. As long as ordinary people have the right and the responsibility to determine the fate of their fellow citizens accused of crimes, the power of government rulers is restricted. The jury trial system is the bulwark of our freedom, the highest wall of defense for our liberties.

Trial by Jury. Our jury system can be traced back to the Roman Republic[63] (508 to 27 BC) and before that to Ancient Greece (600 to 133 BC).[64] One of the most fascinating moments of my life took place during a visit to the Museum of Athens in Greece a few years ago, where I saw ancient bronze ballot disks used by Greek jurors to cast their votes of guilty or not guilty in criminal cases.

The practice of dictators eliminating jury trials in order to wield absolute power has continued in more recent times. In Russia, Tsar Alexander II introduced jury trials as a reforming measure in 1864 to provide greater freedom to his subjects, but when the communists came to power in 1917, they immediately threw out the jury trial system. Thus, Stalin and other socialist dictators were free to control the criminal justice system, and they used it at various times to wreak absolute terror on their political enemies and subjects. The jury trial system was reintroduced in 1993 in Russia following the collapse of the Soviet Union, although it has been recently limited to a certain extent.[65]

In 2007, I had the opportunity to travel to Singapore as an officer of the International Bar Association's Criminal Law Committee. In the streets, many people approached me with written petitions or whispers in the hopes that we would let the world know about their plight as subjects living in a police state. Singapore has been under one-party rule since 1969, and while Singaporeans had enjoyed the right to trial by jury under the British Commonwealth system, when dictator Lee Kuan Yew came into power, one of the first things he did was to throw out the jury system, declaring it to be an "Anglo-Saxon" concept irrelevant in Asia.[66]

One evening, I spoke with a local Singapore attorney who reflected that, although his country had made great material strides in the past generation—Singapore is full of upscale restaurants, gleaming skyscrapers, and fancy shopping malls—"... perhaps we did not have to go so far in surrendering our freedoms." He looked wistfully around the shiny, modern hotel lobby we were sitting in, where you could eat, drink, and shop to your heart's content—but not ask for the liberties of a free citizen without running the risk of being thrown in jail. The dictators who run Singapore will make sure you get convicted for speaking your mind; they control the courts, because there is no jury system to get in their way.

Jury trials also protect the weakest among us. There is no one weaker than someone who is on trial for committing a crime. Unlike the cocky defendants who are depicted on television, literally daring the prosecutor to convict them, my professional experience taken from representing people in American courts is that people are scared to death when they simply enter a courtroom, let alone stand trial. Their liberty is at stake. President Ronald Reagan once said, "Protecting the rights of even the least individual among us is basically the only excuse the government has for even existing."[67]

<u>Speedy Trial.</u> The Sixth Amendment lays out several specific requirements for how jury trials are to be conducted. Today, one of the most difficult issues facing court systems is the ability to provide defendants with "speedy" trials. One thing that drives clients mad is that, in many instances, the court system moves incredibly slowly. It can literally take years for a complex criminal case to go to trial. Constitutionally, courts have an obligation to bring cases quickly to trial when the accused persons are being held in jail, either without bail or because they are so poor that they can't pay the bail in order to get out. These cases come first on the judge's list of cases to try, while other cases and clients wait their turns. At the same time, lawyers and prosecutors take time to prepare cases, juggling busy schedules, and may need time to prepare for trial. Meanwhile, the clients are in a state of limbo, free on bail but psychologically and emotionally imprisoned by having a court appearance hanging over their heads.

I certainly don't purport to have a solution to the problems of court delays. There are times when I may want additional time to investigate matters in my own clients' cases, or there may be strategic reasons why I want a client's case not to go to trial too quickly, especially if I need to gather evidence or want time to negotiate a deal in a case where the evidence of my client's guilt is overwhelming. Ironically, many times it is the prosecutors' cases that are harmed by long delays between the time a crime allegedly occurred and trial. After all, the prosecutor has the burden of proof—he or she is the one who has to present evidence—and prosecutors' cases don't get better with age. Witnesses move, evidence can get lost, and memories fade. The victims of serious crimes pay probably the highest price for the delays in our jury system, in my opinion. They want justice for a loved one killed, or property lost, and they may suffer as much as, or more than, the accused as both sides wait for their day in court.

Impartial Jury. The concept of a trial by an impartial jury means that the jurors hearing any case should be objective and unbiased in their decision-making process. Reality does not always live up to this ideal, because jurors, at times, bring their preexisting prejudices, emotions, and biases with them into the courtroom—jurors are people, after all, not computers. At the same time, the process of jury selection is used to help discover which jurors will be most objective in their reasoning and have the least personal interest in the outcome. Hence, a person who is good friends with the investigating police officer of the case should not sit on the jury, nor should a friend of the defendant or the defendant's family. The system is not perfect, but in my experience, jurors take this aspect of their job very seriously and work hard to remain objective, unbiased listeners and deciders of the facts in the case in which they hear evidence and render a verdict. In short, juries tend to get it right.

Trial Where the Crime Was Committed. The Sixth Amendment requires that an accused person be tried in the community (or at least in the state) where the crime occurred. This is important for many reasons. If the defendant is from the community, then a jury of fellow members of his community will decide his or her fate. Provided they can be impartial, this is normally to the advantage of the defendant and avoids the issue of "rendition," which means essentially transporting a person far from home to be prosecuted in a foreign state or land.

On the other hand, what if the defendant is not a citizen of the community in which the crime occurred? Perhaps, for example, the accused is from Florida, but the prosecutor is alleging that he committed a murder in California. The California jurors are more likely to be familiar with the surroundings in which the crime allegedly occurred, and the jurors also have a vested interest in their community, and, hence, they will take the time to carefully listen to the evidence. In cases where the accused is an outsider, and there exists a genuine danger that this fact will prejudice the jury, the defense lawyer can ask the judge to move the trial to another locale. The interesting thing about this section of the Sixth Amendment is that it does protect the accused, but it also gives the victims—and the citizens of the community where the crime occurred—closure by letting them have the case heard in their own locale and, in most cases, render judgment over the guilt or innocence of a member of their own community.

Information About the Accusation. This aspect of the Sixth Amendment is one that we looked at during our discussion of the functions of the grand jury. The concept is a simple but essential element of our liberties as free people. Basically, if government officials are going to arrest and prosecute you for committing a crime, they have to tell you specifically how they believe you broke the law. This allows you and your lawyer to prepare your defense and to understand whether you, the accused, actually broke the law. Being arrested without knowing why has happened to people in times past, and still does in many parts of the world today. A person wakes up to a knock on the door, and then is hauled away without ever being informed as to the charges. Many times what the accused really did was tick off the local king or baron or dictator who ruled over the country. The fact that the monarch or local despot was upset was enough to get them arrested. No other reason had to be given except they are under arrest by "order of the King."

One of the groups that do a remarkably good job in our country of ensuring we, as free citizens, are informed of what we are being arrested for is the police. Most police officers I have met over the years take this aspect of their jobs very seriously. They work hard to know the laws that they have the responsibility of enforcing, and they make it a point to inform the person they are arresting specifically under what laws, and for what conduct, he or she is being arrested. Yes, there are exceptions. There are bad cops as well as good ones. But, all in all, the police do an excellent job of fulfilling this vital function of their job. We can hardly imagine a police officer stopping our car and telling us we are under arrest "by order of the governor" or some other nonsense. In this way, the police uphold not only law and order, but our liberties as well.

The Confrontation Clause. The Sixth Amendment also gives the accused the right "to be confronted with the witnesses against him." Known as the "Confrontation Clause," this provision is based on the ancient principles of Roman and English law. The basic idea is that a person accused of committing a crime has a right to look his accuser in the eye.[68] English law also developed the right of cross-examination, which in our American jury system means that both the prosecutor and defense lawyers have the right to question the truthfulness and accuracy of the other side's witnesses. (We are all familiar with television crime dramas involving dramatic cross-examinations.) In this respect, the courtroom, through the practice of skilled lawyers asking pointed questions to the other side's witnesses, becomes a virtual lie detector machine.

Long before the invention of electric lie detector machines, people understood that the best way to get at the truth and accuracy of a situation was to put everyone in a courtroom. The courtroom is well designed for this purpose. As a witness, a person first must walk from the pews, where the audience sits in the back of the courtroom, past the lawyers and the defendant seated at the counsel tables, and past the jury, seated as a group on the side of the courtroom. The witness then sits in a chair raised up a foot or so, the effect of which is to put the witness on display right in front of the jury. The judge sits high up on the bench in a black robe and is positioned so he or she is literally looking down over the witness. A court deputy then orders the witness to put his or her hand on the Bible and swear, or affirm, to tell the whole truth and nothing but the truth. The witness is then approached by each lawyer in turn and asked to answer questions in this intimidating and awe-inspiring environment.

The lawyer who called the witness to testify does "direct examination," which is, typically, friendly questioning. Cross examination is adversarial questioning meant to show the falseness, lack of credibility, and/or lack of accuracy of the witness's testimony during the direct examination. This adversarial setting of cross examination is one of the reasons why television audiences love courtroom dramas. In real life, the testimony can also be dramatic, as a skilled lawyer pounds away during the cross examination of a witness.

Modern-day lie detector tests don't really detect lying. What they measure are physiological responses inside a person's body to questions being asked. When people lie, their blood pressure may go up slightly, their heartbeats may quicken, their sweat glands may secrete more fluids, or their breathing rhythms may change. Electronic measuring devices attached to the skin measure these physiological changes. A witness may show the same type of signs under the stress of cross examination in a courtroom. The courtroom atmosphere is intimidating and the jurors are sitting just a few feet away, watching the witness's every movement, listening to every inflection of speech, and observing the person's bodily postures and movements. A single bead of sweat appearing on the witness's brow, or the fact that he nervously folds his arms or starts breathing more heavily, can be physical cues the jury can pick up on.

Unlike a machine, however, the jurors are also listening to the person's responses and deciding whether the witness's answers make sense and are logical and truthful. The person may have a criminal history that shows dishonesty in the past, he may not be able to explain simple details about an event he claims to have witnessed, or he may have some type of personal or financial interest in the case that he had not disclosed until confronted during cross examination. The jurors' observation of the physical responses of the witness, combined with their listening ability and use of their own common sense and logic, turn the courtroom and the art of "confronting witnesses" into what eighteenth-century Justice Blackstone called "the single most important engine for getting at the truth ever devised by man."[69]

Compulsory Process. The Sixth Amendment requirement of "compulsory process for obtaining witnesses in [the defendant's] favor" is accomplished by the use of the subpoena. A subpoena is a written order directing a person to appear as a witness in court. If the person fails to appear, he or she can be arrested and brought to court to testify and can be held in contempt of court—and potentially jailed—if he or she defies the order of the court.

This critical function of liberty has been undermined on a practical basis in modern times by two basic logistical problems. The first is the simple fact that people move around the country—and even the world—much more now than they did two hundred years ago. Two hundred years ago, if a crime occurred within a community, the chances were that all of the witnesses for the prosecution and the defense could be easily found, as they all lived within the same town or village, had been born there, and probably were never going to move away from there. Today, many of us move around a lot. This, coupled with the fact that a criminal case may literally take years before the case comes to trial, means that key eyewitnesses may have moved away, left the state, or even left the country. This means that the defense has to work ever harder to bring witnesses to court. The process of getting witnesses into court involves time and expense and, on a practical level, can be extremely frustrating or even downright damaging to an accused person's defense. The prosecution is faced with the same problem, although to a lesser extent, as they have the full power of the government to support their efforts. The criminally accused person is either relying on the normally understaffed and underfunded local public defender to try to track down witnesses or is paying for the securing of witnesses through the use of a private attorney and, perhaps, a private investigator. Either way, this clause of the Sixth Amendment is an area where the reality of getting people properly subpoenaed and into court falls short of the ideal.

There is no simple solution to this problem. The Internet has been helpful, however, in keeping better track of people through public records, social media accounts, e-mail addresses, and cell phone information. These "locations" are becoming more "permanent" than people's physical residences. But judges, lawyers, and public policy makers need to develop updated forms of securing witnesses for the accused at trial that are in line with the realities of life in twenty-first-century America. Otherwise, this important clause of the Sixth Amendment is in danger of becoming a hollow promise.

<u>*Assistance of Counsel.*</u> Nowhere is the reality of life less in line with the constitutional ideal than the Sixth Amendment promise of right to counsel. Historically, the need for trained counsel was not absolutely necessary, as trials were often prosecuted and defended by private parties. Beginning in the 1930s, the U.S. Supreme Court decided a series of cases that ultimately guaranteed all criminal defendants in state and federal courts the right to counsel if they could not afford to hire their own.[70] In 1963, the Supreme Court ruled that in order for the Sixth Amendment right to assistance of counsel clause to have any real meaning, counsel had to be appointed and paid for by the government.[71]

At the state level, public defenders' offices are systematically understaffed, overwhelmed, and underfunded. If a county does not have a public defender's office, the judge will appoint a lawyer to represent a defendant in need of one. The lawyer may be well trained, but the county may set the pay scale so low that it is virtually impossible for the lawyer to properly represent the person and eat at the same time. At the federal level, things are noticeably better, as the federal public defender's office is generally well funded, and the pay rate for appointed attorneys is not terrible. But even at the federal level, the workload is immense, so even the most well-intentioned lawyer is often overwhelmed and underpaid.

There is a pernicious philosophy among state legislatures that they should fund public defenders' offices just well enough so they can give the *appearance* of providing counsel to the poor, without truly helping out. In Georgia, the state legislature, in an enlightened mood, actually provided adequate funding for criminal defendants facing the death penalty several years ago. They did so because they were hoping it would end some of the mistakes that underfunded and/or undertrained defense lawyers were making in death penalty trials. After all, death penalty defense is extraordinarily complex, and is very much a specialty practice within criminal law.

The Georgia state legislature hoped that by providing proper counsel for criminal defendants facing the death penalty, they would cut down on costly appeals after a jury rendered a death sentence. (Jurors in Georgia decide life or death in death penalty cases.) What happened, instead, was that the defense lawyers—now that they were provided with funding similar to what prosecutors receive for prosecuting death penalty cases—started to persuade jurors to not impose the death penalty. The state legislature was enraged, and they immediately cut the funding—not because the defense lawyers were doing a bad job, but because they were doing their job too well and actually winning cases! This type of backward thinking makes a mockery out of the Sixth Amendment's promise of right to counsel for poor Americans.

So what's the solution? At the risk of self-promotion, my recommendation is to hire a private lawyer if you can in any way raise the funds to do so. The situation is not going to change concerning public defenders. In fact, with the recent economic turndown it is only getting worse. Look for resources from family and friends and find a private lawyer who practices criminal defense or, even better, *specializes in* criminal defense. Your liberty is worth the cost.

Bail, Fines, and Punishments—The Eighth Amendment

Excessive bail shall not be required, nor excessive fines imposed, nor cruel and unusual punishments inflicted.

<u>Making Bail.</u> If you or someone you love is arrested, you have a constitutionally recognized right to reasonable bail. "Reasonable" means it must be an amount that is proportional to the offense, that you can afford, and that will ensure that you will return to court as directed by the judge throughout your case.

Bail can be denied if the government can show that the accused person is a flight risk, is likely to commit other crimes, or presents a risk of harming members of the community or influencing witnesses in the case. In serious felony cases, the issue of whether someone receives bail may be hotly disputed between the prosecution and the defense. For nonviolent offenses and less serious crimes, bail is generally allowed so that the accused person can be released from jail, provided the person does not have an extensive criminal record that shows evidence that he or she may commit new crimes while out on bail.

Bail can be posted with the court in three general ways. Suppose, for example, that on a case of possession of cocaine the judge sets a "bond" of $5,000 dollars. The accused person can pay $5,000—in cash or with a postal money order—directly to the front desk of the jail, which will hold the money and then return it when the person's case is resolved. Or the person can post property, such as the title to a house or land worth—at a minimum—the amount of the bond, sometimes up to double the amount of the bond. In this case, the person would usually file the deed to the property with the jail.[72] The person can also pay a bail bonding company a fee, generally around 10 percent of the actual bail amount ($500 in the above example) to "stand" on the person's bond. (The person doesn't get this money back, as it is considered the fee for doing business with the bail bondsman.) The bail bondsman is then on the hook for paying the $5,000 if the accused person does not show up in court. If that happens, the bondsmen can call in a bounty hunter (the extreme of which would be the reality TV character "Dog the Bounty Hunter") who is paid by the bail bonding company to track down the not-so-smart alleged cocaine possessor who decided he didn't feel like showing up in court, and drag him back to jail.

Finally, in some cases, the judge will allow an accused person a "signature bond." This means the person signs an IOU to the court for the bail amount (such as the $5,000 in the above example), promising to pay the court in the event he or she does not show up. These bonds are obviously most favorable to the accused and are generally available to persons who are accused of nonviolent crimes when they have both no criminal record *and* a good lawyer who will negotiate this bond for them. (Bonds can come with all kinds of onerous conditions these days, though, as we discussed in Chapter Six.)

No Excessive Fines or Cruel and Unusual Punishment. The Eighth Amendment clause prohibiting "excessive fines" and "cruel and unusual punishments" dates back to the English common law of the Middle Ages. In fact, it was lifted, more or less word for word, from the English Bill of Rights of 1689.

Throughout history, criminal justice systems have come up with all manner of ways to punish those persons convicted of crimes—many of which might fall into the categories of both "cruel" and "unusual." They have been beaten with sticks or canes (still popular today in Singapore); mutilated, such as by having their hands, ears, nose, genitals, or feet cut off (still very popular with the Taliban in Afghanistan today); or branded with a hot iron or forced to wear a letter or other symbol on their clothing.[73]

They have been stoned (recently a Somalia court ordered a woman convicted of adultery be stoned to death); drawn and quartered (each arm and leg is tied to a different horse, and then the horses are sent running simultaneously off in four different directions, ripping off the person's legs and arms at the sockets); pressed (by having slabs of rocks piled on top of them); whipped (whips could be made of horsehair or other materials, sometimes with metal tips); burned (usually while tied to a stake—a punishment popular at one time for convictions of witchcraft). They have been poisoned (this remains one method of imposing the death penalty in the United States, where poison is injected into the person's veins, causing death); gassed (popular with Americans for a period of time and a preferred method of killing by the Nazis); or electrocuted (popular in the United States during most of the twentieth century).

They have been shot by firing squad (perhaps the most dignified way to go, as long as the executioners can shoot straight); hanged by rope around the neck; beheaded by sword, axe, or guillotine (especially popular during the French Revolution, where huge crowds showed up for the guillotining of political prisoners and fashionable ladies wore earrings in the shape of the guillotine). They have been fed to hungry animals (the early Christians were thrown to the lions by the Romans for refusing to worship the Roman dictator as a god); starved (as through the use of the gibbet, which was a steel cage just tall enough for a person to crouch or sit in; the convicted person was locked into the cage, the cage was set on a pole, usually right outside the city walls, and the person starved to death or died of exposure to the elements; the body was then left to rot as a public warning to any other would-be breakers of the law).

And, of course, perhaps the most famous form of criminal punishment in history: crucifixion (the person's feet and hands are nailed to a cross and the person is left to hang from it, and the person suffocates to death as the lungs wear out under the weight of the suspended body; the ancient Romans used this type of punishment, primarily for persons convicted of political offenses such as inciting public riot and treason— which, of course, were the types of crimes for which Jesus of Nazareth was convicted before he was sentenced to death).

The drafters of the U.S. Constitution were familiar with the various types of creative and dreadful punishments devised by governments for use against convicted criminals over the centuries. The Eighth Amendment's clause disallowing cruel and unusual punishments was their attempt to limit these excesses. Over the years, there has been much debate in U.S. courts over what constitutes cruel and unusual punishment. One thing is for certain: because the language of the clause is so general, there will always be disagreement about what exactly is a "cruel and unusual" punishment, as opposed to a just and usual punishment.

The word "cruel," for example, speaks to whatever a contemporary society's understanding of cruel means. If you asked a Roman citizen at the time of Jesus whether crucifixion was cruel, he might well say no. But if we started nailing people to crosses today, most Americans would argue that this type of punishment was cruel and unjust.

On the other hand, the term "unusual" seems to point in the exact opposite direction for guidance—it suggests that traditional or long-standing punishments *should* be acceptable. This reasoning infuriates opponents of the death penalty, for example. In truth, the death penalty has been a longstanding and traditional form of punishment in America. The debate over the death penalty has played out in our nation's highest court, as some Supreme Court justices have argued that contemporary standards prohibit the use of the death penalty to punish certain heinous crimes, while others have argued that tradition and history should hold sway over what constitutes cruel and unusual punishment.

For me, this debate shows the genius of our founding fathers. They wrote this clause trying to ensure that our criminal justice system punished convicted persons in ways that were severe enough to mete out justice, but not so severe as to be barbarous and cruel. By using one term that refers to our present-day perceptions to guide our judgment: "cruel," and another term that looks to history and tradition to guide our judgment: "unusual," they left the whole issue open for debate. There is no right answer, but surely our founding fathers understood that as long as American citizens were free to think and write and speak their minds, each generation could decide for themselves what constitutes cruel and unusual punishment. This is exactly what each American generation has done, down to the present day.

Final Thoughts on the Bill of Rights

One of the fascinating things about the first ten amendments to the United States Constitution is just how many of them deal with criminal law. The first two amendments address criminal law indirectly by outlining large areas of human behavior that cannot be outlawed or even legally restrained in any excessive way by the American government or its people. In 1787, when the Constitution was first written, criticizing the government in the press, worshipping differently from how the government told you to worship, and speaking out against the government or other powerful entities were crimes in most nations, yet the First Amendment makes it clear that none of these acts can be criminalized. And the Second Amendment ensures that the government cannot criminalize the ownership of guns, which are some of the first things dictators try to take away from their citizens so that they can't fight back and overthrow the dictator.

The Fourth, Fifth, Sixth, and Eighth Amendments all deal with how to ensure that due process in criminal law is fair and just for American citizens. Thus, six out of the ten amendments contained in the Bill of Rights focus either directly or indirectly on criminal law. Why?

The answer is simple: the criminal justice system is the most potent form of power any government possesses over its citizens. Once a particular type of behavior is declared "criminal," the government can arrest any people doing (or merely *accused of* doing) that behavior and then shackle and handcuff them, stuff them into a steel cage, and deprive them of their liberty (and, in extreme cases, their life), all within the bounds of the law. The founding fathers knew that all governments attempt to increase their power first and foremost by expanding criminal laws, both in scope and by severity of punishment. One of the great and terrible issues of our time, as I discussed in Part II, is the question: "How many types of behavior that different portions of our population dislike and find contemptible are we going to use the awesome power of the criminal justice system to punish?"

This is not a right-wing/left-wing issue or, if you prefer, red-state/blue-state issue. Groups on the left want to see people punished for a variety of acts and behaviors they view as dangerous to society or morally contemptible. Groups on the right see other acts and behaviors as dangerous to society and morally contemptible. One group may want to expand upon the definition of—and severely punish those who commit—environmental crimes, crimes involving guns, or crimes against animals. Another group may want to outlaw abortion, ban pornography, or rigorously enforce drug and marijuana laws. Sometimes the left and right converge on issues—for example, they may agree on the expansion of severe punishment for certain white-collar crimes, sex crimes, or crimes against children.

Recently, I heard a leader of an anti-smoking group demanding that cigarettes be banned. The gentleman who made this statement wants to use the awesome power of America's criminal justice system to lock up the manufacturers of cigarettes and their customers. Great—for criminal defense lawyers, that is—a whole new group of clients to defend! Unfortunately, making cigarettes illegal would be not so great for anyone else and certainly not great for our civil liberties, as we would simply be further destroying our freedom to choose how to live. Besides, we tried this with alcohol in the 1920s, and the only people who seriously benefited from making alcohol illegal were members of organized crime and, of course, the lawyers who got paid well to defend them.

The bigger issues are: Just how much behavior should we declare illegal? How rigorously should the laws be enforced? And what types of punishment are just and usual versus cruel and unusual? There are no absolute right or wrong answers. In my opinion, in the Bill of Rights, the founding fathers gave us a signpost that reads:

> *Be wary of using the criminal justice system to solve too many of your perceived societal ills. By bringing down the power of the criminal justice system on your fellow citizens, you are invoking its awesome power against yourself and your loved ones, too. Tread carefully, cautiously, and judiciously: the more you use government to gain security for yourself over others, the less liberty you retain for yourself in the bargain.*

CHAPTER NINE

BASIC PRINCIPLES OF CRIMINAL DEFENSE

Now that you have a basic understanding of your constitutional rights, we can look at some of the general principles of criminal defense and some of the basic tools used by criminal defense lawyers. Before I begin this chapter, I want to seriously caution you that this chapter—as well as the rest of this book—**is in no way intended to be, nor does it constitute, legal advice**.

This chapter is written to give you a very general perspective on how criminal defense lawyers do their work. As I have said throughout this book, if you have been arrested or are being investigated for a crime, you should meet with a lawyer of your own choosing and discuss the matter with him or her. The law is not a "do it yourself," friendly profession. As the old saying goes, "He who represents himself has a fool for a client." Beyond the fact that this book is in no way intended to be used as legal advice, it is also—for the most part—simply my opinion. Other lawyers may have other opinions on what types of actions they should take or not take as criminal defense lawyers on behalf of their clients. This is why there is another old saying in the law: "If you ask three different lawyers the same question, you will get at least four opinions."

Beyond all of this, the practice of criminal law, in my opinion, is not so much a science as an art. And therefore, it is open to differing opinions, contrasting styles, and a variety of approaches to solving the myriad complex legal problems each client's case poses to a practicing attorney. So please read this chapter as you have the rest of this book:

to gain some general knowledge, be entertained, and develop a sense of perspective and some basic insight. If you truly need legal help with a criminal matter, call a criminal defense lawyer and go see him or her so that you can get legal advice tailored specifically for your particular case.

Criminal Investigation—Fiction versus Fact

In Part I of this book, we discussed how, for the past decade or more, Americans have been fed a steady diet of television shows featuring police officers and prosecutors investigating crimes. Television shows such as *Law & Order* and its spin-offs, *CSI: Crime Scene Investigation* and *its* spin-offs, and other police dramas have all depicted the investigation of criminal cases in more or less the same way.

In the first few minutes of the show, a crime is committed—usually a murder. The police arrive at the crime scene to find a dead body. The police then spend the rest of the one-hour show figuring out who committed the crime. In some shows, such as the *CSI* dynasty, the police do most of the work themselves. In the *Law & Order* franchise, the police and the prosecutors team up to find the killer. In each show, the police follow every lead, interview countless witnesses, check alibis, run fingerprints, pull phone and computer records, and spend lots of time sitting around discussing different theories of the case. In some shows, four or five detectives all work the case, drawing up elaborate theories on chalkboards. They send blood and hair and fiber samples to the crime lab where, in the *CSI* shows, a team of forensic scientists working out of a state-of-the-art crime lab tracks down all sorts of scientific evidence to support the investigation. The lab results come back in a few days or even mere hours. Thus, the police, crime lab technicians, and prosecutors are all shown to work tirelessly until they finally crack the case and nab the bad guy. Other cases never distract them. The crime lab is always available for testing any and all types of evidence, and all the manpower and technological resources needed are put to use to find the killer.

I love these shows. They are lots of fun to watch. How realistic they are, though, is another thing. Granted, most of these cases do deal with murders, and it makes sense that the police would spend a lot of time investigating those most serious of crimes. Federal cases, too—that is, those criminal matters investigated not by local, county, or state police, but by the FBI—may involve many, many hours of investigation. That being said, for most criminal case investigations, especially those involving the city, county, and state police, the enormous amount of human and material resources the police seem to be able to devote to each case in these television shows is over the top.

As I discussed in Part I of this book, the real world simply does not work like this. The truth of the matter is that police officers, detectives, and prosecutors are overworked, are underpaid, carry huge case loads, and most of all, are human. That's not to say there are not many good, hardworking police officers, detectives, and prosecutors—of course there are. But there are also lazy, dishonest, even corrupt police officers, detectives, and prosecutors. Of course, even the most well-intentioned of them have nowhere near the time or resources they probably need to dedicate to each individual case they handle, and especially not for cases that are less serious than the murder investigations portrayed endlessly on television.

Beyond all this, the police work in an enormous government bureaucracy that carries with it all the inefficiency, political pressure, infighting, rivalries, red tape, and other problems inherent to government bureaucracies. I always find it ironic that many hard-core law-and-order types—who tend to be politically conservative and, thus, deeply distrustful of the ability of government to solve our nation's problems—never admit that the police departments and prosecutor's offices of our country have all the same problems of any other government agencies.

As a nation, we live in dangerous times, so we naturally want protection from the bad guys. This is why there is such appeal in the television shows that depict police and prosecutors having all the time and technological tools they need to do their jobs flawlessly. Beyond this, I believe that—as I discussed in Part II of this book—our national desire to be "tough on crime," coupled with the popularity of zero tolerance crime policies in the past generation, has also heavily influenced contemporary crime-fighting television shows.

When clients come to me, they are often frustrated with how the police department and the court system work. They tell me the police didn't listen to their side of the story, or that they have important information that will prove to the police and prosecutor that they are innocent,[74] or that the whole situation was a misunderstanding, or that it's not as bad as it appears to be. They and their families are frustrated when I explain that it may take months or years to resolve their cases. Raised on law-and-order television shows, they mistakenly assume the criminal justice system operates the way it is depicted on television.

At this point, I tell them there is a television show that does more accurately depict the way most criminal cases are investigated—they are probably just too young to remember it. I tell them to go home and rent an old episode of *Perry Mason*, a show about a criminal defense attorney practicing law in Los Angeles during the 1950s and '60s.

When I was a young boy growing up in Baltimore in the late 1960s, reruns of *Perry Mason* were on television all of the time. *Perry Mason* did portray the jobs that police, prosecutors, and private defense attorneys normally perform in their real, day-to-day, professional lives. In the politically correct, law-and-order, zero tolerance, twenty-first-century world of today, I don't think *Perry Mason* would ever have been produced. Nevertheless, the show is a great lesson for anyone who wants to understand how things really work in America's criminal justice system.

Episodes of *Perry Mason* always start the same way: somebody is murdered. The police are summoned to the scene and a rumpled detective, Lieutenant Tragg, takes over the investigation. Tragg scratches his head and looks at the body—to makes sure it's dead. He may go interview a witness or two, or dust for fingerprints. He then finds out who was nearby when the victim was killed or who had a motive to kill the victim or who owned the murder weapon and arrests that person. That is the end of the investigation—case closed. When the case gets to trial, District Attorney Hamilton Burger handles it. He doesn't do any additional investigation; he simply uses whatever evidence the detective gathered as his case, end of story.[75]

The accused then, of course, goes out and hires Perry Mason, a private defense attorney. (He often accepts the case for free, which I'm sorry to say is also not a real-world scenario, since lawyers do have to make a living, just like everyone else.) Perry Mason then gets to work defending his new client by investigating the case. He uses the services of his private investigator, Paul Drake, who works with Mason to track down possible leads, locate potential witnesses, discover physical evidence, and find other information important to the case. Thus, it is the defense lawyer, Perry Mason, and his legal team who take the time to work the case, investigate the crime, and look into all possible issues—not the police or the prosecutor.

"Wait a minute!" I can hear everyone saying. "That's not right! That's ridiculous! I want Benson and Stabler, Crockett and Tubbs, hell, I'd even settle for Starsky and Hutch investigating criminal cases, not some privately hired, suit-wearing criminal defense attorney representing the person accused of committing the crime!" My response is: "Sorry, but we don't live in the fantasy land of television. We live in the real world, and the people who do much of the investigation on criminal cases—and frequently almost the *entire* investigation on criminal cases—are privately hired criminal defense lawyers and their staffs."

There is a rule that applies to almost all criminal cases: the more serious or "high profile" the crime is, the more time and resources the police department and the prosecutor's office give to the case. High-profile cases are in the public eye and, because they garner media attention, police departments and prosecutor's offices have a vested interest in working these cases. For one thing, as we saw in Part I of this book, many times elected officials run police and prosecutor's offices.[76] Plus, most citizens naturally want the police to use their limited resources to investigate the most serious crimes, such as murder, rape, international drug trafficking, crimes against children, and major fraud and swindles, to name several. Crimes handled by the FBI and other federal police agencies may also be thoroughly investigated.[77]

In the vast majority of criminal cases, however—and even in many cases concerning major crimes that are not high-profile cases—the amount of police investigation can be little (or practically none at all). This is one of the reasons the police work so hard to get suspects to confess to a crime: it eliminates the need to do any further investigation. But even in cases where the police have done some investigation, there is still investigating for the defense lawyers to do. The police, after all, are looking at the evidence from the point of view of making an arrest. They may have skipped over or ignored information that is important and relevant, but does not help them make their case against the person they believe most likely committed the crime. Regardless of how much, or how little, investigation law enforcement has done on a particular case, the defense lawyer's investigation is equally important—after all, it is the key to building a client's defense.

Meeting With Your Lawyer

The first thing that will happen when you hire a defense lawyer is that you will be interviewed. This may sound simple, but the initial interview is very important because it helps to set the course of the defense. The interview may take place during one meeting, or it may take several meetings for your lawyer to learn everything about the case from your perspective. One of the most important reasons for the initial interview is that it gives you, the accused, the chance to finally have someone who is not an adversary listen to your side of the story.

For some lawyers, listening to their clients can be difficult. They want to launch into giving legal advice, and they may have predetermined notions about what the clients did or did not do. By simply listening, your defense lawyer can learn much about both you and your case. The information that you provide to your criminal defense lawyer is generally "privileged," meaning that the lawyer cannot share the information with anyone without your prior approval. If you find yourself in a meeting with a defense lawyer, ask the lawyer about the specific rules for privilege in his or her jurisdiction. Then, provided your privilege is secure, open up and tell your lawyer what happened. Your lawyer can then begin to frame a defense strategy around your side of the story.

Building Your Defense—Gathering Factual Evidence

Once your defense lawyer has interviewed you, he or she can then begin to gather evidence through an independent investigation. In order to gather factual evidence, your lawyer may begin by reviewing the police report on the case, witness statements, and other written materials that the police or prosecutor have in their possession. He or she may also see if there are DVDs, videotapes, or audiotapes important to the case. Increasingly, whenever you are pulled over in your car by the police, the police cruiser will have a digital video and audio camera mounted on the dash or hood of the car that captures the entire interaction between the police officer and you, the driver of the vehicle the police officer pulled over. Also, digital video surveillance cameras routinely monitor more and more businesses, commercial buildings, and public areas, so there may be filmed footage of the alleged crime that could help your defense.

Your defense lawyer may also interview witnesses or have his investigator interview witnesses. These witnesses may be people the prosecution plans to call as witnesses to testify against you, or they may be witnesses that you believe can help your defense but who were not interviewed by the police. Perhaps there is a witness who can provide helpful information about the alleged victim, or who saw another person commit the crime, or who has knowledge about a particular police officer that could be useful to show that the officer has some bias against you or has had disciplinary issues in the past. Once again, the list of potentially important witness interviews that may be conducted on your behalf is only limited by the particular set of circumstances in your case and the professional discretion of your lawyer.

Your lawyer may also want to subpoena public or private records of different types, or gather school records, police records, and other types of information that is important to the case through "open records" acts.[78] These types of records are especially useful to find out more about the alleged victim in a case, members of the alleged victim's family, or witnesses who may testify for the prosecution, such as police officers or private citizens. For example, a police officer may have had a misconduct report filed against her during the investigation of a case similar to yours that may raise questions about the truthfulness, or accuracy, of her investigation of your case.

Performing Forensic Audits of Factual Evidence

Your lawyer may also recommend gathering factual evidence through "forensic audits" performed by an expert in a particular professional field. These forensic audits can be used to independently examine and/or test different types of evidence gathered by the police during their investigation, or they may be used to gather and examine other evidence that you and your lawyer feel is important to your case but that was never gathered or reviewed by the police.

Forensic audits can also be used to determine whether the police actually gathered, tested, or analyzed different types of evidence in accordance with proper police procedures, generally accepted scientific standards, or the standards expected for a particular profession (such as generally accepted accounting principles when reviewing business or financial records). The types of possible forensic audits are practically endless, but some of the more common ones involve hiring an accountant or bookkeeper to gather and review important financial documents; using a doctor to gather and review medical records; having a psychiatrist or psychologist review psychological records; or asking a ballistics expert to review a gun or bullets used in an armed assault case. The types of forensic audits, or forensic investigations, that may be useful in a criminal defense lawyer's investigation are only limited by the types of evidence and the set of circumstances surrounding your individual case.

Strengthening Your Defense—Gathering Mitigation Evidence

Your lawyer may also focus on gathering "evidence in mitigation" on your behalf. What is evidence in mitigation? Evidence in mitigation is what I call "good guy" or "good gal" evidence. It is evidence that may not directly relate to the facts of your case, but may help improve your character in the eyes of the police, prosecutor, and judge handling your case. For example, if you have been charged with the possession of cocaine, it may be helpful to your case to show that you are willing to enter a drug treatment program to get help for your substance-abuse problem. It may also be helpful to show that you were in no way selling cocaine or other drugs (generally selling illegal substances is viewed by prosecutors and judges as much worse than being the user of the drugs). It may be useful to show that you have routinely done charitable work in your community or, if you are a student or recent graduate, that you have done well in school. Your lawyer may advise you to gather friends, employers, employees, clients, or other people who are supportive of you and know you well—such as members of your church congregation, community, or workplace—to write letters on your behalf to present to the judge or prosecutor.

Your lawyer may also instruct you to undertake some type of counseling or psychological examination, for instance, if you are charged with possession of cocaine, to illustrate—by way of the testimony of a medical expert—that you are really in need of medical treatment and counseling, rather than being punished by being locked up in jail or prison.

Your lawyer may also suggest you take a private lie detector test, which he or she may then present to the prosecutor as evidence of your innocence, or to show that you are at least telling the truth about your side of the story. Lie detector tests are not considered "scientific" tests and cannot, generally, be used at trial. But a prosecutor can still take into account the results of a lie detector test when making decisions about how and whether to prosecute a case, and a judge can consider the test results when deciding a person's punishment.[79] I recommend that you never take a lie detector test sponsored by the government, because a lie detector test only detects nervousness, and, in many ways, it can only hurt your case. If you fail it, the police will immediately arrest you. If you pass it, they will probably arrest you, anyway, as it is not a scientific test. As such, it is a lose/lose for you and a win/win for the police.

You may also have information concerning the commission of other crimes by other people. Or you may know information about the criminal actions of another person arrested at the same time you were and charged with committing the same crime. This information should be shared with your lawyer, first, so that you and he can decide together whether it might be worthwhile to share this information with the prosecutor, or the police, in order to help your defense.

When I talk to a client about evidence in mitigation, I explain that until we gather this kind of information on his behalf, all he is is a name on a cardboard file sitting on a prosecutor or police officer's desk, along with a bunch of other names on other cardboard files. (Or, today, in the twenty-first century, a digitized entry on a computer screen.) Evidence in mitigation helps to illustrate for the prosecutor and the judge, and at times also the jury, that you are neither a hardened criminal nor just a faceless number on a file needing "to be processed," but a flesh-and-blood human being who is either wrongfully accused or—if you are proven guilty—a good person who made a mistake and is more in need of rehabilitation, help, and mercy than ruthless justice and harsh punishment.

As I discussed in Part I of this book, many people end up arrested because they did something dumb. Usually the arrest is the last domino to drop in a long series of mistakes, missteps, and bad personal choices that finally led to arrest. A defense lawyer needs to help each client to demonstrate to the court that he or she has not only learned from these mistakes, but also will not repeat them, while also highlighting all the good things the client has done in his or her life. In cases where the client is wrongly accused, evidence in mitigation is also important, because the client's good actions can help to prove it is unlikely that he or she committed the crime.

Two Baskets of Evidence for Your Defense

By the time your lawyer is done investigating your case, he or she should have two "baskets" of evidence. The first basket is **factual evidence** that helps support your innocence. Factual evidence reveals problems with the prosecutor's case and shows it is not likely—or at least it is less likely—that you actually committed the crime for which you are accused. Your lawyer's second basket consists of **evidence in mitigation**—"good guy" evidence—that shows why you are generally a good person, regardless of whether or not you actually committed the crime you are accused of committing.

As your defense lawyer works through your investigation, gathering both factual evidence and evidence in mitigation, he or she weighs the strength of each piece of factual evidence and each piece of evidence in mitigation that is ultimately going to be placed in the two evidence "baskets." Each piece of evidence is weighed and judged by your lawyer as to its strength and persuasiveness to either help or harm your defense. When gathering evidence in mitigation, for example, a letter from your mother is probably going to carry less weight in convincing a prosecutor that you are a generally good person than a letter from your former employer. Likewise, if you are accused of bank robbery, and the gun used to commit the robbery was found in your car, this may be a more harmful piece of factual evidence to your defense than if the gun was found in another person's car.

The specific pieces of factual evidence and evidence in mitigation that may be important to each client's defense are case specific. That is, each accused person's case is unique, and each piece of factual evidence and evidence in mitigation that is important to that individual case is also unique to that case. It is the defense lawyer's job to comprehend what pieces of both types of evidence are going to be helpful to his or her client's defense and to gather these pieces of evidence together to build the best defense for the client.

One of the things that criminal defense lawyers do is look at the facts to try to determine what really happened. The truth of the matter is that no one knows for sure *exactly* what happened in most criminal cases. Even if there are eyewitnesses to a crime, their memories may be inaccurate or they may have reasons for not being completely truthful when interviewed. Victims sometimes lie or don't accurately remember the details. Even the person accused of committing a crime may not understand why she was charged with a particular crime or whether she has a viable defense to the charge. Criminal cases are really history stories. That is, each case is an attempt by people—working both sides of the case—to try to gather the evidence of an event that happened in the past.

As with history, everyone is relying on his or her memories and pieces of information about a past event that can be interpreted in different ways or be flawed in some way. This is one of the main reasons why our system is based upon an adversarial system of justice, as I described in Part I of this book. Adversaries—the police and prosecutors on one side, and the defense lawyer representing the accused on the other side—will often look at the same pieces of evidence quite differently. Nether side knows the whole truth—many times not even the accused or the alleged victim does—but it is the investigation by the defense lawyer that balances out the investigation by the police.

Taking Your Case to the Prosecutor

Once your defense lawyer has completed the investigation into your case, he or she will decide whether the results of the investigation are strong enough to take to the prosecutor before the case goes to trial. There are, in essence, two ways to try a case. The first is in the privacy of the prosecutor's office. The second is the way most people are familiar with: in a courtroom with a jury (or, in some very limited instances, in front of only a judge). Jury trials are the staple of television and movie dramas, as they make for great television. In real life, the defense lawyer's first job is to decide whether to discuss the case with the prosecutor before the trial, and to see if the prosecutor can be convinced to either drop the charges completely or to negotiate a settlement that both the prosecutor and the lawyer's client can live with. This decision is made as the defense lawyer conducts his investigation.

Some of the goals your defense lawyer can strive for during these negotiations with the prosecutor are: (1) to make sure that whatever evidence he is showing the prosecutor is true and accurate (presenting false information is not only unethical but can really hurt you, the client); (2) to be prepared to listen to any offers of settlement that the prosecutor is prepared to make to resolve your case before you go to trial, so that he, as your lawyer, can communicate them to you, the client; and, (3) to know the facts and the evidence of the case better than the prosecutor. (As a defense lawyer, I work hard to be in a position to educate the prosecutor on all of the important facts of the case and all of the important background information about my client, so that the prosecutor can learn more about the case than just the information provided by the overworked police officer or the detective who made the arrest.)

By doing these three things, your lawyer makes it much more likely that the prosecutor will be willing to resolve the case in a way that will be favorable to you. Or, if your lawyer is able to demonstrate evidence of major weaknesses in the prosecutor's case, he or she may even convince the prosecutor to dismiss the charges altogether before trial. There is no right or wrong answer to this game of negotiation—each case calls for its own unique strategy. Ultimately, it is up to your lawyer—in collaboration with you, the client—to decide the best course of action during these pretrial negotiations.

Pre-Arrest and Pre-Indictment Investigation

Depending upon the circumstances of your case, the same evidence-gathering investigation techniques and pretrial negotiation tactics discussed above may be utilized by your lawyer *prior to* you being indicted by a grand jury, formally accused, or even arrested by the police. Your defense lawyer's systematic gathering of factual evidence and evidence in mitigation on your behalf is conducted in the same way, whether you have been approached by the FBI or local police for questioning, but not yet arrested, or you have been arrested but not yet indicted and formally accused.

There may be benefits to your lawyer intervening and negotiating on your behalf even before you have been arrested or indicted, depending upon the individual facts and circumstances surrounding your case. For example, in the state of Georgia, it is generally much easier to get a case expunged (or "sealed," which is the term used in New York State) and removed from public records, before you have been indicted by a grand jury or the prosecutor has filed a formal written accusation against you.[80] And, of course, if you can avoid being arrested altogether, that is pretty much always a good thing! Whether it is best for your lawyer to reach out to the police or FBI while you are under investigation, but have not yet been arrested; or whether it is best for your lawyer to reach out to the prosecutor after you have been arrested, but before you have been indicted or formally accused, is a decision for you and your lawyer to make together.

The idea of prosecutors and defense lawyers meeting privately and resolving cases "behind closed doors" drives some people nuts. A good defense lawyer could walk into a prosecutor's office or go down to the police station and convince the prosecutor or the detective to drop the case or cut a good deal for the defense lawyer's client before the case ever gets to court. I've had people at cocktail parties get all red in the face and even start frothing at the mouth (depending upon how many drinks they've had) as they bluster on about "guilty people going free" and "slimy defense lawyer tactics" and victims being "denied their day in court" and wishy-washy prosecutors "letting the bad guys off the hook" and, well, you know, blah, blah, blah.

Hey, guess what? A good defense lawyer does not care about any of that, and neither should you. A guilty person has not gone free when a prosecutor dismisses a case for lack of evidence, or because the police choose not to arrest someone because of a lack of evidence. A guilty person did not go free, **because the person was never guilty to begin with**. In our justice system, as set up in the Constitution, a man or woman accused of a crime is **always innocent until proven guilty—if a person is never convicted, there can be no presumption of guilt.**

The same type of fury can also come from the other side. Some champions for leniency (many times the families of the accused) argue that by negotiating with the prosecutor before trial, the defense lawyer is "selling their client down the river without a paddle." They scream about how the accused was denied a day in court, or how the defense lawyer should have forced the prosecutor to his knees at trial and ripped the victim to shreds through cross-examination.

Both of these views are flawed, assuming that both the prosecutor and the defense lawyer do their jobs. The defense lawyer's job is to devote time to investigating each case in a way that the overwhelmed and underfunded police and prosecutors are not always able to do. The job of the prosecutor is to review all of the evidence provided by both the police and the defense lawyer and then to decide what the proper outcome—one that ensures that justice is done—should be.

On to the Jury—If Necessary

In close cases, when the defense lawyer and the prosecutor cannot reach an agreement that is acceptable to the accused, the matter goes to trial where a jury makes the decision of guilt or innocence. By investigating the case thoroughly before it ever gets to court, the defense lawyer will be ready to go to trial, if necessary, while also being in the strongest possible position to negotiate a settlement of the case prior to trial. Again, the key for the defense lawyer is to be like Perry Mason: to investigate the client's case, and then decide on the best approach for negotiating with the prosecutor on behalf of the client.

The reason why the jury system works so well is that prosecutors know they can't get around the jury in order to convict a person accused of a crime. If they believe they do not have enough evidence to prove the accused person's guilt beyond all reasonable doubt at trial, prosecutors tend to drop the case or offer a deal so favorable to the accused that he or she may want to accept the deal rather than risk having the prosecutor "throw it up to the jury to see if it sticks."[81] (After all, it just might "stick.") Juries keep both sides honest in criminal cases, because both sides know that they ultimately have to be able to present the facts and the evidence to a group of fellow citizens who don't have a personal stake in the case, and who get to make the final decision of guilt or innocence.

In my opinion, jury trials in criminal cases should be reserved for those cases where the facts are close—that is, when reasonable people can see the case in different ways after reviewing the evidence—or where the prosecutor refuses to dismiss a case he or she objectively knows is weak factually because of political pressure, media exposure, pressure from the victim or the victim's family, or lack of professional experience. In those situations, we have our juries to decide the innocence or guilt of the accused person. And this is how it should be. As I have said, in my experience, juries, after hearing all the facts and evidence, tend to get it right. This is truly justice at its best. It is a system of justice that is more than 2,500 years old, and it is still the best way of deciding a person's guilt or innocence ever devised by man.

Let's now take a look at seven different hypothetical, fact-based scenarios to see how various issues arising in different hypothetical criminal cases may be handled by defense lawyers working on behalf of their clients.

CHAPTER TEN

DEFENSE LAWYERS IN ACTION—
SEVEN CRIMINAL CASE STUDIES

The seven hypothetical—yet fact-based—"case studies" in this chapter are composites of some of the types of cases that criminal defense lawyers routinely handle in criminal courts in the United States today. I am providing them to give you a general perspective on how criminal defense lawyers work—hopefully while keeping the chapter entertaining, interesting, and easy to follow. After all, this book is written for everyone, but especially for Americans who are *not* lawyers.

Once again, I want to stress that *neither this chapter nor any other part of this book constitutes legal advice—nor is this book a substitute for legal advice.* The only way to get legal advice specific to your criminal case is to talk to a criminal defense lawyer. I emphasize this point, as I did in the preceding chapter, especially because of the nature of the "information age" in which we live. For good or bad, consumers today can surf the Web for information on all sorts of products and services. With a few clicks of a mouse, anyone can look up vast amounts of information and spend endless hours reading about a particular topic. In my opinion, we all suffer from information overload, because we can research any topic endlessly. The problem is, when it comes to professional and technical fields such as the law, most of us don't have the background to really make sense of the vast stores of information available to us.

For example, I have had two major knee surgeries in the past ten years. I went to an excellent surgeon who has spent decades training in medical school and then working as a knee surgeon. He did a great job, and both my knees are fine today. I remember one night, though, I stayed up researching knee surgery on the Web and drove myself completely crazy trying to make sense of the data I found. By the time I turned off the computer, I was utterly confused and scared to death. Thankfully, I finally hit the off button and went to sleep. I then went and had my knee surgery and let the surgeon do his job—and everything was fine.

In short, my advice is simple: you can drive yourself nuts trying to "be your own lawyer." But, in the end, you can't do it, nor should you try. Please use this book as a way to gain a *general* perspective on how criminal cases may be handled—not as a "how to" guide.

What I also do *not* want to do in this chapter is to sound like I am telling you, "This is how you should defend this type of case, here are the steps your lawyer should follow, just listen to me . . . ." Each person's criminal case is unique. There are different ways to craft a defense for each person's case. The law drives lots of people crazy for the very reason that it is filled with shades of gray and little is black and white. If you have a problem with the criminal law, by all means read the rest of this book to get a general perspective; but then go talk to a criminal defense lawyer, explain your case, and listen to what your lawyer has to say. It is your criminal defense lawyer's job to provide you with legal advice.

My intention in this chapter is also not to tell a bunch of "war stories." Instead, I have written these composite case studies to help illustrate some of the tools criminal defense lawyers are able to use while defending clients. To keep this from becoming a very long chapter, I have limited my analysis to focus on just a few specific legal defense issues—either problems or possible solutions—that could come up in each type of case. By the end of the chapter, I hope that you will have a good general understanding of how lawyers work when defending their clients against different types of criminal charges. Again, the following case studies are *absolutely not* intended as legal advice or to be used as a blueprint for how a particular criminal case should be defended.

With all of that in mind, let's start with Sarah, a teenage girl who finds herself busted for drug possession.

1. Drug Use and Possession: Sarah's Story—Where privacy and "presence" are discussed

The phone rings at two in the morning. An anxious father sleepily answers the phone, only to hear his eighteen-year-old daughter crying and pleading for help.

"Daddy, it's Sarah. Please help me! I'm at the police station and I've been arrested!"

"What?" Dad sits bolt upright in bed, one of his worst fears as a parent has come to pass. "Wait, you're supposed to be at Emily's house. You were going to have a party and sleep over."

"I know, I know," cries Sarah, "we were. But Emily's boyfriend brought over some pot and beer, and then two guys got in a fight in the backyard. A neighbor called the police and they came and arrested everyone in the house."

"Wait a minute, for what? What were you arrested for?"

"The police said we were arrested for underage drinking and the possession of marijuana."

"Sarah, you promised there wouldn't be any alcohol at the party," Dad responds, partly in anger and partly in parental exasperation.

"I know, but I didn't bring the beer. Emily's boyfriend did, along with the pot. Please help me! I'm terrified, and I don't know what's going to happen."

Dad stumbles out of bed. Mom is now awake, too, of course. Panic, adrenaline, anger, fear, and guilt all course through both of them. Dad's mind is racing, as he thinks, *Damn daughter, can't trust her! Shit, what if someone hurts her? If only I'd been a better parent. I wonder if she found those old Led Zeppelin concert photos in my high school scrapbook!*

Mom looks at Dad. "We've got to help her!"

Dad says, "Yeah, I know, I know, but maybe we should let her stay in there and learn a lesson, first."

Mom stares angrily at Dad. "Are you crazy? Our daughter's in jail! There are *criminals* in jail!"

Dad's anger turns to blind panic as he realizes his worst fears are coming to pass. "My baby's in jail, my precious little girl. Oh my God, oh my God, we've got to get her out!"

The first step in Sarah's criminal case begins right after her parents go down to the jail at two in the morning to collect their daughter. Sarah may be able to make bail and get out that night, once her parents spend several hours running around to cash machines to get the money needed to post her bail, or Sarah may be released on her own recognizance by signing a signature bond (as discussed in Chapter Eight). When—and if—she is released, she will receive a copy of her charges, cry a lot, and go home.

Sarah's parents will call the parents of Emily, the girl who had the party, only to find out they got arrested, too, for furnishing alcohol to minors. (Thanks to zero-tolerance policing policies, parents who try to supervise their underage children by allowing their eighteen-, nineteen-, and twenty-year-old children to have parties at home with alcohol—let alone pot—can get busted for furnishing alcohol to minors.) Emily's parents have already talked to their lawyer, who has told them to keep quiet, because they could also get sued by the parents of the other kids who were arrested. So Emily's parents can't give Sarah's parents any information on what happened at the great "pot and beer" bust at Emily's parents' suburban ranch house.[82]

What Sarah's parents finally figure out is that, yes, Sarah was drinking, but she was not tested for marijuana consumption, and the marijuana was actually found in one of the bedrooms where a bunch of the teenagers were using a bong. When the police came into the house, Sarah was in the living room, holding a beer—not in the bedroom.

Sarah and her parents go to talk with a criminal defense lawyer, Sally Shield, the next day, and she discusses a legal concept called "mere presence." Under the theory of mere presence, someone cannot be found to be in possession of an illegal substance—or to be found guilty of a crime generally—if that person is merely present and not actively participating. On the other hand, if an illegal substance is in "plain view" so that everyone has "equal access" to it, then anyone might be found guilty of possession of the illegal substance under the "totality of the circumstances."

According to the police report, the police noted that when they arrested Sarah they detected a "strong odor of alcohol and marijuana." The problem is, of course, that marijuana smoke pretty much smells up wherever it is being smoked, and so Sarah may have simply smelled like marijuana because everything in the house smelled like marijuana from the people doing bong hits all night in the back bedroom. Also, according to the facts in evidence: the police found no marijuana on Sarah, she was not caught smoking marijuana, there was no marijuana in the living room (only in the back bedroom), Sarah did not admit to the police she was smoking marijuana, and the police did not ask her to provide a urine sample to perform a chemical analysis to detect the presence of marijuana.

Ms. Shield meets with Sarah privately to find out what happened. She asks Sarah if she would pass a urine test. Sarah says no. The lawyer explains that even if she could pass the test, it would not be a total defense, because you don't have to use marijuana to be in possession of it—which is the charge Sarah is facing. Sarah tells the lawyer that she has a court date the following week in the local city court (the type of court that typically handles this type of case).

A more serious problem arises when Sarah's lawyer more closely reads the charges and discovers that the amount of marijuana confiscated was over an ounce, which is a felony in her state, which means that Sarah now faces a potential felony charge.

Sarah freaks out. "What? It wasn't even my pot. Shit! I'm accepted into college in the fall. What am I going to do?"

When Sarah's parents hear about this, they freak out, as well.

Sarah's attorney says, "Look, here's how we will handle this. You have a court date in the local city court right up the street. We need to handle your case there before it goes to superior court, where you could be indicted for felony pot possession. You got caught red-handed with the beer, so there's no use fighting that. After all, you are only eighteen and the legal age for consuming alcohol is twenty-one. But the pot charge is a hard charge for the prosecutor to prove, and I can make his life a big headache by filing a bunch of motions arguing that the police had no probable cause to search the house and that the possession charge against you should be thrown out for lack of evidence.

"The city court has a diversion program where you have to listen to a sermon from the prosecutor about the dangers of drinking, write an essay, take an alcohol-awareness class, and then perform twenty hours of community service," Ms. Shield continues. "In exchange, the prosecutor would dismiss the pot charge, the case would stay in the local city court, and after one year the arrest could be expunged from your record by court order and agreement of the prosecutor."

"OK," Sarah says. She and her parents agree that sounds good.

When Sarah, her parents, and Ms. Shield go to court, the prosecutor meets with Ms. Shield in his office and reviews the case with her. He agrees with Ms. Shield that the marijuana charge is really weak and drops the felony charge in exchange for Sarah agreeing to complete the city court's alcohol awareness program.

Sarah goes on to college and her parents get some sleep. Oh . . . and Sarah's parents put the Led Zeppelin concert photos in storage, along with their high school yearbooks.

2. **Shoplifting: Sasha's Story—Where the past meets up with the present**

We met Sasha at the very beginning of the book. As you remember, she is on scholarship to an exclusive private college. Under pressure to conform to the lifestyles of her wealthier friends, she succumbs to the pressure to shoplift a party dress "just this once."

Sasha walks into a high-end boutique and takes several items off the racks. She then goes into the changing room and carefully conceals one of the dresses under her own clothing the way her sorority sisters told her how to do it. She then leaves the other items in the changing area and tries to look calm and casual as she heads for the store exit. In fact, her adrenaline is through the roof, she is breathing heavily, and her heart feels like it's going to explode out of her chest. As she heads toward the exit, she calms herself by recalling a scene from that old movie *Animal House*, where the dorky freshman Delta House pledge shoplifts a bunch of food from a grocery store by putting it under his sweater and gets stopped by the female cashier. Not only does the cashier in the movie not "rat him out" to the store manager, she even agrees to come to the frat party that night with him.

"No big deal," Sasha tells herself, "it's just a harmless prank. Even if I get caught, they'll just make me put the dress back."

Instead, she is stopped by security and hauled to the back of the store, where there appears to be the retail version of a Homeland Security stakeout going on. A man is sitting in front of a bank of video monitors conducting surveillance of every nook and cranny of the store. A burly, unsmiling female guard approaches Sasha.

The security guard recovers the dress, slaps down a piece of paper, and bellows at Sasha, "Write down your confession, *NOW*! You smarty-pants college kids think it's OK to steal in *MY* store? Humph!"

"I'm sorry," Sasha cries, tears rolling down her face.

"Listen, young lady," the female security guard snarls, "you're in a heap of shit! You better start writing if you know what's best for you."

Sasha, scared and ashamed, dutifully starts to write her confession.

After she writes out her confession, the security guard calls the local county police and a uniformed officer comes to arrest Sasha. The dress was priced at a little over $500, and the value of the dress makes stealing it a felony in her state. Sasha is taken to jail and booked in, and she makes bail after spending the night in jail. Sasha calls her parents, who now have to go to family members to pool money together to hire a lawyer named Mr. Liberty, who practices in the college town.

Sasha explains everything to Mr. Liberty, but is surprised when he asks, "Have you ever done this before?"

"No, never," Sasha says unconvincingly. "I would never shoplift."

"Uh, you just did," replies Mr. Liberty, a bit dryly.

"Oh, yeah, but only that one time... well, maybe one other time, just some perfume."

"It's interesting," Mr. Liberty responds. "The problem with shoplifting is that it can become habit forming. It is also one of the few crimes that in the majority of cases involves women perpetrators, at least in my experience. I end up representing a lot more female shoplifters than male shoplifters."

"Why is that?" Sasha asks, now curious.

"You understand, I'm just a criminal defense lawyer, not a shrink or a sociologist. But in my opinion the physiological reaction a person gets when they shoplift—the adrenaline high, if you will—is highly similar to the high people who are addicted to gambling experience. That adrenaline high is a huge dopamine rush that can become, well, addictive. And shopping is one of the few socially acceptable activities that a woman, especially a young woman, can do alone in public. I mean, you probably wouldn't go sit in a bar alone would you?"

"No way, absolutely not," replies Sasha. "I only go out to bars with my girlfriends or on a date."

"Exactly. Would you go to a casino, or a racetrack—or even a movie theater alone?"

"Maybe a movie theater, that's OK, but I've never been to a racetrack and I have only been to a casino on a road trip with my sorority sisters."

"Right, so you see my point. Shopping is an activity a woman can do in public alone, without getting hassled or judged, so many women go shopping as a way to deal with everyday stress, the same way a man might stop at the local tavern for a beer after work."

"OK," Sasha replies, "so what's the problem? I like to shop. All my girlfriends do."

"There is nothing wrong with shopping," Mr. Liberty responds. "But the problem is, if you start shoplifting, it can become addictive relatively easily. The adrenaline rush from shoplifting is very powerful, and it's also tempting because society tells young woman that they are supposed to be well dressed and have the newest styles and all that kind of stuff. So you combine a socially acceptable outlet for stress for women—shopping—with the constant marketing message aimed at young women to "buy this and wear that," and you add the adrenaline high that comes from stealing something and not getting caught, and *bingo*, you have a potential path to very destructive behavior."

"OK, so maybe I have shoplifted a few times, just little stuff, but I really needed that dress."

"Here is what I want you to do," says Mr. Liberty. "Go get lots of reference letters from your professors. My guess is that you have very good grades."

"I'm a straight-A student, Mr. Liberty, but how'd you know that?"

"I didn't, but it does not surprise me. You're not alone. Many of the women I've represented on shoplifting charges over the years are high achievers. They perform well in all areas of their lives, and shoplifting is their own little private rebellion."

"I admit, it's fun to get away with it. I mean, why should the rich, bitchy girls get all the cool stuff and I get stuck with the totally random bargain-basement crap?"

"OK, so based on that remark, I recommend that you enroll in private counseling. I can recommend someone, or you can see someone from the university, provided it is absolutely confidential."

"I'd like you to recommend someone, please."

"I will. In the meantime, I am going to look at the police report and find out more about your case."

"Hey, I signed a confession, and they didn't read me my *Miranda* warnings."

"That doesn't matter. *Miranda* only applies when it is a government law enforcement officer interrogating you. The security guard is a private employee of Rambo Security Inc., which is the loss prevention company the boutique you shoplifted from contracts with to provide their in-house security. Plus, you're probably on video. All those cute little blue glass bubbles you probably noticed in the ceiling are security cameras."

"Hey, I saw a guard watching all the video monitors when they dragged me into the back of the store."

"That's right. Shoplifting is a big problem for retail stores, so whenever you walk into a store you are probably under electronic surveillance the whole time you're in there, except for when you are in the changing areas."

Sasha leaves Mr. Liberty's office. Her court date is not yet scheduled. She goes back to college and enrolls in weekly therapy classes.

Meanwhile, Mr. Liberty goes down to the county criminal courthouse to talk to the local prosecutor handling the case. He asks the prosecutor, Mr. Mean Jeans, to drop the case or reduce it to a municipal, civil ordinance violation so that Sasha's record can be sealed after a year.

"No way," Mr. Mean Jeans huffs. "The retail stores in this town are fed up with these damn college kids stealing stuff. They want zero tolerance. She's going to get slapped with at least two years probation, a fine, and a weekend in jail. The best I'll offer is she can plead as a 'first offender' so she doesn't have to become a convicted felon, provided she completes her probation properly."

"But the arrest will still appear on her record. It will be there for the rest of her life," replies Mr. Liberty.

"She should have thought of that before," snaps Mr. Mean Jeans.

"OK, I'll get back to you," replies Mr. Liberty.

Mr. Liberty gets the government's witness list and he runs a criminal background check on the female security guard who questioned Sasha. He also obtains her police personnel file from the state police licensing board on the hunch that she is an ex–police officer. It turns out that the security guard used to be a county police officer. She was fired from her job three years earlier for beating up a young man with her flashlight after a minor arrest and for using a Taser on another man who was *not* resisting arrest. She was fired, and her police officer's badge was suspended by the state.

Armed with this new information, Mr. Liberty goes back to Mr. Mean Jeans and presents him with his findings.

"Turns out Rambo Security Inc. didn't do their homework on the gal who stopped my client in the store," he says. "The guard has a history of disciplinary problems involving assault. My client says she was treated roughly—she indicated to me that she felt like this security guard was groping her when she was trying to uncover the stolen merchandise."

"Hmm, that could be a problem for the store," admits Mr. Mean Jeans.

"You sure the boutique won't let you reduce this charge down to a civil ordinance violation and let the arrest get sealed? My client's doing counseling, and here are five letters of reference from her college professors, all stating that she is a star student and a nice person."

"Oh, OK," sighs Mr. Mean Jeans. "We'll go with that. She can plead to a violation and pay a fine, and we'll seal it in a year if she stays out of trouble and shows proof of six months of counseling."

"Done!" replies Mr. Liberty.

3. Domestic Violence: Jim and Janet—Where private matters go public

Jim and Janet have been married for fifteen years. Jim is becoming suspicious, because Janet keeps staying out late. One night when she comes home after midnight, he angrily declares, "Janet, I've had it. I know you're having an affair. Tell me what you're up to!"

"Nothing!" she cries. "Besides, what do you care, you never even look at me, anymore!"

They argue back and forth. Finally, enraged, Jim grabs Janet by the arms and shakes her, shouting, "I want answers, damn you!"

Janet strikes back, scratching his face with her fingernails until he lets go. In a fury, he picks up a vase and slams it against the wall, shattering it and leaving a gaping hole in the wall. Janet picks up a book and hurls it at Jim, knocking a picture off the wall. Jim grabs her again and knocks her to the floor, tearing her blouse, and then stalks into the bedroom and slams the door.

Furious, Janet calls the police, asking them to come quickly.

Suddenly, Jim comes out of the bedroom and asks, "Janet do you still love me?"

"With all my heart," she responds. "It's just that you've been so angry lately, so I go hide over at Rhonda's house. You can ask her. We've been watching movies and eating popcorn all night."

"Oh, sweetheart," Jim says. "I'm sorry I've been so angry lately. I love you so much."

"Oh, Jimmy, I love you, too. I'm so sorry you were worried," cries Janet.

They embrace, kiss, and head off to the bedroom together.

Then there's a banging on the front door.

"Who's there?" Jim calls out.

"It's the police, sir. Open up, or we'll have to break in the door."

"What?" Jim turns to Janet. "You called the police?"

"Oh crap, I forgot! Yes, I did, honey—you were so angry. I'm so sorry!"

"Shit!" cries Jim. "We better let them in."

Jim opens the door and there are three police officers, two men and a woman. They walk into the living room. The police officers immediately note the living room is a mess, with books thrown about, a broken vase, a gaping hole in the wall, and a picture on the floor. Janet's blouse is torn, and Jim has a huge scratch with dried blood on his cheek.

"Hmm, looks like you two have had quite a night," replies Officer Strong. "What happened?"

The police separate Jim and Janet and question them separately.

Both Jim and Janet explain how the fight started and then explain they have made up and everything is OK now. Janet asks if they want coffee or cookies. Officer Strong politely refuses.

"Thank you so much for coming, Officer Strong," Jim and Janet both say to him and his fellow officers. "We appreciate you checking on us. We're OK. You can leave now. Sure we can't make you some coffee for the road?"

"Uh, sorry, ma'am," replies Officer Strong politely but firmly. "Both you and your husband are under arrest for battery under the state's domestic violence act."

"But I love her!" Jim cries as he is stuffed into the back of the police cruiser.

"But it's all my fault!" Janet screams as she is led away in handcuffs.

The next day, after they make bail, they both go to see a lawyer. The first problem is, as the lawyer explains, "I can't represent both of you; there is a conflict."

"But there is no conflict between us. That's the whole point, we've made up!" Jim and Janet reply.

"Yeah, I know, and that's truly wonderful, but *legally* there is a conflict. You each have a potential self-defense claim against the other. You also have the issue of spousal privilege, meaning you can't be forced to testify against the other, and each of you will need to make the decisions about your potential defenses and privileges individually and with separate counsel. I can only meet with one of you. I can recommend other lawyers for the other one of you to meet with."

"Honey, you meet with him," says Jim. "I will wait outside." Jim goes out to the reception area.

Janet asks Lawyer Number One, "If we both refuse to testify against the other, then can't we just force the government to drop the charges?"

"Not necessarily," says Lawyer Number One. "The 911 call may come into evidence because it can be shown to be the reason the police had to come to your home. Plus, the police saw the damage you guys caused to the home—and each other—and they may be able to get in your admissions that you inflicted harm on each other if you refuse to testify. Without either one of you willingly testifying against the other, it will be difficult for the state to go forward, but not impossible."

"But this is crazy," Janet gasps. "Why can't we just both agree to drop the charges?"

"Because, in the 1990s, the federal government created a zero-tolerance program under then–President Clinton to prosecute domestic violence cases. Former President George W. Bush renewed the mandate for that legislation. So, the state prosecutors and police can't drop domestic violence cases on the alleged victim's wishes, the way they used to in the old days. The concern comes from the idea that domestic violence can escalate between couples. The police have to arrest someone whenever there is a domestic disturbance call where they see physical signs of domestic violence, because it is better to stop domestic violence early before it gets out of control. When you called the police, you brought the government into your home. Under zero-tolerance domestic violence policies, it's not easy getting the government *out* of your home once you've let them in. Now, the decision to prosecute your husband or for him to prosecute you is not up to you and your husband, it's up to the prosecutor's office—and their hands have been tied by the federal government."

"Well, it's all my fault," says Janet. "I started it, and I called the police. Jim shouldn't be punished."

"Unfortunately, if you told the police officers that, you probably sounded like a battered spouse to them. People who are victims of domestic violence often blame themselves for the violent conduct perpetrated against them by their spouses or partners. They blame themselves when they are actually the victims."

"Well, he did grab me first and shake me," Janet sheepishly admits.

"OK," the lawyer responds, "so Jim was the initial aggressor."

"Yeah, but I scratched his face so hard it bled," Janet responds apologetically.

"But you could argue it was in self-defense, or that you simply reacted without intending to cause him harm. In order to batter someone, you have to act with intent to do the act."

"I don't care. I want my husband back. I love him and I never should have called the police. I won't testify against him."

After they leave the office of Lawyer Number One, Jim goes to see another lawyer.

"I don't want to prosecute my wife," Jim states flatly.

"It's not up to you, it's up to the government," replies Lawyer Number Two. "Besides, from what you've told me, she has a good defense. Her scratching you was in self-defense."

"I thought she was cheating on me, so I shook her to get some answers out of her," Jim shoots back.

"Well, if this was fifty or a hundred years ago, that would be a fine defense, but not in a twenty-first-century world. A hundred years ago, a man's home was his castle and he was the king. Now, under the zero-tolerance domestic violence laws, all that stuff's out the window."

"But she doesn't want to prosecute me and I don't want to prosecute her. We just want this to go away. Can't it just go away?"

"No, it can't," says Lawyer Number Two. She then explains, "The state will prosecute it regardless of what you guys want. The two of you may be able to do counseling for anger management, and then the state may eventually agree to allow you to plead to a lesser charge. I may be able to get your case sealed, too, provided I can negotiate a deal with the judge. Or, you guys could choose to push it to trial, and the case may fall apart for the government because of spousal privilege, but it's not a guarantee. The prosecutors lock onto these DV cases harder than a dog on a bone. Otherwise, they'll lose their federal funding."

Jim looks crestfallen. "Isn't there any good news?"

"Absolutely," responds Lawyer Number Two. "Be glad your wife loves you and does not want to prosecute you, because you would lose."

Stunned, Jim stammers, "Why?"

"There are two reasons," Lawyer Number Two explains. "One, legally she has a valid defense—self-defense—in my professional opinion."

"OK," says Jim. "I understand that. What's reason number two?"

"You have a natural disadvantage in domestic violence courts, although no prosecutor or judge would ever admit it."

"What's that?" Jim asks.

"You've got a penis," she replies.

4. Driving Under the Influence: Carlton's Case—Where "influence" is both good and bad

Carlton is a commercial contractor, family man, and staunch supporter of his local law-and-order politicians. Pulled over one evening for failing to stop completely at a stop sign, he failed a Breathalyzer test and found himself in court on a charge for DUI, or "driving under the influence."[83]

After bonding out of jail, Carlton goes and meets with his defense lawyer, Mr. Innocent. Mr. Innocent has been recommended by Carlton's friend. Carlton arrives at the office with the bundle of papers he received from the police window when he was released on bail the night before, but he is not in a good mood. Not only was he arrested—right in his own neighborhood—but the cops impounded his car, and it took him half the day getting it out of the impound lot run by Take It Away Towing, Inc., located on the "other" side of town.

Carlton marches into the lawyer's office. "I don't get why I was arrested!" he bellows at his defense lawyer

"Please have a seat, Carlton," says Mr. Innocent. "Tell me what happened."

"I had a few drinks at the club and some wine with dinner, like I always do, and then drove home, like I always do, and this local cop pulled me over for not stopping at a stop sign."

"Did you stop at the stop sign?"

"I performed my customary rolling stop. It's at the intersection of Dogleg Court and Blue Blood Drive. It was ten o'clock at night. There's never anybody at that intersection that time of night. Hell, it's in *my* neighborhood!"

"I see. OK, so let me take a look at the paperwork the police gave you."

Mr. Innocent examines the citations and the other paperwork. "Well, it says here that you agreed to perform all the field sobriety tests—the one-leg stand, the nine steps back and forth, and the HGN[84]—plus you performed a breath test at the scene and then again back at the station. Is all this accurate?"

"Yes, that much is accurate. I've got nothing to hide. But after I took all of the tests, and I blew into that little contraption the officer handed me on the side of the road, he handcuffed me and took me to jail like some sort of common criminal. Then, when I blew at the station on the machine they had there, he gave me that piece of paper that's got a lot of numbers on it, then he stuck me in the holding cell. I mean, the nerve! I pay big taxes to keep these police officers on the streets to catch *criminals*, not to lock up good, decent, tax-paying citizens like me!"

Mr. Innocent responds, "Well, according to your breath test results, you blew a .16 at the station. That's twice the legal limit for BAC."

"Speak English! What's BAC?"

"Blood alcohol concentration."

"Well, look, I had a few drinks, like I always do, but I can hold my liquor. I was out with my friends and business colleagues at my club, not sitting in some dingy bar downing shots of tequila or acting like some wino on the street corner. Hell, all we had was single-malt Scotch, and a decent bottle of merlot with dinner."

"How many Scotches?'"

"Well, let me think, one, maybe two."

"How much wine?"

"One or two."

"Glasses or bottles?"

"Glasses! Well, we ordered a couple of bottles, but there were four of us having dinner together in the club dining room."

"Anything after dinner?"

"Just my usual nightcap."

"What's that?"

"Cognac—Hennessy."

"How many?"

"Uh, just one, if I remember correctly."

"OK, well, here's the thing, Carlton. You agreed to perform all the tests, plus you admitted to the officer that you had been drinking when he pulled you over."

"I told him I had had two drinks, that's all!"

"OK, but the second you admit you've been drinking and you agree to do the field sobriety tests, you are agreeing to let the police officer gather evidence against you to arrest and prosecute you for DUI. Plus, you also agreed to do the breath test at the station, and it says you were twice the legal limit of .08 BAC."

"So, I should have refused to take any of the tests, shouldn't I?"

"There is no clear right or wrong answer to that question. Opinions can differ. For instance, if you had refused the breath test, then the officer would have put down 'refused' on his report, and you could have faced a potential yearlong license suspension."

"The officer did give me my license back, because I was polite."

"That's fine, but we better send a letter to the DMV, just to be sure there's not a license suspension petition filed. That's a fairly high blow on the breath test."

"Look," Carlton leans forward in his chair and leans onto the lawyer's desk. Lowering his voice, he says, "I know that county prosecutor has been trying to get into our club for a while. Problem is he doesn't get paid squat and he's having a hard time coming up with the entrance fee. Why don't you just go have a drink with that prosecutor and tell him I will take care of his entrance fee if he just makes this thing go away? I mean, I don't want this on my record—it could hurt my business reputation if this gets out. Not that I was drunk, but you know how people talk."

Mr. Innocent sits back in his chair and responds sternly, "That would be both unethical and a crime—bribing a public official. I can't help you there, Carlton."

"Well, what if *I* do it?"

"At this point, I have to warn you that although everything you tell me is normally privileged, there is an exception, and that is if I have good grounds to believe that a client of mine is planning to actually commit a future crime. If I believe the client is really serious, I have a duty as an officer of the court to report it to the authorities, so I really do hope you are talking out of your ass, here. You are kidding, aren't you, Carlton?"

Carlton leans back from the desk and thinks for a moment. "Uh, well, hell, of course I am. Just joking around. I would never really pull a stunt like that."

"OK, good. Furthermore, just FYI, I don't believe it would work."

"Why not?"

"One, I don't think you're giving either the judge or the prosecutor's office credit for their integrity. I know both the judge and the prosecutor, and they are tough, but they're also honest, hardworking public officials. Two, even if you had a corkscrew prosecutor or judge, your case is going to be tracked by a very powerful lobbying group."

"Who's that?"

"In the defense world, we jokingly refer to them as the 'MADD Mothers'—Mothers Against Drunk Driving. They are extraordinarily powerful and they are zealous about the enforcement of drunk-driving laws. The judge and prosecutor would be crazy to try to bury your case with MADD around."

"So MADD gets to decide who gets prosecuted?"

"No, but they exert a lot of influence; some good, some not so good, in my opinion. But regardless of how you feel about them, they are out there watching over judges and prosecutors to make sure they enforce DUI laws."

"So, what do I need you for? Might as well just give up and pay a fine and get it over with."

"It's not that simple. You face not only a fine, but also mandatory jail time, probation after that, community service, drug and alcohol evaluations, urine screenings, DUI and driver safety classes, and a possible license suspension. Oh, and your insurance premiums could shoot through the roof."

"Hell, that's ridiculous. I'm an upstanding member of my community, not some junkie or wino."

"No, but you did drive, if the test was accurate, way over the legal limit. If the test was accurate, you were definitely a less-safe driver, if not downright dangerous."

"Hey, you're a *criminal* defense lawyer. You're supposed to get me off the hook, that's what you guys do. So go work the system and get me off, like you guys get all those *criminals* off the hook!"

"Well, you may get off. I will file a bunch of motions and try to get the evidence thrown out. The breath machine may not have been properly maintained or operated, or the results could be off. Plus, we can see if the officer had you perform the field sobriety tests correctly. There's a lot we can do to fight it, and we may just win; but by admitting you were drinking and agreeing to perform the field sobriety tests and the breath test, you have given the prosecutor a lot of evidence to work with."

"So I should have refused those stupid tests, especially that breath test? That machine's gotta be rigged. Do you agree?"

"Well look, Carlton, this is my professional opinion. If someone has had a little to drink—one or two drinks—meaning single drinks, not the four- or five-shot drinks they pour at a lot of bars, but two ounces of alcohol, and then they get pulled over, if they do the breath test and fail, then they should ask for an independent blood test, which is considered to be more accurate. Or, say they agree to do the field sobriety tests and feel like the cop screwed them. I mean, the field sobriety tests—FSTs—are basically set up for the driver to fail. They make you stand on one foot in the middle of the street, which is almost never level, and most streets and sidewalks have some sort of unevenness to them. The wind may be blowing, or it may be cold. Plus, most people are scared out of their minds and nervous, so the tests are really just evidence-gathering tools to make you look guilty. But suppose you are in good physical health, with decent coordination, and you do them anyway—you walk the imaginary straight line heel to toe, you recite the alphabet backwards or *d* through *u* or whatever, you stand on one foot properly—and the cop still says you fail. *Then* you refuse the breath test.

"DUI juries are interesting and somewhat unique," Mr. Innocent continues. "Unlike jurors in a bank robbery case, just as an example, jurors in a DUI case tend to actually put themselves in the accused person's shoes during the trial—at least some of them do. Why? Because they drink and drive sometimes, too. Plus, it is perfectly *legal* to drink and drive in our country, for now, anyways, as long as you are not impaired to the point that you are less safe. So juries will understand if you went through all the gymnastics for the officer by the side of the road and you did pretty well, but the cop didn't let you go, so you refused to take the breath test.

"Also, juries rely on their own common sense. They don't leave it outside the courtroom, nor should they. So if you really *did* have two glasses of wine at dinner over the course of two or three hours and the cop still tries to haul you down to the station to take the breath test, then the jury will get it and use their common sense to make their decision as to whether you were intoxicated. The whole thing is probably on video, so we can look at the video—and so can the jury. If you look and act drunk or impaired, they will convict you. But if you look sober, then they may acquit.

"My experience," continued Mr. Innocent, "is that juries want to be able to drink socially and get home without having to run a police gauntlet every time they have dinner or drinks out. At the same time, juries don't want drunks on the road, and they worry about their children being injured or killed while driving while impaired, or hurting or killing someone else. So juries tend to be fair and to pay special, close attention to any video. If we can get the breath test tossed, or we can legitimately challenge its accuracy—and you did decently on the field sobriety tests—then the jury may find you not guilty. If, on the other hand, the breath test appears to be more or less accurate, and if on the video you look drunk—or at least impaired in your speech and coordination—and if you didn't do well on the FSTs, then they're likely to convict you. Juries, like I said, don't leave their common sense at the door, despite all of the political hullabaloo from an organization like MADD. Juries actually tend to do justice in these cases."

"Hmm. OK," sighs Carlton. "I want to see that video and then fight the hell out of this thing."

"Let's do it!" replies Mr. Innocent.

"How much are you going to cost me?" asks Carlton.

Mr. Innocent slides a written fee agreement across the desk for Carlton to review and sign.

"What?" hollers Carlton, looking at the lawyer's fee. "That's ridiculous! This is a DUI, not a murder case."

"Yeah, but there's a lot of forensic work and negotiation in DUI defense before we even decide whether it's worth taking your case to a jury. And you know, it's funny, Carlton. Years ago, as a young lawyer, I said the same thing to a judge when he was threatening to toss my client in jail for a DUI. I said, 'Heck, Judge, it's just a DUI. It's not like this is murder or anything.'"

"What did the judge say?"

"He glared down at me and said, 'Counselor, that's like saying shooting off a gun in a crowded movie theater is just a misdemeanor assault. When you are intoxicated and driving a one- or two-ton vehicle under the influence of alcohol, you are basically driving around in a huge weapon without the ability to properly control the damn thing.'"

"Well, I see his point."

"I do, too. I have children myself, and DUI is a serious problem."

"So, any *good* news, counselor?"

"Yeah, maybe next time you feel you're anywhere close to impaired, you'll have someone who has *not* been drinking drive you home. For what you're paying me, you could have bought a lot of taxi rides."

"Anything else I should be feeling *thankful for* right now, Counselor?" Carlton snorts back.

"Yeah. Thank God you didn't hit anybody—jogger, dog walker, mom and her kid, or some other driver—when you performed your 'rolling stop.' Worst-case scenario, you'd be looking at major prison time and, of course, a lifetime of guilt. You're a good man, Carlton, not a sociopath, so, if you had injured or killed someone, that would have been on your conscience forever."

"Well, I have to admit you have a point there, Counselor."

"Yup, the MADD Mothers aren't all bad."

5. Murder: Jason's Story—Where it's all relative

Three young men are at a gas station late at night. All three men are wearing baggy blue jeans and T-shirts: one man's T-shirt is yellow, the second man's T-shirt is dark blue, and the third man's T-shirt is black. All three men are wearing sneakers. A heated argument starts up. The gas station attendant comes out of the front office and tells the three men to stop yelling at each other.

In response, the young man wearing the yellow T-shirt turns to the attendant and screams, "Fuck you, old man! Get your fat ass back inside the office before I bust a cap in your ass, motherfucker!"

The gas station attendant, now terrified, races back inside, locks the door to his office, and hides behind the counter and dials the police.

Suddenly, two shots ring out.

The gas station attendant grabs the .38-caliber revolver he keeps stashed under the counter for just such nightmares, waits, and prays. It takes about five minutes for the police to get there. When they arrive, the police find the young man with the yellow T-shirt lying face down on the pavement next to the gas pump, his shirt soaked in blood. He is dead. No one else is there.

At seven the next morning, Jason is sleeping in his grandmother's house, which he shares with his mother and his older brother Sean, in a low-income neighborhood. He recently finished an eighteen-month prison stretch, followed by three years of probation for selling three twenty-dollar bags of crack cocaine. He has another prior felony for sale of marijuana. He hears tussling around downstairs, but figures it's just his brother stumbling up the stairs to bed, either drunk or high or both.

Then he hears heavy boots on the stairs, moving fast, and then a booming voice calls out, "Red Dog Patrol, Red Dog Patrol, everybody down!"

"Oh, shit," Jason cries to himself, "not the Red Dogs!"

Jason reaches for the trousers hanging off the edge of the bed. Just then, his bedroom door is smashed open, literally flying off its hinges, and three men in full military fatigues with rifles and scopes and flashlights level their guns inches from his face.

"Down on the ground, motherfucker, down on the ground! Hands! Hands! Let me see those hands, now!"

Jason hits the floor face down, spreading his hands and legs out as far as he possibly can. He's been here before and knows the Red Dog Patrol doesn't like to give orders twice. The Red Dogs, the Police Department's military-style drug task force unit, is well known to anyone who lives in low-income neighborhoods and public housing projects in the city.

"Looks like it's back to prison for you, Jason," one of the Red Dogs half-jokes, "but this time for good. You're under arrest for murder."

"What?" Jason screams.

Jason is held without bail, both because of the seriousness of the charge and because he is on probation. The state puts a "probation hold" on his case, meaning that even if he is granted a bond, he will be held in jail for violating the terms of his probation—one of which is to not get arrested while on probation.

Jason meets with the attorney his parents and grandparents have been able to retain after maxing out their credit cards and pulling money from the equity in his grandmother's home. The attorney, Mr. Justice, comes and meets with Jason at the jail.

"I did not do this," states Jason flatly.

"OK. What happened the night the victim, D'Jamal, was gunned down at the gas station?"

"I have no idea. I wasn't there."

"Where were you? Do you have an alibi?"

"No, not really. I was with my brother Sean and some guy named Sly, but they dropped me off at the Dreamy Doughnuts, and I bought some doughnuts and a Coke and then walked home."

"What time were you at the Dreamy Doughnuts? You pay cash or credit there? What time did you get home? Anybody see you walking home or see you enter your house? Was your grandmother there when you got home?"

"That's a lot of questions. Lemme think."

"Think *hard* Jason. We've gotta establish a time line here."

"I got dropped off at the Dreamy Doughnuts around midnight. We all went to a movie together and we were hitting some gin and juice at this girl Latisha's house. We were there until about midnight. Then Sean and this guy, Sly, wanted to meet up with Heavy D and get some decent weed and X, and I said, 'Fuck you, I'm on probation, just got out of jail, drop me off at the Dreamy Doughnuts.' So my brother Sean did, then him and Sly took off for whatever."

"Heavy D is D'Jamal Jackson, the same guy who got shot and killed at the gas station—who the police are now saying you and your brother Sean murdered. Is that right?"

"Yeah, that's right, but it's fucked up. I did not kill anyone. I was home."

"The police report says the shooting took place at 1:35 a.m., were you home by then?"

"Yeah, I think so. I bought my doughnuts with cash, then walked home. It takes me, like, thirty minutes to walk home. Then I went in and went to bed. Next thing I know, the Red Dogs are shoving a piece the size of a cannon in my face, accusing me of something I didn't do."

"You know who did it? They arrested your brother, too, but the other guy got away. Could you point him out or give info on your brother?"

"No, I can't, and I won't fuck my own brother. Fuck you! I was *not there!*"

"OK, OK, calm down. Just asking. Between only us, who's the other guy? The guy the police could not find."

"You want me to get my fucking head blown off? I kind of like my head in one piece."

"True, but your head, along with the rest of you, is going to prison pretty much forever. You've already got two felony drug convictions, you're twenty-two years old, and this is murder. You get convicted now and you're gone for good—or at least for a very, very long time."

"I don't know him, he's new around here. Like I said, he goes by Sly."

"OK, so back to you walking home. Anybody see you walking home?"

"Hey, yes! Fat Joe, he's a wino that hangs out on the corner down from my grandmama's place. I gave him a doughnut and a couple of bucks for beer."

"What time was that?"

"Maybe 12:45 or 1:00 a.m."

"OK, only problem is the gas station is just a ten-minute drive from your home. What about when you got home? Was your grandmother home?"

"Man, she runs a cleaning company, Bright Lights Cleaners. She's up working downtown in office buildings from five in the afternoon until six or seven in the morning. That's how she bought her house. She's got me working for her now. No damn way I'm going back into the drug business. I'm supposed to be working with her tonight. Eventually I'm going to run the business. My grandmama needs a damn rest—she's been working full-time since she was sixteen."

"Did you log onto a computer? Click on cable? Make a cell phone call, anything from your home that we could track via an electronic signal maybe to show you were home?"

"Nah, man, we don't own a computer. The cable's been out all month because grandma lost a customer last month, and I loaned my brother my cell phone because his was broke. I just ate my doughnuts and went to sleep."

"They found the gun they think was the weapon near the gas pumps. It's going to take probably six months to a year before the forensics come back from the lab."

"So, I gotta sit here for a fucking year while the police look at the gun? That's bullshit. What about all the *CSI* shit on TV?"

ARRESTED   219

"That's bullshit, Jason. Plus the court system is so backed up you may be in here for two, three years before your case goes to trial."

"Fuck that! I wasn't even there. I did not do this!"

"Well, for now let me see what me and my investigator can find out. What were you wearing that night?"

"Jeans, sneakers, and a T-shirt."

"What color shirt?"

"Red."

With that, Mr. Justice and his investigator, Mr. Cochran, start working the case.

"Investigator Cochran," Mr. Justice asks, "can you go ask around and find out what really went on that night? Check out this Fat Joe guy and see if you can track down this guy named Sly. See if the gas station had a video or the station attendant remembers anything. I will call Jason's brother's lawyer, see if he's willing to let Sean vouch for Jason."

The investigator shakes his head. "It wouldn't matter anyway. Sean's got plenty of shit on his rap sheet, too. Prosecutor's not gonna drop the charge just because Sean says Jason wasn't there. Plus, Sean's lawyer will never let you near him."

"I know, I know, probably not a snowball's chance in hell, but I gotta try."

"Whatever. While you're at it, why don't you get his grandmama to write a nice letter telling everybody what a great employee Jason is?" replies Investigator Cochran, laughing as he walks out the door.

Over the course of the next few months, Mr. Justice and Investigator Cochran work the case. As they do, several things become clear. One, there is no video of the shooting; the camera was broken the night it took place. Two, the convenience store manager remembers almost nothing. He was scared to death. But he does recall that the dead man was wearing a bright yellow shirt and the other two men were wearing dark blue or black tee shirts and blue jeans. He recalls that they were young black men in their early twenties, medium height, he thinks, and medium-build. He only remembers the one car at the gas pumps, the one ultimately traced by the police back to the deceased, D'Jamal—Heavy D—who was a well-known drug dealer in the neighborhood.

The third guy, Sly, is never found. A couple of guys in the neighborhood had heard about him, maybe from Jacksonville, Florida, but nobody knows for sure. The ballistics finally comes back on the gun found next to the gas pumps, and they show it was the murder weapon. The police also trace the gun's serial number and determine the gun was stolen from a guy living in Savannah, Georgia, two weeks earlier. This is about the time the man named Sly seems to have come to Atlanta, based upon witness statements.

The best piece of evidence for the prosecution comes from an alleged eyewitness who claims he was standing across the street about 100 feet away, and saw the whole thing. He says three men got in a fight and were fussing and arguing at the gas station. Then he saw a man shoot and kill Heavy D, who staggered, pulled out a gun, squeezed off a shot, and fell to the ground. The eyewitness, Martin, says he took off after he heard the shots fired.

Investigator Cochran goes and stands where Martin says he saw the whole thing. Then he goes and tries to interview Martin. At first, Martin won't talk to Investigator Cochran, but he finally agrees to talk to him. Afterward, Investigator Cochran goes back to the crime scene and, using the police notes and the witness statement, figures out more or less where Martin claims to have been standing when the shots were fired. Then he reports his findings to the defense lawyer.

"OK, Mr. Justice. I've got some interesting information."

"Whatcha got? Anything good?"

"Maybe. I got the supposed eyewitness, Martin, to talk to me."

"You did? That's fucking awesome. I have no doubt you properly identified yourself as a private investigator working for my office. Isn't that correct, Mr. Cochran?"

"Absolutely," replies the investigator. "And, in the course of my investigation, witness Martin told me he was standing at the corner of Dead End Avenue and No Jobs Road, right in front of the Cheapo Liquor Store. Problem is, in the police report, he told the police he was standing at the intersection right across the street from the gas station where the shooting occurred. But the intersection he told *me* he was standing at is the next block down, more than 250 feet from the gas station. Plus, you can't see the gas pumps from there, because the convenience store at the gas station is in your line of sight from that intersection, and there's also a big metal trash dumpster in the way. Both the convenience store and the trash dumpster block your view of the gas pumps where the shooting occurred.

"I also tracked down the wino, Fat Joe. He says he remembers Jason giving him a doughnut at some point, but he can't remember when or what Jason was wearing. Plus, he's a big drunk who lives at the homeless shelter when he's not panhandling on the streets."

"So who is this guy, Martin? Any ideas?"

"That's interesting, too. He's got a rap sheet a mile long, including a pending charge in the same county for forgery. Plus, I talked to his neighbors. His family moved up from Jacksonville a couple of years ago."

"That's a big help, Investigator Cochran. Great work. Also, Jason confirmed he was wearing a red T-shirt and boxer shorts when he was arrested."

Mr. Justice goes and talks to the prosecutor, Ms. Vader. She is known to be ambitious, and is seeking a judgeship in the next election cycle.

Mr. Justice explains his case and his findings to her. "There is absolutely no evidence linking Jason with this crime. No gun, no ID, no forensics or physical evidence, no blood spatters, gunpowder residue, gun, nothing. My client has a partial alibi . . ."

"Yeah, a wino that doesn't know what year it is," Ms. Vader interrupts.

Mr. Justice continues, ". . . plus your eyewitness is crap and may even be suborning justice by covering for a relative nicknamed Sly, who according to several witnesses in the neighborhood, showed up from Jacksonville about two weeks before the murder, and your eyewitness's whole family is from Jacksonville. So you may be able to get a lead on the third guy at the station."

Ms. Vader looks at the two-foot-high pile of files on her desk. "Yeah, sure, Mr. Justice, I'll get right on that."

"You are actually going to take this case to trial? The jury will acquit in a heartbeat. You've got nothing, nada, zippo, on Jason."

"He's got priors. Two drug convictions. Both felonies."

"The jury will never hear about them, you know that, Ms. Vader."

"C'mon, this was a drug deal gone bad. Your client, or his brother Sean, pulled the trigger!" Ms. Vader shoots back.

"The drug convictions won't come in. The judge won't let them in, not similar priors. You know that."

"Yeah, but Sean has a prior aggravated assault with a handgun. I'll tell you what, Mr. Justice, you go tell your client he can plead to ten and serve two years, aggravated assault. He's got a year and a half already in the system, he's paroled out in six months, tops."

"Not necessarily, after he gets revoked on his probation. He's got three years on that."

"That's his problem."

Mr. Justice goes back to see Jason and explains the prosecutor's offer to settle the case.

"No fucking way," Jason responds. "I am innocent!"

Four months later, the trial begins.

When Ms. Vader walks into the courtroom, she walks up to Mr. Justice and asks, "Well, Counselor, has Jason come to his senses? The deal is still open."

Mr. Justice goes to the courtroom's jail holding area and talks to Jason. "It's up to you, Jason, it's your life. You can take the deal or go to trial. You have a good case for trial, in my professional opinion, and you could win, but of course it is a risk—a big, big risk. If you take the deal, you'll be home in two to three years, max. It's your call—I go home either way. If you're found guilty of murder by the jury, you don't. I respect whatever you decide to do. What's it going to be?"

Jason stares straight at Mr. Justice. "Trial! I did not do this!"

Mr. Justice gives the prosecutor Jason's reply: "Jury trial."

Just then, the judge calls Ms. Vader and Mr. Justice back into his chambers. "So, Counselors, are both sides ready? We need to move this case. Are both sides ready?"

"Defense is ready, Your Honor," replies Mr. Justice.

Ms. Vader hesitates and then replies, "Your Honor, before you call in jurors for selection, the state has an announcement."

"What's that?" replies the judge.

"We've decided to dismiss all charges against Jason for lack of evidence. The state is moving forward to trial, however, on his brother Sean."

"Very well," responds the judge, "all charges against Jason are dismissed. We will proceed to trial on the charges against Sean. Mr. Justice, you and your client are excused from court."

6. Sex Crimes: Candace's Story—Where we uncover the age of innocence

Candace is twenty years old and lives at home with her parents. One day, the police arrive at her parents' house and ask to speak with their daughter.

"What's this about?" Mom and Dad ask the police.

"Your daughter is an adult, ma'am. We can only discuss this with her."

Candace comes out of her bedroom. "Mom, Dad, what's going on?"

The police say, "Candace, we need you to come down to the station to talk with us. There are some things we really need you to clear up for us."

Candace immediately agrees, "OK, if you insist."

"Wait, dear, we want to come with you," Candace's parents tell their daughter.

"Your daughter's an adult. She needs to come down on her own."

"Is she under arrest?" her parents press the officer.

"No, ma'am, your daughter is not under arrest, we just need to talk to her about some things and have her help us clear some things up."

Mom and Dad are somewhat relieved to hear this. They are good, law-abiding citizens who give annually to the local police office's "Toys for Tots" program at Christmas.

"Oh, Mom and Dad," Candace says, rolling her eyes, "I'm old enough to handle this myself."

"OK, dear, call us if you need anything."

Mom and Dad stand in the doorway as the police walk Candace to the police cruiser, help her into the back of the car, and drive away.

"Maybe we should call a lawyer," Dad says. "I don't like this at all."

"Yeah, but then it will look like were not cooperating with the police, and that would certainly be bad," says Mom. "Plus, the officer promised he would call us once they were done talking with Candace."

"Yeah, I guess you're right," sighs Dad. "Let's wait until we hear from the police officer so we can find out what this is all about."

A few hours later, they get a call from the same police officer.

"Good evening, ma'am. I have to inform you that we have taken your daughter into custody. She's being charged with aggravated child molestation, child molestation, and enticing a minor for indecent purposes."

"What?" both parents shriek. "How can that be? This is ridiculous! Can you tell us what all this about?"

"No, ma'am, this is official police business at this point. Your daughter is being taken to the county detention center. You can call them for more information."

Mom and Dad immediately start calling lawyers. They get one on the phone.

"What's the penalty for these charges, and what do they involve?" they ask.

The lawyer, Ms. Darrow, takes a deep breath and replies, "The more serious of the two is aggravated child molestation. If your daughter is convicted of aggravated child molestation, it carries a mandatory minimum sentence of twenty-five years to life in prison."

Dad stands there, stunned into silence as if he's just been kicked in the gut. Mom collapses on the floor and wails.

Ms. Darrow's first step is to get a bond hearing for Candace. Due to the serious nature of the charges, she has to file a formal written document with the superior court judge requesting that a bond be set. Unlike in less serious criminal cases, only the presiding judge can set bail and grant bond to a person accused of serious felony charges such as aggravated child molestation or child molestation.[85] This process takes several weeks, so Candace spends several weeks in the county jail until she finally gets out on bond. She has to wear, and pay for, an ankle

ARRESTED

monitor, and she has a strict curfew attached to her bond conditions that states she must be home by 7:00 p.m. and not leave the house again until 7:00 a.m. This allows her to try to find a new job, which she has to do because she had immediately lost her previous job working as a receptionist for a local business when the arrest was reported on the front page of the local newspaper under the headline "Woman Arrested for Sexually Molesting a Local Teenage Boy."

After finally getting out on bail, three weeks after her arrest, Candace—and her parents—meet with Ms. Darrow at the attorney's office. By the time they finally meet at her office, Ms. Darrow has a pretty good idea of what happened based on what she has read in the police report, from the charges filed, and from speaking with Candace. Her investigator has already started looking into the background of the alleged victim, a fifteen-year-old boy from across town who was posting on Facebook saying that he was eighteen years old.

"So, let me make sure I've got all the details correct. You met this boy at a pool party last summer, and then you guys 'friended' each other on Facebook, is that right?"

"Yes, that's right," replies Candace.

"Then, at some point, he asked you out on a date?"

"Well, not really a date. We just decided to meet up at the mall and hang out together. Then we went back to his place and his parents weren't home and . . . ," Candace pauses. "Uh, do my parents need to hear all this, especially my Dad?"

"Do you want your parents to leave? We talked about this before. Your parents do not have to be here, and it is totally up to you. You are the client."

"Uh, Mom, Dad, can you guys please leave?"

"OK," Mom and Dad say. They walk out reluctantly.

"So what happened, exactly, Candace?"

"We drove back to his place. I drove because he said he lost his license for DUI and couldn't drive. I should have known better, but I had just broken up with my boyfriend and was angry and hurt. My ex-boyfriend was a jerk, plus he dumped me, and Billy was just a really decent guy. He told me he was eighteen and I believed him. He is, like, six-foot-five and weighs way over 200 pounds, he even had a beard—well, at least he was scruffy. Anyway, he wanted to have sex and I said 'No way, absolutely not.' But he talked me into giving him a blowjob, which I did, and then he wanted to go down on me and I was like, 'Well, OK'—I mean why should he have all the fun? So I let him. We texted some after that, but then I met another guy near my work—he works in the electrical supply factory—and we started dating. I stopped texting with Billy after that."

"So then what happened?"

"Billy got angry and then he sent me several angry text messages. I told him to forget about it, and then I un-friended him on Facebook. I was already dating my new boyfriend. He's twenty-four, drives a really cool Mustang, and is *way* hotter."

"I'm glad you have met a young man is who is age appropriate."

"A week later, the cops showed up at my house. They were nice to me at the station, at first. They told me they had some paperwork to sign before they could talk to me, so I signed a *Miranda* Rights Waiver Form. There were a bunch of boxes for me to check off and to initial next to each box, and then I signed it at the bottom. I wasn't really sure what I was signing, but I got the sense I had better sign it or I was gonna really piss them off."

"The police are definitely well trained at getting people to waive their Miranda Rights."

"Look I'm not some whacko slut who hangs out around the high school trying to pick up boys. He said he was a senior. I just turned twenty three weeks ago. I graduated from high school a year late because my dad was in the military and we moved a lot. I mean, doesn't it matter that I'm a girl? I thought girls got cut some slack on this kind of thing. You always hear boys getting into trouble at school for dating young girls. The girl's dad finds out and doesn't like the boy she's dating and calls the cops—that happened to at least two or three boys I can remember when I was in high school. But I'm a girl, doesn't that help?"

"Not really, it might even hurt you."

"Why?"

"Well, these cases are funny—funny meaning 'weird.' It is true that lots of boys get in trouble now. About fifteen years ago, our state legislature raised the age of sexual consent for teenagers from fourteen to sixteen years of age. It had been fourteen since the early nineteenth century, but various social and political groups lobbied hard to raise the age of consent to sixteen, and so you have lots of boys getting into trouble and being arrested for dating girls who are in high school but are fourteen or fifteen years old. They put on Facebook that they are sixteen or seventeen, or even eighteen, to get guys to date them, but then their parents find out and call the cops and have the older boy arrested."

"Well, sure, all my girlfriends said they were older than they really were. If you didn't, the cooler older guys wouldn't like you. That's totally normal. That's why I figured Billy was telling the truth—it would be totally random for a *boy* to do that, or at least I thought so until now."

"Yes, it looks like boys are catching up to girls in the deception department, although last time I checked there's still plenty to go around. The problem you've got is that the prosecutor in your case might want to make an example out of you. You are, in a way, what the writer Tom Wolfe described in his classic novel from the 1980s as the 'great white defendant.'"[86]

"Uh, Miss Darrow, you're talking way, way over my head. I don't read a lot, and I was born in 1993. *A great white what?*"

"OK, hmm, let me try and explain. In this book, a rich white guy driving a sports car runs over a black guy and kills him. The prosecutor who handles the case wants to make an example out of the white guy, who is arrested for murdering the black guy. Why? Because the prosecutor works in the Bronx, in New York, and spends most of his time prosecuting and locking up poor and working-class black guys. So, by prosecuting the rich white guy, the prosecutor looks super fair and can win political popularity in the Bronx and maybe run for public office, like mayor or something. He wants to make an example out of the white guy to show that justice is blind—that is, fair and equal—to all members of his community, regardless of their financial background or skin color."

"OK, I think I see where you're going with this. The prosecutor handling my case, what's his name?"

"Tom Law."

"Right, Mr. Law will want to lock me up because I am a girl and he spends most of his time locking up guys for this kind of thing. Is that it?"

"Bingo! You got it."

"That, like, sucks. That's bullshit."

"Yes, and there's another name for it, too: politics."

"Can my parents come in now? I really want my parents to understand what is going on. Just *please* don't mention the blowjob part. My dad will hit the fucking roof!"

"Absolutely."

Ms. Darrow walks to the door. "Please come back in and rejoin your daughter. She has explained what happened, and I can lay out for you the first steps we need to take in your daughter's defense."

Mom and Dad nervously sit down beside their daughter.

"The good news is we have some useful information on the alleged victim, Billy. He put on his Facebook page that he was eighteen, and he led your daughter to believe he was eighteen years of age."

"OK, good," says Dad, "that means my daughter's innocent."

"No, I am afraid not."

"Why the hell not?"

"Because, an adult—your daughter being the adult—cannot use as a defense the fact that she was misled by a child—that being the alleged victim—to believe he was of age to sexually consent."

"Why not? That's the stupidest thing I've ever heard. Plus, my daughter's not an adult. Hell, she's not old enough to *buy beer* yet. She still has a restricted driver's license!" bellows Dad.

"I know, I know. I realize this is frustrating and terrifying."

"Isn't him lying about his age a crime? It should be," Dad presses, clearly frustrated.

"No, it's not a crime for a child to lie about his age to attempt to gain sexual interest from an adult."

"Why the hell not? What about his parents, shouldn't they get

ARRESTED

arrested?" Dad asks angrily. "Wait a minute, my daughter turned twenty just three weeks before she went out with this guy. Does that make a difference?"

"It would if she had gone out with the boy when she was still nineteen, but since she was twenty years of age at the time of the alleged incident she is charged with a felony under the sex crimes laws of our state—as an adult."

Mom gulps. "By *felony*, you mean the part of the law that says my daughter may go to prison for twenty-five years to life in prison?"

"That's correct."

Dad joins in. "So, what would have been the potential punishment if she had done something with this Billy kid, I mean, I'm not saying my little girl did *anything*, I'm sure she didn't, but just supposing for a minute she *did* do something when she was nineteen, would that change the charge?"

"Yes, then she would be charged under what's known as the 'Romeo and Juliet' section of the same law and that would make it a misdemeanor."

"What would the punishment have been then, the worst?"

"Twelve months in jail."

"WHAT?" Dad shoots out of his chair like a firecracker just went off under his seat. "You're telling me that the law says that the difference of three weeks is the difference between twelve months in jail and twenty-five years to life in prison?!?"

Ms. Darrow clears her throat. "That is correct."

"Wait a minute," Mom pipes in. "The boy, Billy, he was almost sixteen, wasn't he? He was just a couple of months shy of his sixteenth birthday? Does that make a difference?"

"Not really. No."

"Wait a minute," says Dad in response. "What would the law say if he was sixteen when he and my daughter went out?"

"Then it would not be a crime at all. Any relations Billy and your daughter may have had would have been perfectly legal."

Dad takes a deep breath, then says, "So what you are seriously telling us is that the law says that if my daughter is a month or so younger it's a misde ...,misdem ..."

"A misdemeanor—a minor crime punishable by no more than twelve months in jail."

"Right, a misdemeanor. And if the boy, Billy, was two months older, then the law says there's no crime at all?"

"That's correct."

"So, the difference of about a month in my girl's age and two months in the boy's age is the difference between no crime, twelve months in jail, and twenty-five years to life in prison? That's the actual law?"

"Yep, you pretty much nailed it right on the head."

Dad and Mom sit back, looking like they have just seen a pink pig fly across the room.

Mom leans forwards in her chair. "Isn't that just a little bit nuts?"

"Yes, you could certainly say that."

"Well, what the hell do we do?" asks Dad.

"The first thing I'm going to do is have my investigator pull all of Billy's Facebook information off of the internet along with anything else we can find under social media sites. Along with the fact he was advertising himself as eighteen we may find other embarrassing information out there about him that he posted as images, videos or written content. This type of information is not a defense, but it can help mitigate the situation with the prosecutor and the judge both of whom might agree to deal lightly with your daughter's case. It is also potentially embarrassing to Billy and his parents and so could slow them down once they learn that potentially embarrassing information is going to come out publically about their son.

"Then, I want to have my forensics expert—he is a former FBI agent—take a look at your daughter's computer and cell phone and see if there is anything potentially helpful or harmful to your daughter's case on these devices. If there is helpful information, we can image your daughter's hard drive on her computer and phone, so that we have proof of what was and was not on your daughter's computer and phone right now, at this date and time, shortly after her arrest. We may also want to subpoena Billy's school records to see if he has a history of disciplinary problems and run criminal background checks on his parents to see if they have any dirt under their fingernails."

"By doing these things we may make Billy and his parents look like the bad guys in all this, to some extent. It's not a defense, but it is definitely what we call 'evidence in mitigation.' We need to get this case down to some sort of charge that severely restricts any time your daughter will have to spend on the sex offender registry or, under the best-case scenario, keeps her off it altogether."

"THE SEX OFFENDER REGISTRY?" Mom, Dad, and Candace gasp in unison.

Now Dad goes completely ballistic. "My daughter's not some pervert. She's a normal girl who likes boys. This is completely crazy. That registry is for sex nuts and perverts."

"I know, I know," replies Ms. Darrow, "and I agree with you. But it will take a lot of work to keep your daughter off the registry completely or at least simply get it down to a minimum number of years. If she is convicted of either aggravated child molestation or child molestation, she could end up on there for life."

"What are we going to do?" asks Candace, obviously in a state of shock.

"We will need to gather a lot of evidence in mitigation on your behalf: a psychosexual evaluation, possibly a polygraph, and letters of good character, for starters. In the meantime, we need to go after the victim, use his own actions against him and his family to get them to back off, and then also attack the case, both legally and factually."

"But, you know, Candace," Ms. Darrow adds, "I really wish you had insisted on talking to a lawyer before you went anywhere with those police officers."

Dad looks at Mom. "See, I told you we *should have called a lawyer* when those cops came to the house. I told you!"

"Your Dad's right on that one, Candace," says Ms. Darrow. "Without your confession and cooperation, all the cops have got is a weak case with an outcry from the boy and his parents and very little, if any, evidence to back it up."

"What the heck is a 'psychosexual evaluation'?" asks Mom.

"We can discuss all that tomorrow. Let me call my forensics investigator so he can start his investigation, so we can try and gain some leverage on Billy and his parents. I will then go try to talk sense to the local prosecutor. He's not a bad prosecutor. My hope is he will see this for what it is: another stupid case involving young people who have been trapped in the wonderfully messed-up web of our state's sex crimes laws."

7. Corporate Embezzlement: Chuck's Story—Where confession may actually be good for the body and soul

Chuck, a vice president for a large manufacturing company, is sitting in his office, talking on the phone with one of the company's clients and negotiating payment for a large overseas order. He's talking on the speakerphone with the client, lost in the details of his phone conversation, when his assistant, Mary, walks in with a worried look on her face. Chuck looks up at her from across his desk with the typical "What is it? I'm busy with a customer" look he always has whenever she interrupts an important call. She slides a scribbled note across the desk that says, "The president needs to see you ASAP," and Chuck scribbles back, "All right, as soon as I am done with this call." Mary nods and walks out, closing the door to Chuck's office behind her. Chuck goes back to the call and finishes it about a half hour later. With the sale completed, and having downed the last of his mid-morning coffee, he strides down the hall to the corner office and tells the boss's assistant he has been asked to come see the president.

"Mr. Perry will see you now," says the assistant, and Chuck walks into Mason Perry's office.

"What's up, Mason? Mary says you need to see me. Sorry to take a while, but I just got off the phone with our client in Singapore. They just put in their annual spring order with us—deal's done," Chuck says with obvious satisfaction. He is known as the "go-to guy" at his company, the one who brings in the big deals. It's the main reason he is vice president of international sales at the age of thirty-six.

"That's great, Chuck. Fantastic job. You always land the big ones!" responds Mason, shaking Chuck's hand and ushering him over to the sitting area in Mason's executive office with the view overlooking the downtown skyline. Chuck settles into the leather sofa, while Mason takes a seat on one of the straight-backed chairs across from the mahogany coffee table.

"Do you want some coffee?"

"No, thanks, just had mine. What's this about, Mason?"

"Chuck, we've got a problem."

"OK," replies Chuck, "sounds serious. What's up?"

"It turns out our office manager, Martha, has been stealing from the company for years."

"Martha?" Chuck asks in disbelief. "Are you sure, Mason? I mean, Martha has been with us for, what, twelve, maybe fifteen years. Heck, she brings in fresh-baked cookies every time we have a holiday party and helps out at our annual fundraiser. Seems impossible to believe she would be stealing from the company."

"I know, I know," replies Mason, "it's hard for me to wrap my brain around, too. I never would have suspected Martha of doing such a thing. She's like the den mother around here. Hell, everybody loves her and trusts her completely. But we switched accountants last year, and the new firm was looking over our books, just to make sure everything is shipshape, and they saw two sets of expenses from the last four fiscal quarters that didn't look right."

"What are those?"

"The first were charges on a company credit card that was linked to an employee who left seven years ago. There was an open credit card in his name on the books with regular expenses on it for things like lunches, dinners, gas, even some retail purchases from clothing stores and the like. The card was active and had been paid every month, like clockwork. The accountant says it averaged several hundred a month. The second are airline tickets, mostly to California, Las Vegas, and Miami, along with a couple of trips to Costa Rica and the Bahamas, plus all the expenses for the trips—meals, drinks, hotels, the works."

Chuck runs through the client list in his brain. "We *do* have clients in those places."

"That's right, we do. Only problem is that when you go back through the company records for business trips by our salespeople or executives, and through the expense reports, there's no record of anyone from the company traveling to those locations on those dates, nor are there any expense reports filed for those dates. And, it just so happens that the trips all match up with vacation and sick leave Martha took over the past seven years."

"Oops, that's not good," sighs Chuck. "Hey, wait a minute. Martha was always driving to South Jersey to see her mom who's been sick a long time. That's where she always told me she was going whenever she took her vacation time or sick leave. To go help out her sick mom."

"Uh, yeah," sighs Mason, frowning. "Turns out Martha's mom has been dead for the past eight years. Our loss-prevention guys checked it out. And guess who approved all the accounts payable invoicing for the trips?"

"Martha?"

"Yep."

"But, wait, she would still need coauthorization from someone in accounting to sign off on those trips. Who else signed off on the travel vouchers?"

"Jim Jackson."

"What? Are you saying he was in on it, too?"

"No, Jim had no clue. Martha had him sign some paperwork, and simply used that to practice signing his name over and over."

"What about his billing authorization code?"

"She had that, too. Hell, you know how sloppy everybody is with those things. He could have left it on his desk, or she may have simply pulled it off his computer."

"Martha was the one person who knew where the hell everything was around here, that's for sure. Heck, everybody went to her whenever they couldn't find things—access codes, phone numbers, hell, the key to the executive washroom!"

"I know, I know. It looks like we gave her a little too much trust and not enough oversight."

"How much are we talking about?"

"It's actually a lot when you add it all up. Over $400,000—going back almost seven years."

"Wow, that's a lot. How do you know any of this is actually true, though? Is it possible it's just a mistake?"

"No, our loss-prevention officer advised us it might be difficult to put all the links back to Martha together, so he confronted her about it—you know, yelled at her, threatened to call the police, then told her he'd go easy on her. You know, the typical way those loss-prevention guys work, and Martha broke down and confessed to the whole scheme. It's all on tape. She's nailed to the cross. We're handing the whole case over to an FBI agent coming over here this afternoon, and the U.S. Attorney's Office will be prosecuting it in federal court. This morning, I spoke to a young assistant United States attorney who is handling the investigation. He says Martha is facing some serious prison time, maybe two and a half to four years, by his estimate."

"Geez. Well I guess she deserves it. Still seems a real shame."

"Whatever," says Mason, "she was robbing us blind. I don't give a rat's ass how many cookies she baked. The woman's a thief, and I hope they throw the book at her! Which is where you come in. We have been advised by the U.S. Attorney's Office and the FBI to have our new accounting firm do a complete audit of the company's books for the past seven years. We need to make sure our books are clean as a whistle. And we've got to move fast, because we can't get this year's private financing together until we are sure our books are cleaner than a virgin's honey pot. Uh, if you know what I mean."

"Sure, sure," sighs Chuck. "And you need everybody who has signing authority on the company's bank accounts and accounts payable invoices to help with the audit, right?"

"You've got it, Chuck. Look, I know you're up to your elbows in alligators with sales—but we are going to need your help, too. This internal audit has got to be a team effort. I mean, how can we go after new financing when it looks like we don't even have enough sense to keep our own employees in line?"

"No, I get it, you're right. Hey, is there any chance of us just letting Martha go? I mean, just fire her or, even better, let her resign quietly? That way it doesn't go public at all. The new investors don't even have to know about it."

"We thought about it," sighs Mason, "but old man White said not a chance in hell. You know how he is. He'd squeeze a penny to make Abe Lincoln shit. We've got to make an example out of her, tar and feather her, and show transparency to our investors and employees. Show them we practice zero tolerance around here. You know the drill."

"Yes," sighs Chuck, "yes I do. OK, I'm in, tell me what to do."

"You meet with loss prevention on Thursday, then the FBI agent and the prosecutor right afterward. They'll need statements from you. Then you can have your assistant help you round up your payment authorization records in order to be ready to sit down with the forensic accounting team next week. They're going to be combing through the books line by line, and they'll need your help—along with the other division VPs—to get through it all."

"OK, I'll get on it. Phew, just what I need right now, more projects."

"I know, I know," Mason shoots Chuck a smile. "It stinks. But look on the bright side: at least you're not Martha."

Chuck smiles back. "At least I'm not Martha." With that, he heads back to his office.

About two hours later, Chuck is sitting in a criminal defense attorney's office across town.

"Thank you for seeing me so quickly, Mr. Process. I really need to talk to you about something."

"Sure, Chuck. You sounded really worried on the phone. What's up?"

"Our office manager just got caught stealing from the company I work for. I'm in charge of corporate sales, and I'm worried."

"Why? Did you have anything to do with her theft?"

"No. I knew nothing about it. The problem is that the company has hired a new accounting firm, and they and the FBI and the U.S. Attorney's Office are all getting involved to audit the company's books."

"OK. Go on."

"Well, I have sign-off authority on invoices billed to the company related to sales—and I am afraid this audit might turn up something."

"What's that?"

"A few years ago, I got into a problem with gambling. At first, it was no big deal, but then I started to bet on football games a lot. I started to use a bookie that a friend of mine knew, and it got out of control, and I ended up blowing a lot of money and really going into debt. This bookie is not the kind of guy you want to owe money to, if you know what I mean, so I set up a consulting company on the side and started invoicing the company for its services. I sent the invoices from a post office box I set up and then had the payments sent there, too. Then I deposited the checks in an account I set up in the consulting company's name and used the money to pay back my bookie."

"OK."

"So, I finally stopped gambling—I went and got professional counseling for the problem. And I put an end to the consulting company about a year ago. I was really proud of myself. I got my act together, stopped the gambling, and stopped the invoicing."

"How much are we talking about? What's the general dollar amount?"

"Oh, over six years, probably close to a million."

"Do you know if it's over or under a million?"

"Not totally sure. Does it matter?"

"It could. There are guidelines concerning punishment for wire and mail fraud that apply in this kind of criminal case. These are generally federal charges investigated and prosecuted by the U.S. Attorney's Office because they involve bank transactions, which are considered interstate commerce and are regulated by federal statute. For example, my guess is Martha's case is also being investigated by the U.S. Attorney's Office, is that right?"

"Yes, that's correct. That's what my boss told me this morning."

"Okay, so you have some idea what you'd be dealing with. Now, did you perform any work for these fees you paid yourself that could be considered legitimate services, and do you have any authorization to independently hire vendors for the company?"

"Would that excuse it?"

"Honestly? It could very well get you fired if they find out. I doubt you're allowed to do this under your employment contract, and it definitely shows bad faith. But whether it is criminal fraud or not may be in question."

"Well, when you put it like that, yes, I have to get authorization, but I got it from my boss, Mason. He signed off on it. I explained how the consulting company could help us, and he trusted my judgment. My company's sales have gone through the roof since I took over the international sales department. He'd pretty much sign off on anything I gave him. The thing is, I am paid to sell, that's my job description, but the truth of the matter is the partners are always asking me for advice on what trade shows we exhibit at and which trade publications and PR approaches are best to boost company sales. I worked for a marketing and PR firm before I joined my present company, and so I know all that stuff, and I don't get paid a dime for it. They just assume it's mine to give them for free since I work for them—but it is independent knowledge that I built up over five years of doing marketing research for my prior employer. I even thought about starting my own consulting business when I was younger, but chickened out and took this job in sales. I mean, I get paid OK, but it's always ticked me off that I am basically providing them with free consulting services for product marketing and public relations advice just because, oh you know, 'good old Chuck, just go to him, he'll know what to do,' that kind of bullshit. Truth be told, it pisses me off!"

"The only problem is that you never bothered to tell your boss you were the one billing the company for the consulting services and taking the proceeds, correct?"

"Yes, that is true."

"Did you report the income on your tax forms?"

"Yes. I was afraid not to. It is a sole proprietorship for tax purposes, so the profits just flowed through to me on my personal tax return. That way my bosses never saw them. Oh, shit, what am I going to do? Old man White, that's the senior partner, he's hanging Martha out to dry for a couple of trips to the Bahamas and a few hundred grand. He's going to string me up by the balls if he finds out! The fucking auditors are sniffing through the corporation's books like bloodhounds. I am fucked!"

"Well," Mr. Process sits forward and leans on his desk, "it seems to me, Chuck, you've got a choice to make."

"OK, what is it? Choose cyanide or pick a rope to hang myself with?"

"No," Mr. Process smiles patiently. "No, Chuck, by a choice I mean you can choose to do nothing and see if the auditors catch it—it's what in the defense world we call 'whistling past the graveyard,' or you can disclose it and try to work a deal with your bosses. If you choose the first one—and they find out—you're probably going to be investigated, and there's a very good chance you'll get indicted on mail and wire fraud charges. If the loss amount is around a million, you could be looking at some serious prison time. Of course, if you disclose it and they still want to prosecute you, they can. But, the fact that you disclosed it early on before they found out could earn you some points with the judge and the United States prosecutor in federal court, and that could earn you a sentence lower than the federal sentencing guidelines range."

Chuck raised a questioning eyebrow.

"In federal court, there is a big book called the 'federal sentencing guidelines' that basically guides the judge as to what a recommended sentence should be in a particular type of criminal case," Mr. Process explains. "In recent years, the U.S. Supreme Court has declared the federal sentencing guidelines 'merely advisory,' meaning that the judge can depart from the recommended sentence. In your case, suppose the recommended sentence for mail fraud is sixty months, the judge could depart downward and give you less time."

"Oh, God, what a fucking idiot I am. What am I going to do?"

"There is another thing to consider, too. If you disclose everything, the prosecutor can let you plead to one charge only—such as one count of mail fraud. But, if you fight it or really piss off the prosecutor, then he can charge you *separately*—for *every single check* you cashed and every invoice you sent to the company, basically stacking all the counts up. How many invoices did you send?"

"One a month, for about four and a half years."

"So that's fifty-four counts or so right there. The federal prosecutors can get really creative if they want to, and they have enormous power. Federal fraud statutes are incredibly broad, meaning a good U.S. attorney can really jack someone up on the indictment if they want to."

"Do I have a defense? That I billed for legitimate services?"

"It's a real stretch. But, arguably, you do—maybe. Did your invoices detail what you were actually doing for the company to earn the consulting fees?"

"*Yes*! Yes, they did. I basically detailed whatever work I had done that month that involved providing marketing and public relations advice and work to the company—that is *not* part of my job description—and billed the company for my time."

"OK, so the consulting you did was valuable to the company, was it not?"

"Yes, it was extremely valuable. Mason's always telling me, 'thanks for the great input, Chuck; boy, you really know how to structure our marketing approach; great choice on the trade show last month; great PR work,' all that kind of stuff."

"And you are their top seller?"

"Yes, absolutely."

"Is there any dirt under your boss's fingernails—or old man White's—that we need to consider as leverage?'"

"Not that I know of. Truth is, it's a great company. I'm the shithead, here. Me and Martha, I guess, although I'm way worse than Martha."

"How do you think the company's investors would feel about another disclosure of company funds 'mismanaged,' so to speak, to the tune of a million or so dollars, right on top of the Martha affair?"

"Hmm," Chuck chews on this a bit. "I mean, even the million is a spit in the ocean, sort of. The company had sales of close to $75 million last year alone, and old man White is terrified of getting caught with his pants down in front of his rich financing buddies. Hell, he's the one who plays golf with those rich old farts every month. At the very least, he'd be embarrassed."

"How much do you make, Chuck?"

ARRESTED 241

"About 250K a year."

"Any savings?"

"Some, stock and equity in my home. My wife inherited a beach house we're supposed to sell soon and maybe clear three or four hundred grand after taxes."

"So, if you, their top seller—whom they probably don't want to lose—come forward and explain the situation, even this Mr. White might come around, right? You can settle on an amount to pay back—or maybe you can simply explain *why* the consulting services were legit, despite the fact that you were paying yourself. Then maybe, just maybe, the company's partners will agree with you and then they will all agree that the company was not deprived of anything of value, but in fact received valuable marketing and public relations services from you that you were authorized to bill for. You did get authorization from your boss, and you did provide the services. You may very well get fired or forced to resign, but you might just avoid criminal prosecution especially if you can offer to pay a good chunk of the money back. The defense stinks, of course, in my opinion. In court, if it looks and quacks like a duck, it's generally a duck. And this looks and quacks like mail fraud, so to a federal judge or jury, it's probably mail fraud. But it's at least enough of a defense to make it a bit of a pain in the rump for whatever assistant federal prosecutor gets stuck with it.

"On the other hand," the lawyer continues, "if you don't say anything, it may go unnoticed. You did stop the billing a year ago. Your boss approved the consulting services, and he signed off on the invoices. You are a company star in sales, and they're not looking at you during this audit. Plus, it's an old vendor no longer used by the company, so your auditor may gloss over it. Of course, if you are asked questions about it by the feds and you lie, then you could get hit with other criminal charges—such as lying to a federal prosecutor and obstruction of justice—which also carry federal prison sentences. And then you could still get hammered for mail fraud, too."

"What the hell do I do? The right thing to do is to go tell them—and maybe it's the smart thing to do. On the other hand, if I try to *whistle past the graveyard*, as you put it, I just might make it past. Then the past is buried and it's as if nothing ever happened. Shit, what a terrible choice to have to make."

"Yes, it is. But you have to make it, and it sounds like you need to make it in the next couple of days, at least based upon when you are supposed to meet with the auditors. My advice is to go home and sleep on it, and then let me know how you want to proceed. If you are going to disclose your activities, then we need to get you prepared. Either way, you need legal counsel."

"I'm not sure I am going to sleep much tonight."

"I understand, Chuck," Mr. Process says as he leans back in his chair. "And, in that respect, I can assure you, you are just like anyone else who has found themselves in the grip of *The Beast*—America's criminal justice system."

ENDNOTES

1 Public Broadcasting System, "Clotaire Rapaille Reptilian Marketing" (Excerpt), video clip [n.d.], http://wn.com/PBS_Excerpt_Clotaire_Rapaille_Reptilian_Marketing.

2 For a detailed discussion of this issue, see Joanna Cohn Weiss, "Tough on Crime: How Campaigns for State Judiciary Violate Criminal Defendants' Due Process Rights," *New York University Law Review* 81 (June 2006): 1101.

3 "Do prosecutors have to take an oath?" *Answers.com*, http://wiki.answers.com/Q/Do_prosecutors_have_to_take_an_oath.

4 For a detailed discussion of this topic, see William Ayers, Bernardine Dohrn, Rick Ayers, eds., *Zero Tolerance: Resisting the Drive for Punishment in Our Schools*, foreword by Rev. Jesse L. Jackson (New York: The New Press, 2001).

5 For further reading on this topic, see Eric Schlosser, "The Prison-Industrial Complex: Crime is Down, But the Prison Biz is Booming," *Atlantic Monthly*, (December 1998).

6 *American Heritage Dictionary of the English Language*, 4th ed., s.v. "zero tolerance," http://dictionary.reference.com/browse/Zero%20Tolerance; Brian James Schoonover, *Zero Tolerance Discipline Policies: The History, Implementation, and Controversy of Zero Tolerance Policies in Student Codes of Conduct* (New York: iUniverse, Inc., 2009).

7   "Zero tolerance," *Wikipedia, The Free Encyclopedia*, http://en.wikipedia.org/wiki/Zero_tolerance.

8   James Q. Wilson, *Thinking About Crime* (New York: Basic Books, Inc., 1975).

9   James Q. Wilson, *Thinking About Crime* (New York: Basic Books, Inc., 1975).

10 James Q. Wilson, *Thinking About Crime*, rev. ed. (New York: Basic Books Inc., 1983): inside jacket cover.

11 George L. Kelling and James Q. Wilson, "Broken Windows: The police and neighborhood safety," *Atlantic Monthly* (March 1982), http://www.theatlantic.com/ideastour/archive/windows.html.

12 George L. Kelling and James Q. Wilson, "Broken Windows: The Police & Neighborhood Safety," in Wilson, *Thinking About Crime*, rev. ed., 75.

13 Ibid.

14 Ibid.

15 Ibid., 76.

16 Ibid.

17 Ibid.

18 Ibid.

19 Ibid., 77–78.

20 Ibid., 78. (Emphasis added)

21 Ibid., 78–79.

22 Ibid., 89.

23 Ibid., 77.

24 Ibid., 84–85.

25 Ibid., 85.

26 Ibid., 84.

27 Ibid., 83.

28 Ibid., 84

29 Ibid., 84–85.

30 "Zero tolerance," ch. 4, n.7, *Wikipedia: The Free Encyclopedia*, http://en.wikipedia.org/wiki/Zero_tolerance; Criminology Center,

31 Kelling reportedly used the term "no tolerance," which then became "zero tolerance." "Zero Tolerance," (citing G. L. Kelling, M. Julian, and S. Miller, "Managing 'Squeegeeing': A Problem Solving Exercise," New York: NYPD, 1994; and Norman Dennis and George Erdos, *Cultures & Crimes* (2005)). See also: George L. Kelling, "How to Run A Police Department," *City Journal* (Autumn 1995), http://www.city-journal.org/html/5_4_how_to_run.html; and, more recently, "Return of the Squeegee Men," *New York Press* (July 26, 2006), http://www.nypress.com/article-14010-return-of-the-squeegee-men.html.

32 "What is a Task Force?" *WiseGEEK*, http://www.wisegeek.com/what-is-a-task-force.htm.

33 "Task Force," *Wikipedia, The Free Encyclopedia*, http://en.wikipedia.org/wiki/Task_Force.

34 Barbara Tuchman, *A Distant Mirror: The Calamitous 14th Century* (New York: Ballantine Books, 1978).

35 "Rough Justice: America Locks Up Too Many People, Some for Acts That Should Not Even Be Criminal," *Economist* (July 22, 2010): 26–29.

36 *Blakely v. Washington*, 542 U.S. 296 (2004); *United States v. Booker*, 543 U.S. 220 (2005); and *Booker*'s progeny.

37 The scope of mandatory minimum sentences is too vast to describe in detail in this book, but they are found in most areas of criminal law today, from DUI/DWI laws to sex crimes and from white collar crimes to drug crimes and violent crimes. For detailed discussions on mandatory minimum sentencing, see the following: "America's Unjust Sex Laws: An Even Harsher Approach Is Doing More Harm Than Good, but it is being copied around the world," *Economist* (August 8, 2009): 21–23; "Rough Justice;" Christian Parenti, *Lockdown America: Police and Prisons in the Age of Crisis*, new ed. (Brooklyn, NY: Verso Publishing, 2008); and Jeffrey Reiman, *The Rich Get Richer, and the Poor Get Prison: Ideology, Class, and Criminal Justice*, 8th ed. (New York: Pearson Publishing, 2006).

38 Wilson, *Thinking About Crime*, rev. ed., 256.

39 Ibid., 253.

40 Greg Bluestein, "Georgia Softens Once-Lauded Strict Sex Offender Law," *Atlanta Journal-Constitution* (July 19, 2010), http://www.law.com/jsp/article.jsp?id=1202463693327&slreturn=1&hbxlogin=1.

41 "Rough Justice."

42 See "America's Unjust Sex Laws;" "Rough Justice;" Parenti, *Lockdown America*; and Reiman, *The Rich Get Richer, and the Poor Get Prison*.

43 Brian Innes, *The History of Torture* (New York: St. Martin's Press, 1998), 57–61.

44 Nathaniel Hawthorne, *The Scarlet Letter* (1850; reprinted New York: Tribeca Books, 2011).

45 OFFICIAL CODE OF GEORGIA §42-1-12 (2010).

46 Ian Freedman et al., "Creating a More Deliberative Sentencing Process for Sex Offenders," *The Champion* (December 2009); "America's Unjust Sex Laws;" Bluestein, "Georgia Softens Once-Lauded Strict Sex Offender Law."

47 Official Code of Georgia §42-1-15; "America's Unjust Sex Laws;" Bluestein, "Georgia Softens Once-Lauded Strict Sex Offender Law."

48 http://newyork.cbslocal.com/2011/04/17/ny-legislators-propose-domestic-violence-registry/.

49 For a full discussion of this issue, see David Garland, *The Culture of Control: Crime and Social Order in Contemporary Society* (Chicago: University of Chicago Press, 2002).

50 Stanton E. Samenow, *Inside the Criminal Mind*, Rev. ed. (New York: Crown Publishers, 2004), 83.

51 Wilson, *Thinking About Crime*, rev. ed., 253.

52 Some may feel my depiction of someone accused of a crime as being the prey of the police and prosecutors is simply too extreme. In my opinion, it is not. In a recent New York City reality series, one of the police officers stares into the camera and announces to the camera, "I love to hunt," by which he means investigate and arrest people he believes have committed crimes. (The series was pulled off the air because of the controversy it stirred in New York.) When federal investigators and prosecutors are investigating a person, they routinely describe that person as "a target." Thus, both the police and prosecutors use hunting terminology when describing their pursuit and prosecution of persons they believe have committed crimes. This leads to only one logical conclusion: a person who is a *target* of the police or the prosecutor's office is clearly their *prey*.

53 Clinton Rossiter, *1787: The Grand Convention* (New York: W.W. Norton & Co., 1987).

54 See *Griswold v. Connecticut*, 381 U.S. 479 (1965), and its progeny.

55 *District of Columbia v. Heller*, 554 U.S. 570 (2008).

56 *Semayne's Case*, 5 Co. Rep. 91a, 91b, 77 Eng. Rep. 194, 195 (K.B. 1603).

57 Mark Bowden, "Tales of the Tyrant," *Atlantic Monthly* (May 2002): 35.

58   Sikkink, K., "From Pariah State to Global Human Rights Protagonist: Argentina and the Struggle for International Human Rights," *Latin American Politics and Society* 50, no. 1 (Spring 2008): 1–29.

59   *Miranda v. Arizona*, 384 U.S. 436 (1966).

60   Anthony Everitt, *Cicero: The Life and Times of Rome's Greatest Politician* (New York: Random House, 2001).

61   Rossiter, *1787: The Grand Convention*; Everitt, *Cicero*, preface; David McCullough, *John Adams* (New York: Simon & Schuster, 2001), 34, 46, 48, 121, and 375.

62   Cicero, *De Legibus (On the Laws)*; Also emblazoned on a coffee mug given out for Emory University's Law School's Law Day a few years ago.

63   See generally Everitt, *Cicero*; Thomas R. Martin, *Ancient Greece: From Prehistoric to Hellenistic Times* (New Haven: Yale University Press, 1996).

64   Ibid.

65   *Jury Trials in Russia*, http://www.prison.org/english/rpsjur.htm.

66   "Jury Trial," *Wikipedia, The Free Encyclopedia*, http://en.wikipedia.org/wiki/Jury_trial#Singapore .

67   http://www.brainyquote.com/quotes/quotes/r/ronaldreag169552.html.

68   Acts 25:16, *Holy Bible* (Authorized King James Version), reports the Roman governor Porcius Festus, discussing the proper treatment of his prisoner Paul, to have said: "It is not the manner of the Romans to deliver any man to die, before he that is accused have the accusers face to face, and have license to answer for himself concerning the crime laid against him." Also see Sir William Blackstone, *Commentaries on the Laws of England* (Oxford: Clarendon Press, 1765–69; modern ed. *Blackstone's Commentaries on the Laws of England*; edited by Wayne Morrison. 4 vols. Published: London: Routledge-Cavendish; London, England: 2001).

69 The *Commentaries on the Laws of England* are an influential eighteenth-century treatise on the common law of England by Sir William Blackstone, originally published by the Clarendon Press at Oxford, 1765–1769. The work is divided into four volumes: the rights of persons, the rights of things, of private wrongs, and of public wrongs.

70 See, for example, *Powell v. Alabama*, 287 U.S. 45 (1932); *Johnson v. Zerbst*, 304 U.S. 458 (1938); *Hamilton v. Alabama*, 368 U.S. 52 (1961); *Gideon v. Wainwright*, 372 U.S. 335 (1963).

71 *Gideon v. Wainwright*, 372 U.S. 335 (1963).

72 The "worth" of the land or property may be valued as the amount of *equity* the title holder has in the land. For example, if a person owns a home valued at $100,000 dollars, but has a mortgage of $80,000 owed to a bank, their *equity* is worth $20,000 dollars. If you want to post property as bail, talk to the person at the bail window at the jail and they can explain the specific requirements to you.

73 The examples of torture techniques in the next several paragraphs come from Innes, *The History of Torture*. See Stanley Karnow, *Paris in the Fifties* (New York: Three Rivers Press, 1999): 155–173, for a discussion of the use of the Guillotine during the French revolution. See also Larry Helm Spalding, "Florida's 1997 Chemical Castration Law: A Return to the Dark Ages." *Florida State University Law Review* (1998), http://www.law.fsu.edu/journals/lawreview/frames/252/spaltxt.html.

74 I use the term "innocent," here, in the way anyone who is not a lawyer uses the term. By telling me they are innocent, my clients are claiming they did not commit whatever crimes they are being investigated or prosecuted for doing. I then explain to my clients that they *are innocent* as far as the law goes, because—in America—accused persons are innocent under the law until they are convicted by a judge or jury (or admit guilt in open court during a guilty plea hearing). I know, I know, this sounds like so much lawyer speak. But refer back to Chapter Eight, where I discuss

the Sixth Amendment to the United States Constitution. This is not "slick Rick" lawyer talk. This is one of your most important constitutional rights as an American.

75   OK, I may be exaggerating a little bit. Hopefully the real police do more investigation than Lt. Tragg usually did, but I suspect they do not always do more than he did. There are many, many cases, especially in state courts (as opposed to the federal courts) where the only evidence in a case is a perfunctory police report with little or no evidence, and with no investigation having been conducted at all.

76   "Rough Justice;" Weiss, "Tough on Crime."

77   I use the terms *serious crimes* and also *major crimes* many times in this chapter. By using these terms, I mean to refer to crimes that are felonies (punishable by a year or more in prison) and capital crimes (felonies punishable by life imprisonment or death). Obviously, though, for my clients—as for anyone accused of a crime be it a misdemeanor or a felony—their crimes are utterly serious and of major importance to them and their family and friends.

78   "Open records acts" are laws that give lawyers and other members of the public the right to obtain information about a person or an institution from a government agency by simply writing a letter requesting the information under the legal authority of the "open records" law. A "subpoena" is a document legally compelling the keeper of a certain type of record to bring the records to court to be reviewed by the judge and/or for use during a trial.

79   I never recommend that a person being investigated or accused of a crime take a lie detector test administered by the police, FBI, or other government or prosecutorial agency. If you do decide to take one, I recommend that you do so confidentially and privately. This is a decision you will need to make with your lawyer, but the government cannot force you to take a lie detector test.

80 In felony cases, the accused generally must be indicted by a grand jury; in misdemeanor cases, the arrested person can be generally "accused" by the prosecutor, meaning that the prosecutor will write up an "accusation," which looks a lot like an indictment but is not presented to a grand jury to vote on. Instead, the prosecutor is allowed to simply draft the accusation and then file it with the clerk of court, who formally accuses the person with the alleged commission of a misdemeanor crime. Check your local county or state court's websites to learn more about the rules in your community, or speak with a lawyer familiar with state or county's local rules.

81 This is a common phrase used by prosecutors when they try a case with not particularly "good facts" for their side—that is, facts that will convince a jury that the accused is guilty beyond a reasonable doubt.

82 Of course, Emily's parents will probably also be publically humiliated, because their arrest will be in the local newspaper and on the web, where they will be the subject of endless tongue wagging by social busybodies and bloggers.

83 In some states this charge is called DWI (Driving While Intoxicated) and in other states it's called DUI (Driving Under the Influence).

84 HGN is a common acronym for Horizontal Gaze Nystagmus, which is a field sobriety test sometimes administered by police officers to drivers they suspect to be under the influence of alcohol. The officer holds his finger or a pen in front of your face and tells you to hold your head still while tracking the movement of his finger or pen with your eyes. He then moves the pen to about a forty-five-degree angle to each side of your face and tells you to keep your head facing forward while focusing your eyes on his finger or pen. If your eyeballs twitch involuntarily, this supposedly indicates that you may have been drinking. (To see what the twitching might look like, get a friend to let you spin her in circles while standing in one spot, then look at her eyes, which will probably be twitching involuntarily.) With the HGN test, the idea is that the alcohol in your system inhibits muscle control and some of the first muscles you

lose control of when you drink alcohol are your fine motor coordination skills—such as those eye muscles, which allow your eyes to remain smoothly focused on an object such as the officer's finger or pen.

85 The rules differ from state to state and between state and federal cases (criminal cases prosecuted by the United States Attorney's Office on behalf of the People of the United States are considered to be federal criminal cases). As with all laws, you should check your own local laws or ask an attorney in your state so that you can better understand what rules apply in your state.

86 Tom Wolfe, *Bonfire of the Vanities* (New York: Picador, 2008).

BIBLIOGRAPHY

"America's Unjust Sex Laws: An Even Harsher Approach Is Doing More Harm Than Good." *Economist* (August 8, 2009): 21–23.

Answers.com. "Do prosecutors have to take an oath?" accessed May 5, 2011. http://wiki.answers.com/Q/Do_prosecutors_have_to_take_an_oath.

Axelrod, Alan. *Little-Known Wars of Great and Lasting Impact: The Turning Points in Our History We Should Know More About*. Beverly, MA: Fair Winds Press, 2009.

Ayers, William, Bernardine Dohrn, Rick Ayers, eds. *Zero Tolerance: Resisting the Drive for Punishment in Our Schools*. New York: The New Press, 2001.

Blackstone, Sir William. *Commentaries on the Laws of England*. Oxford: Clarendon Press, 1765–1769. Modern ed. *Blackstone's Commentaries on the Laws of England*; edited by Wayne Morrison. 4 vols. London: Routledge-Cavendish, 2001.

Bluestein, Greg. "Georgia Softens Once-Lauded Strict Sex Offender Law." *Atlanta Journal Constitution*, July 19, 2010. http://www.law.com/jsp/article.jsp?id=1202463693327&slreturn=1&hbxlogin=1.

Bowden, Mark. "Tales of the Tyrant." *Atlantic Monthly*, May 2002.

Byrne, Robert. *The 2,548 Best Things Anybody Ever Said*. New York: Simon and Schuster, 2002.

Darrow, Clarence. *The Story of My Life*. New York: Da Capo Press, 1996.

Dershowitz, Alan M. *Contrary to Popular Opinion*. New York: Pharos Books, 1992.

Ellis, Alan and Mark H. Allenbaugh. "Standards of Proof at Sentencing." *GP Solo* 27, no. 2 (March 2010): 24.

Eugenics Archive, accessed May 2011. http://www.eugenicsarchive.org/html/eugenics/static/themes.

Evans, Richard J. *The Third Reich in Power, 1933–1939*. New York: Penguin Books, 2005.

Everitt, Anthony. *Cicero: The Life and Times of Rome's Greatest Politician*. New York: Random House, 2001.

Ezoe, Hiromasa. *Where is the Justice? Media Attacks, Prosecutorial Abuse, and My 13 Years in Japanese Court*. Tokyo: Kodansha International Ltd., 2010.

Frampton, Mary Louise, Ian Haney Lopez, and Jonathan Simon, eds. *After the War on Crime: Race, Democracy, and a New Reconstruction*. New York: New York University Press, 2008.

Freedman, Ian, Roger Pimentel, Kristena W. Supler, and Robert Weiss. "Creating a More Deliberative Sentencing Process for Sex Offenders." *The Champion* (December 2009): 21.

Garland, David. *The Culture of Control: Crime and Social Order in Contemporary Society*. Chicago: University of Chicago Press, 2002.

Gibbon, Edward. *The Decline and Fall of the Roman Empire*. New York: Everyman's Library, 1994.

Hawthorne, Nathaniel. *The Scarlet Letter*. 1850; reprint, New York: Tribeca Books, 2011.

Heck, Mathais H., Jr. "Sexting: Balancing the Law and Bad Choices." *Criminal Justice Section Newsletter, American Bar Assoc.* 18, no. 1 (Fall 2009): 1.

Hickey, Thomas A. *Taking Sides: Clashing Views in Crime and Criminology*. 9th ed. New York: McGraw-Hill, 2009.

Holy Bible. Authorized King James Version.

Innes, Brian. *The History of Torture*. New York: St. Martin's Press, 1998.

Joseph, Lawrence B., ed. *Crime, Communities, and Public Policy*. Chicago: University of Chicago, 1995.

Kairys, David. *The Politics of Law: A Progressive Critique*. 3rd ed. New York: Basic Books, 1998.

Karnow, Stanley. *Paris in the Fifties*. New York: Three Rivers Press, 1999.

Kelling, George L. "How to Run a Police Department." *City Journal* (Autumn 1995). http://www.city-journal-.org/html.

——— and James Q. Wilson. "Broken Windows: The police & neighborhood safety." *Atlantic Monthly* (March 1982): 29–38.

Ketchum, Richard M. *Faces from the Past*. New York: American Heritage Press, 1970.

Martin, Thomas R. *Ancient Greece: From Prehistoric to Hellenistic Times*. New Haven: Yale University Press, 1996.

McCullough, David. *John Adams*. New York: Simon & Schuster, 2001.

Muldoon, Gary. *Handling a Criminal Case in New York*. 2009–2010 ed. Rochester, NY: Lawyers Cooperative Publishing, 2009.

Murphy, Wendy. *And Justice for Some: An Expose of the Lawyers and Judges Who Let Dangerous Criminals Go Free*. New York: Sentinel, 2007.

New York Police Department. "Crime Prevention: Citywide Vandals Task Force—Mission," accessed May 2011. http://www.nyc.gov/html/nypd/html/crime_prevention/citywide_vandals_taskforce.shtml.

New York Press. "Return of the Squeegee Men," accessed July 2010. http://www.nypress.com/article-14010-return-of-the-squeegee-men.html.

Parascandola, Rocco, Kerry Burke, and Bill Hutchinson. *New York Daily News* (August 5, 2010): 3.

Parenti, Christian. *Lockdown America: Police and Prisons in the Age of Crisis*. New ed. Brooklyn, NY: Verso Publishing, 2008.

Public Broadcasting System, "Clotaire Rapaille Reptilian Marketing" (excerpt), video clip [n.d.], accessed July 2010. http://wn.com/PBS_Excerpt_Clotaire_Rapaille_Reptilian_Marketing.

Reiman, Jeffrey. *The Rich Get Richer, and the Poor Get Prison: Ideology, Class, and Criminal Justice*. 8th ed. New York: Pearson Publishing, 2006.

Rosenbaum, Thane. *The Myth of Moral Justice: Why Our Legal System Fails to Do What's Right*. New York: HarperCollins, 2004.

Rossiter, Clinton. *1787: The Grand Convention*. New York: W.W. Norton & Co., 1987.

"Rough Justice: America Locks Up Too Many People, Some for Acts That Should Not Even Be Criminal." *Economist* (July 22, 2010): 241.

Samenow, Stanton E. *Inside the Criminal Mind*. Rev. ed. New York: Crown Publishers, 2004.

Schlosser, Eric. "The Prison-Industrial Complex: Crime Is Down, But the Prison Biz is Booming." *Atlantic Monthly* (December 1998): 35.

Schoonover, Brian James. *Zero Tolerance Discipline Policies: The History, Implementation, and Controversy of Zero Tolerance Policies in Student Codes of Conduct*. New York: iUniverse, Inc., 2009.

Sikkink, K. "From Pariah State to Global Human Rights Protagonist: Argentina and the Struggle for International Human Rights." *Latin American Politics and Society* 50, no. 1 (Spring 2008): 1–29.

Simon, Jonathan. *Governing Through Crime: How the War on Crime Transformed American Democracy and Created a Culture of Fear*. Oxford: Oxford University Press, 2007.

Spalding, Larry Helm. "Florida's 1997 Chemical Castration Law: A Return to the Dark Ages." *Florida State University Law Review*, 1998, accessed July 2011. http://www.law.fsu.edu/journals/lawreview/frames/252/spaltxt.html.

Sullivan, Robert, ed. *The Most Notorious Crimes in American History*. New York: Time Home Entertainment, 2007.

Tuchman, Barbara. *A Distant Mirror: The Calamitous 14th Century*. New York: Ballantine Books, 1978.

Vitale, Alex S. *City of Disorder: How the Quality of Life Campaign Transformed New York Politics*. New York: New York University Press, 2008.

Weiss, Joanna Cohn. "Tough on Crime: How Campaigns for State Judiciary Violate Criminal Defendants' Due Process Rights." 81 *New York University Law Review* (June 2006): 1101.

Wikipedia, The Free Encyclopedia. "Jury Trial," accessed August 2011. http://en.wikipedia.org/wiki/Jury_trial#Singapore.

———. "Task Force," accessed August 2011. http://en.wikipedia.org/wiki/Task_Force.

———. "Zero Tolerance," accessed August 2011. http://en.wikipedia.org/wiki/Zero_tolerance.

Wilson, James Q. *Thinking About Crime*. New York: Basic Books, Inc., 1975.

———. *Thinking About Crime*. Rev. ed. New York: Basic Books, Inc., 1983.

Wines, Michael. "China Keeps 7 Million Tireless Eyes on Its People." *New York Times*, August 3, 2010.

WiseGEEK. "What is a Task Force?" accessed August 2011, http://www.wisegeek.com/what-is-a-task-force.htm.

Wolfe, Tom. *Bonfire of the Vanities*. New York: Picador, 2008.